**REPORT**

**OF THE**

**ASSOCIATION FOR INVESTMENT MANAGEMENT AND RESEARCH**

**CORPORATE INFORMATION COMMITTEE**

*Including*

**EVALUATION**

**OF**

*CORPORATE FINANCIAL REPORTING*

**IN**

**SELECTED INDUSTRIES**

**FOR THE YEAR**

**1991–92**

The Association for Investment Management and Research (AIMR) is a nonprofit professional organization devoted to the advancement of investment management. AIMR combines the functions of the Financial Analysts Federation, founded in 1947, and the Institute of Chartered Financial Analysts, founded in 1962. Sixty-eight local analysts societies in the United States, Canada, The Bahamas, Bermuda, Mexico, Singapore and one international society are affiliated with AIMR. The aggregate membership is more than 22,500. The Corporate Information Committee has reported its evaluations of the adequacy of corporate reporting for investors since 1948.

Association for Investment Management and Research • 200 Park Avenue, New York, NY 10166

212-953-5700

5 Boar's Head Lane, Charlottesville, VA 22903

804-977-6600

December, 1992

Copyright Association for Investment Management and Research 1992

All rights reserved including the right to reproduce this book or portion thereof in any form.

# ASSOCIATION FOR INVESTMENT MANAGEMENT AND RESEARCH

## CORPORATE INFORMATION COMMITTEE

Chairman
Rosario S. Ilacqua, CFA, New York
Rothschild Inc.

Vice Chairman
Thomas P. Moore, Jr., CFA, Boston
State Street Research & Management Co.

George E. Austin, CFA, New York
J. P. Morgan Investment Management Inc.

Anthony T. Cope, CFA, Boston
Wellington Management Company

Stanley H. Harbison, CFA, New York
Scudder, Stevens & Clark, Inc.

Sidney J. Heller, CFA, New York
Lehman Brothers

Richard P. Kost, CFA, Detroit
National Bank of Detroit

Donald Kramer, CFA, New York
Carteret Savings Bank

Peter C. Lincoln, New York
United States Steel and Carnegie Pension Fund

Patricia A. McConnell, New York
Bear, Stearns & Co., Inc.

S. Scott Nicholls, Jr., New York
Nicholls Management Company

Katharine L. Plourde, CFA, New York
Donaldson, Lufkin & Jenrette Securities Corp.

James F. Rothenberg, CFA, Los Angeles
Capital Research Company

Nancy L. Young, CFA, New York
College Retirement Equities Fund

## OFFICERS

*Chairman*
Frederick L. Muller, CFA, Atlanta
Atlanta Capital Management Company

*Vice Chairman*
Charles D. Ellis, CFA, Greenwich
Greenwich Associates

*President*
Darwin M. Bayston, CFA, Charlottesville
Association for Investment Management and Research

---

City indicates location not society.

# INDUSTRY SUBCOMMITTEE CHAIRS

**Airline**
   Candace E. Browning, Merrill Lynch and Co .................................................... New York
**Apparel and Textiles**
   Jay J. Meltzer, CFA, Goldman, Sachs & Co ..................................................... New York
**Auto, Rubber, and Auto Component Manufacturers**
**Banking**
   William J. Welsh, J.P. Morgan Investment Management Inc ............................. New York
**Chemical**
   Brian J. Corvese, Chancellor Capital Management Inc ..................................... New York
**Computer and Electronics**
   Walter C. Price, Jr., CFA, RCM Capital Management ..................................... San Francisco
**Construction**
**Container & Packaging**
   Cornelius W. Thornton, Goldman Sachs & Co .................................................. New York
**Cosmetics and Household Products**
**Diversified Companies**
   Anthony M. Maramarco, CFA, Massachusetts Mutual Life Insurance Co ........... Springfield
**Electrical Equipment**
   Stanley L. Rubin, CFA, Merrill Lynch and Company ....................................... New York
**Environmental Control**
   Marc H. Sulam, Kidder, Peabody & Co., Inc. .................................................. New York
**Financial Services**
   Nancy L. Young, CFA, College Retirement Equities Fund ............................... New York
**Food, Beverage & Tobacco**
   John M. McMillin III, CFA, Prudential Capital Funding .................................. New York
   Roy D. Burry, CFA, Kidder, Peabody & Co. Inc ............................................... New York
**Foreign-Based Oil**
   Todd L. Bergman, CFA, Goldman Sachs & Co. ................................................ New York
**Health Care**
   Kent Blair, Donaldson, Lufkin & Jenrette Securities Corp ............................... New York
**Insurance**
   Myron M. Picoult, Oppenheimer & Co., Inc ..................................................... New York
**International Pharmaceuticals**
   Kenneth R. Kulju, UBS Securities, Inc ............................................................. New York
**Machinery**
   Paul Whelan, Louis Nicoud & Associates ........................................................ New York
**Media**
   Susan L. Decker, CFA, Donaldson, Lufkin & Jenrette Securities Corp ............ San Francisco
**Motor Carrier**
   Remy M. Fisher, Kemper Financial Services, Inc ........................................... Chicago
**Natural Gas**
   Ronald F. Cassinari, M R Beal & Co ............................................................... New York
**Nonferrous and Mining**
   Daniel A. Roling, CFA, CPA, Merrill Lynch Capital Markets ........................ New York
**Paper and Forest Products**
   Kim Williams, Wellington Management Company ......................................... Boston
**Petroleum**
   Janet Rasmussen, Wertheim Schroder & Co. Inc. ........................................... New York
**Railroad**
   Michael H. Lloyd, CFA, County NatWest ....................................................... New York
**Retail Trade**
   Jeffrey M. Feiner, CFA, Salomon Brothers ..................................................... New York
**Saving Institutions**
   Bruce W. Harting, CFA, Salomon Brothers Inc. .............................................. New York
**Software/Data Services**
   Charles E. Phillips, Jr., SoundView Financial Group Inc ................................. Stamford
**Specialty Chemical**
   Stuart M. Pulvirent, Lehman Brothers .............................................................. New York
**Steel**
**Utilities**

The 1991–1992 report of the Corporate Information Committee is in two parts, the first an overview and the second the individual reports of industry subcommittees.

## CONTENTS

**PART I**

| | |
|---|---|
| Introduction | 1 |
| Awards for Excellence | 6 |
| Letters of Commendation | 6 |

**PART II**

Subcommittee Reports:

| | |
|---|---|
| Airline | 7 |
| Apparel and Textiles | 10 |
| Banking | 13 |
| Chemical | 17 |
| Computer and Electronics | 20 |
| Container & Packaging | 25 |
| Diversified Companies | 28 |
| Electrical Equipment | 32 |
| Environmental Control | 35 |
| Financial Services | 39 |
| Food, Beverage & Tobacco | 47 |
| Foreign-Based Oil | 50 |
| Health Care | 53 |
| Insurance | 55 |
| International Pharmaceuticals | 59 |
| Machinery | 61 |
| Media | 63 |
| Natural Gas | 68 |
|    Distribution Companies | 68 |
|    Pipelines | 69 |
| Nonferrous and Mining | 72 |
|    Nonferrous | 73 |
|    Precious Metals | 75 |
|    Coal | 76 |
| Paper and Forest Products | 78 |
| Petroleum | 82 |
|    International Oil Companies | 84 |
|    Domestic Integrated and Independent Refining Companies | 87 |
|    Independent Oil and Gas Producers | 88 |
|    Oil Service and Contract Drilling Companies | 90 |
| Railroad | 93 |
| Retail Trade | 96 |
| Software/Data Services | 100 |
| Specialty Chemical | 105 |
| *Appendix A—Checklist of Criteria for Evaluations | 109 |
| Appendix B—Segment Reporting Georgia-Pacific 1991 Annual Report | 112 |
| Appendix C—Segment Reporting Dexter Corp. 1991 Annual Report | 114 |
| Index of Companies Reviewed | 118 |

*The checklists and criteria sheets of the subcommittees vary from one to many pages. Because of their length, they are not included with the reports that follow. Information copies of the checklists and criteria are available at a cost of twenty-five cents per page from the Association for Investment Management and Research, 200 Park Avenue, New York, NY 10166.

# Introduction

The Corporate Information Committee (CIC) is pleased to reaffirm its long-term objective of enhancing and improving communications between the management of publicly owned corporations and the investment community. While the contributors to this study are by definition exclusively professional securities analysts, the Committee's goal continues to be to improve the quality of the information as well as to speed its dissemination to both the professional and non-professional investor. This effort has taken on an entirely new dimension with the rapid globalization of the business world, the much broader scope of available investment instruments and particularly the growing number of foreign-based corporations whose securities are now available to U.S. investors.

The U.S. investment market remains the premier market in the world and we believe that the disclosure standards required in this country are an important contributor to this position. This Committee would like to see foreign-based companies adopt those disclosure standards expected of U.S. firms. In recognition of the increased globalization of investments, we are pleased to note two new subcommittees dedicated to reviewing foreign-based companies that contributed to this report. Ken Kulju has developed a committee to review foreign-based pharmaceutical companies and Todd L. Bergman has launched a similar effort to focus on foreign-based oil companies. In the next year or so, we look forward to the formation of a group to review a number of Canadian companies as well.

While the goals of this Committee are clearly defined and a specific methodology is made available, as noted in Appendix A, the individual subcommittees continue to enjoy considerable flexibility. This flexibility is evident in several of the subcommittee reports which reflect major modifications and adjusted emphasis to accommodate their specific industries. This is particularly important in comparing companies that have significantly different operations. This year the Subcommittee on Financial Services adjusted its scoring to include foreign operations, segment reporting and supplemental financial data. At the same time, the subcommittee ensured that those companies without foreign operations were not penalized. The Computer and Electronics Subcommittee noted numerous instances in which companies could better define the earnings impact from currency fluctuations, again reflecting the growing importance of international operations.

This year more than 300 analysts reviewed 559 companies and recommended 35 Awards for Excellence in corporate communications and issued 5 letters of commendation for year-to-year improvements. We are pleased that a number of the individual subcommittees noted a trend toward improved communication on the part of many companies, perhaps in response to comments and suggestions made in prior CIC reports. The primary function of this Committee is the enhancement of corporate efforts to keep investors informed through prompt and full disclosure. While many companies are to be commended for meeting this obligation, there is still room for considerable improvement.

We are heartened that comments from the numerous oil industry subcommittees are generally complimentary regarding the quality and timeliness of information made available to investors and the awareness of most managements of their obligation to those who own the company. On the other side of the spectrum are the comments by the Insurance Subcommittee, which we would like to believe are applicable to only a small slice of the corporate world: "In general, comments from subcommittee members showed a growing frustration with the lack of candor and insight into the numerous problems of both the life and property-casualty industries provided by many insurance management teams. There is a sense that too many companies are not being managed in an effective manner." Furthermore, the subcommittee states: "It is hard to believe, but the quality of the industry's reporting to shareholders continues to deteriorate." It is hoped that the work of the Corporate Information Committee can be of some help in improving situations such as those described by the Insurance Subcommittee.

## Committee Operation

### Methodology

Each of the 34 industry and subsector reports that follows addresses the characteristics and issues unique to its industry or sector. General evaluation criteria included as Appendix A to this report provide the basis for individual industry or sector scoresheets. The Corporate Information Committee suggests weightings for scoring the three major communications categories: annual reports and required published material, quarterly reports and other non-required published material, and the various aspects of the investor relations/personal contact area. Individual industry characteristics determine the weightings the different subcommittees use.

The Committee's suggested weightings are:

Annual and required published material (annual reports, 10-Ks, 10-Qs, etc.)  40–50%

Quarterly stockholder reports and other published material not required  30–40%

Investor relations and related aspects  20–30%

Obviously, the Committee's suggested weightings can and should be adjusted to suit specific industry needs. While the annual report remains the primary corporate communication and the quarterly report ranks very high, there is increasing emphasis on "extra efforts" put forth by management. The "factbook" with up to ten-year financial records continues as the most respected extra. Timely and meaningful press releases covering important developments are often cited. Quarterly conference calls and analyst meetings are also becoming more important and may well reflect growing investor concern for short-term "market performance." Many investors cite the absence of a separate fourth quarter report as a continuing sore point. Fax machines are a wonderful tool for the rapid dissemination of hard copy data but this newer means of distribution is often overworked. We stress again that corporate communications should not be confined to the professional investment community but also directed to the general investing public.

The individual subcommittees have considerable leeway in developing pertinent criteria for their specific industry group. We would cite a fine example of this in the excellent report submitted by the Financial Services Subcommittee, chaired by Nancy L. Young. This subcommittee, which reviewed 13 corporations that operate in several different business areas, used a unique approach generally defined by the following categories of communication: Chairman's Letter (1991 weighting, 8.9%), Results of Operations (35.6%), Segment Reporting (15.8%), Foreign Operations (14.9%), Other Public Information (14.9%) and Other Aspects of Investor Relations (9.9%). This subcommittee, which uses an extensive checklist in developing individual scores, concluded that no individual company merited an Award for Excellence, the same decision reached the year before. This subcommittee also developed an evaluation for "Management Integrity." Several reviewers noted that Salomon went to extra lengths in its annual report to try to explain what went wrong (in the Treasury affair) and the steps that had been taken to rectify the situation. A few reviewers also expressed concern about certain companies whose top executives had apparently been misled by lower level management about important business situations. Full and timely disclosure of these happenings are an objective of the CIC.

Two subcommittee chairmen made particular note of a point that this Committee would like to emphasize again and again: Our work is devoted to the improvement of communication between corporations and the investing public and should not be regarded as another point of competition among companies. Janet Rasmussen, Chairman of the overall Petroleum Subcommittee stated: "Our committees have tried repeatedly to make clear that turning this ongoing (evaluation) process into a contest is not the goal or intention of either the industry subcommittees or AIMR. Rather, participation in the evaluation process should emphasize the continuing process of refining written and oral communication between companies and the investment community." William J. Welsh, Chairman of the Banking Subcommittee made a similar comment in defining the purpose of this effort: "Because of the large number of companies reviewed, and the qualitative nature of some of the questions, the subcommittee would not recommend that these findings be used to determine compensation for investor relations professionals."

## 1991 Results

As always, the Committee encourages an interactive dialogue between the companies and the analysts who conduct the evaluation. This should be coordinated through the subcommittee chairmen and could take the form of face to face meetings, teleconferences, and/or written responses to specific inquiries. The 1991 review was conducted by 25 subcommittees, and we are pleased to note that most of the subcommittee chairmen were repeats from the prior year. The subcommittees have the option to take different approaches to the evaluation, all within the guidelines specified by the Corporate Information Committee. Some committees concentrate on a small number of companies with each member evaluating all companies under review. Others use a survey approach with the Chairman tabulating the evaluation reports submitted by the committee members. The ever-growing pressures on almost all investment professionals suggest the need for a larger number of analysts to participate, with each analyst probably reviewing a limited number of companies. In this fashion, the workload on individual analysts could be lightened and our survey capabilities could probably be expanded to companies and industries that have not been subject to review in the past. The Banking Subcommittee, which reviewed the 75 largest publicly owned banks, again covered the largest number of companies. This committee uses an extensive survey approach and then averages the scores submitted by all participants with considerable care for reasonableness in developing comments and final opinions.

While most subcommittees conclude that one of the companies under review has earned an Award for Excellence and many committees suggest that, indeed, more than one company should receive an award, five of the subcommittees made no award recommendations for 1991. Understandably, the two newly formed subcommittees covering foreign-based oils and international pharmaceuticals chose not to make an award based on their initial effort. The chairmen of both committees felt that most companies under review were in the relatively early stages of developing an approach to investor relations, and the committee concentrated instead on establishing a base for future evaluation as well as opening a channel for providing feedback and suggestions for improvement going forward. We are encouraged by the work of these new chairmen, as the CIC looks upon the development of international communication as one of the more important challenges facing the investment community over the next decade.

The following comment by Todd L. Bergman, Chairman of the Foreign-Based Oil Subcommittee, puts into good perspective many of the shortcomings overseas companies have in dealing with investors: "The committee felt that the area where there is most room for improvement was in the frequency and timing of interim reports and communications of business trends to investors on a timely basis. In general, quarterly/semi-annual/annual results are published much later than those of U.S. companies. The French practice, for example, is to release partial data on a timely basis (i.e. less than one month after a period's close), but not to release sector and financial details for one or even two months later. Without details, the initial release is of limited analytical value. Norsk Hydro reports on a very timely basis. Repsol usually reports somewhat on the late side. Both of these latter companies do provide full detail when they release earnings. Most U.K. companies report semi-annually and do so quite awhile after the period has ended. Overall, these practices are in line with those of respective home markets but American investors, used to full detail within three to four weeks of the quarter's close, would prefer quicker and more detailed reports. We realize there is a cost involved with doing this, but feel the market would be better informed and more efficient as a result."

The Environmental Control Subcommittee noted the continued improvement in reporting practices in an industry that is still evolving. While three environmental companies outranked the others, no award was recommended for 1991 in the hope that all companies in this group strive for additional future improvement. The Electrical Equipment Subcommittee's very high standards for corporate communication were not met by any of the companies in its survey. The committee noted that both Honeywell and Cooper Industries are close to achieving an award recommendation and urge the managements to continue their fine efforts. The Financial Services Subcommittee noted that many companies have shown significant improvement in reporting practices but none had yet met the criteria for excellence in reporting and stated: "The analysts and the companies are all seeking an appropriate, cost effective forum for better communication."

## Reporting Highlights

It is impossible to report in any concise fashion all of the viewpoints and suggestions that committee members believe investors seek and need to make informed investment decisions. Most of our subcommittees agree that the annual report will continue as the centerpiece of corporate communication. However, as supplemental information the following suggestions seem appropriate:

- A factbook that provides considerable major background data and preferably a ten-year financial and operating history.
- Segmented financial and operating data, particularly on a quarterly basis, where appropriate both by lines of business and geographic.
- Quarterly reports with timely data presented in a format comparable to that of the annual report.
- Reports should be prepared under a standard format. Companies that use the metric system

should provide appropriate tables for conversion, while companies seeking foreign investors should state appropriate currency exchange rates.
- Segregation of the financial impact from non-recurring items (asset sales, write-offs, etc).
- Prompt communication of significant developments. This includes major changes in strategy as well as business conditions. This would also include full disclosure of the anticipated financial impact from new accounting principals: FAS 107 (Fair Value), FAS 106 (Retiree Health Care), FAS 109 (Income Taxes).
- The investor relations effort is most important and should be handled by someone who is accessible, well informed and empowered to discuss important matters with little restraint.

All of the above seem to be restated in the excellent report prepared by the Insurance Subcommittee chaired by Myron M. Picoult. We repeat the following excerpts: "Capital Holding continues to provide excellent information on a timely basis. Top management is very accessible and travels to meet investors. Commentary is straightforward and they solicit queries from their owners. Information on its basic business, investment portfolio, operational commentary, statistical layout, interim material and analyst sessions continue to be positively cited."

## Examples of Useful Disclosure

In their detailed examination of the financial reporting documents produced by hundreds of corporations evaluated this year, the CIC subcommittee chairmen cited numerous examples of disclosure formats that were particularly useful and insightful. More than one subcommittee, for example, pointed out the utility in trends analysis of having 11 years of historical data made available in a table in the annual report. Still others noted the growing value of factbooks, many of which provide additional layers of detail, not only about a particular company's operations but also about the industry in which the company operates and the broader economic climate as well.

Concluding this report, in Appendices B and C, are two examples of corporate disclosure that address one of the most important needs of the investor: concise and complete segment information. In its 1991 annual report to shareholders, Georgia-Pacific Corporation presented a breakout of sales and operating profit in 13 different forest product sectors. The breakout not only provides current year numbers but also equivalent data for each of the preceding ten years. The Dexter Corporation supplies a multi-year history in its annual report of several separate business lines categorized by seven different measures, such as net sales, r&d, and divestiture/restructuring activities. In addition, Dexter provides a multi-year breakout of net sales, operating income and net assets by geographic area. It was this kind of detailed communication that earned both Dexter and Georgia-Pacific Awards of Excellence for 1991–92.

## Committee Coverage

The staying power of the CIC subcommittee chairmen from year to year continues to be impressive. Two committees did pass the baton for 1992, and we want to acknowledge those changes:

*Machinery*           Paul Whelan
                      succeeded
                      Larry D. Hollis

*Petroleum*           Janet Rasmussen
                      succeeded
                      A. Jack Linder

This year also saw the formation of two new subcommittees: International Pharmaceutical and Foreign-Based Oil. In addition, after many years of work, the Aerospace Subcommittee elected to disband. The Construction Subcommittee will be regrouping under a new chairman following Steven Dobi's resignation after several years of making solid contributions. Also regrouping this year were the Motor Carrier and Savings Institutions subcommittees.

We also want to welcome Nancy Young to service on the Corporate Information Committee, and to acknowledge the dedication and hard work of three individuals who left the Committee this year: Peter Anker, Gerald White and William Williams.

## Committee Activities

The CIC held one business meeting with the subcommittee chairs and one luncheon meeting during 1992. There is a need for additional communication and if business pressures allow, this will be pursued next year. Fortunately, Ray DeAngelo, the head of the AIMR office in New York, has maintained considerable communication with each of the subcommittee chairs and along with his staff performs a crucial function in the performance of the CIC. We are pleased that new committees to review foreign-based oils and pharmaceuticals were launched in the 1991 review. We would like to see similar committees formed to cover foreign-based companies in other industries and would appreciate any suggestions or initiatives along these lines. In our next annual summary, we anticipate reviews of several Canadian industrial sectors.

Over the last twelve months the Chairman and Vice-Chairman of the CIC were invited to meet with the membership of the New York Chapter of the National Investor Relations Institute and a special subcommittee of the American Institute of Certified Public Accountants. Both organizations are obviously very interested in the work performed by the CIC and were thankful for the views and suggestions we made as representatives of the CIC. In the past, copies of the Corporate Information annual report were distributed solely to those who made an active contribution. For the first time, copies of the 1991-1992 report will be distributed to the complete membership of AIMR.

## Acknowledgments

Anyone reviewing this report would quickly recognize a vast amount of time and effort has been poured into its preparation and editing. We would like to recognize and give thanks to the many, many participants including members of the CIC, the subcommittee chairmen, and the numerous members of the industry subcommittees, all of whom are listed in this report. For those who are not listed, we express our thanks for another job well done. This would include Jelena Milinkovic of Rothschild Inc. who helped in the preparation and the New York AIMR staff, under the direction of Ray DeAngelo. Ray is backed up by the industrious Rosalie Poss who makes sure that all of the important work of AIMR is done on time.

Copies of this report will be sent to the executive officers of each of the companies reviewed. In many instances publication of this report follows conferences already held in the fall months with many of the companies as well as letters or telephone calls that have given managements opportunities to discuss subcommittee findings. The Committee's hope is that this report and the management discussions it helps foster will strengthen the dialogue without which strong shareholder/management relations cannot survive.

Rosario S. Ilacqua, CFA
Rothschild Inc.
Chairman, Corporate Information Committee

Thomas P. Moore, Jr., CFA
State Street Research & Management Co.
Vice-Chairman, Corporate Information Committee

## AWARDS FOR EXCELLENCE

| | |
|---|---|
| AIRLINE | AMR Corp. |
| APPAREL AND TEXTILES | |
|    Apparel | VF Corp. |
|    Textiles | Delta Woodside |
| BANKING | First Chicago Corporation |
| | Mellon Bank Corporation |
| CHEMICAL | Rohm and Haas Co. |
| COMPUTER AND ELECTRONICS | International Business Machines Corp. |
| CONTAINER & PACKAGING | Sonoco Products Co. |
| DIVERSIFIED COMPANIES | Harsco Corp. |
| FOOD, BEVERAGE & TOBACCO | PepsiCo, Inc. |
| | General Mills, Inc. |
| HEALTH CARE | Schering-Plough Corporation |
| INSURANCE | Capital Holding Corp. |
| MACHINERY | Dover Corporation |
| MEDIA | Knight-Ridder, Inc. |
| | Gannett Co., Inc. |
| NATURAL GAS | |
|    Distribution Companies | MCN Corporation |
|    Pipelines | Enron Corp. |
| NONFERROUS AND MINING | |
|    Nonferrous | Freeport-McMoRan Copper & Gold |
|    Precious Metals | Amax Gold Inc. |
|    Coal | Ashland Coal Inc. |
| PAPER AND FOREST PRODUCTS | Georgia-Pacific Corporation |
| PETROLEUM | |
|    International Oil Cos. | Mobil Corporation |
|    Domestic Integrated Oil Cos. | Atlantic Richfield Company |
| | Phillips Petroleum Company |
|    Independent Refining Cos. | Ashland Oil, Inc. |
|    Independent Oil & Gas Producers | Enron Oil & Gas Company |
|    Oil Service & Equipment Cos. | Baker Hughes Inc. |
|    Oil & Gas Contract Drilling Cos. | Global Marine, Inc. |
| | Rowan Companies |
| RAILROAD | Consolidated Rail Corporation |
| RETAIL TRADE | Toys "R" Us |
| | The Home Depot, Inc. |
| SOFTWARE/DATA SERVICES | First Financial Management Corp. |
| SPECIALTY CHEMICAL | The Dexter Corporation |

## LETTERS OF COMMENDATION

| | |
|---|---|
| DIVERSIFIED COMPANIES | Allied-Signal Inc. |
| FOOD, BEVERAGE & TOBACCO | UST Inc. |
| | Gerber Products Co. |
| PETROLEUM | |
|    International Oil Cos. | Exxon Corporation |
|    Domestic Integrated Oil Cos. | Occidental Petroleum Corp. |

# Airline

## Summary and Recommendation for Award

The Airline Subcommittee reviewed the corporate reporting practices of eight airlines, the same number as last year. America West, TWA and Continental, which are in Chapter 11 bankruptcy proceedings, were not reviewed, but may be next year pending successful reorganizations.

Although the average overall score dropped 13%, this was mainly due to significant drops by Alaska, British Airways and KLM. Furthermore, the dispersion between companies was greater this year making the rankings more meaningful. In the Annual Report category, the average score declined 10%. While companies, in general, provided better detail on their fleets, with most companies clearly breaking out owned versus leased aircraft, respondents again felt that more detail was needed in the breakdown of revenues and profits by division, particularly since many airlines now have significant overseas operations. The average score declined 15% in the quarterly reporting and other published material category and declined 14% in the analyst relations category.

The subcommittee recommended that the Award for Excellence in Corporate Reporting be awarded to AMR Corp. which scored a first in every category. Southwest, which ranked fourth last year, finished a close second and Delta, which led last year with AMR, finished third.

## Evaluation Procedures

The six members of the subcommittee each reviewed every company, with the exception of Alaska, KLM and USAir which were reviewed by five analysts. The same questionnaire was used this year as last, making the comparisons valid on a year-over-year basis. The questionnaire has three categories and several subcategories.

*Annual Reports* evaluations were based on: (a) the discussion of goals, strategy, and outlook; (b) the current fleet, orders, and capital commitments; (c) the detail of financial statements; and (d) historical data.

*Quarterly Reports* and *Other Published Material* were evaluated with regard to their timeliness, the detail of financial statements, and management comments.

In the *Investor Relations* category, the designated contact, other management meetings, conference calls, and access to senior management were evaluated.

In addition to quantitative ratings, subcommittee members provided extensive written qualitative comments.

A summary of ratings is provided in the table.

## Individual Company Comments

*Alaska* slipped from sixth last year to finish seventh overall. Along with KLM, the company had a 16 point drop in its overall score, the largest year-over-year drop this year. Alaska ranked seventh for its annual report, scoring poorly in the chairman's letter section. Again, while the historical review was thorough and informative, respondents felt that it did not deal enough with long-term issues and strategy. The company ranked sixth in the quarterly reports and other published material. This was largely due to the relatively small amount of other published material available. On the analyst relations front, Alaska also ranked sixth. Respondents had few criticisms other than that the company should be more "forthcoming" with current problems. Also, more meetings with management would be helpful.

*AMR*, first in every category this year and first overall last year, was universally praised as having the best all-around program: an excellent annual report, timely and complete quarterly reporting, and an investor relations program with full support of senior management. With regard to the annual report, suggestions were made that AMR should provide more detail on optioned aircraft. Another suggestion was to improve the amount of information on the non-airline subsidiaries which now generate over $350 million in quarterly revenue (as of 6/92), and to break out revenues and profits generated in Latin America and Europe. In the other published materials area, AMR's Eagle Eye analyst updates were greatly appreciated as were other mailings such as speeches and position papers.

*British Airways* scored sixth overall, down from third last year. In the annual report category, the company ranked sixth as well. The chairman's letter didn't adequately address issues facing the entire airline industry, such as access to capital, or the risks involved in European airline liberalization. Furthermore, a full ten years of historical data are needed for comparative purposes. The company ranked third, its best score, in the quarterly reports and other published materials category largely due to the factbook which was considered very helpful. On a positive note, British Airways does provide a thorough breakout of revenues and profits by division. In the analyst relations category, however, the designated contact scored seventh. Additionally, access to senior management was deemed too limited.

*Delta Air Lines* ranked third overall, slipping from its award-winning finish of the last two years. In the annual report category, Delta scored reasonably well, particularly with regard to the fleet, the detail of the financial statements and the historical data. In the quarterly reporting and other published materials category, Delta tied for second with Southwest. One suggestion was that Delta hold quarterly conference calls following earnings releases, and that traffic release break out European and Pacific operations. In the investor relations category, the designated contact scored high praise for being "knowledgeable," "helpful" and "frank." However, several respondents felt that senior management should be more visible and accessible.

*Southwest* scored second overall, up from fourth last year. The annual report was an excellent description of the company's strategy. One area for improvement is the fleet table, which should have provided a more complete breakdown of owned versus leased aircraft. The company lost some points in the area of other published materials, of which there are few. The designated contact scored the highest in the industry. However, an occasional conference call would be a nice addition.

*KLM* scored last in every category, retaining its last place finish from last year but by an even wider margin this year. The chairman's discussion section of the annual report was criticized for being too brief and not describing in sufficient details KLM's turnaround program. Additionally, the annual report was considered "poorly organized" and "hard to use." Quarterly reports lacked detail and were disseminated poorly. In the investor relations category, the effort in New York was considered not informed, particularly with respect to financial issues. Senior management is considered inaccessible.

*UAL Corp.* scored fourth overall, a small improvement over its fifth place finish last year. The annual report earned good marks in every category, and scored first in the historical data section. The company lost points in the other published materials section but did garner praise for the detail of its quarterly reports. In the analyst relations category, UAL scored fifth, the same as last year. The arrival of a new analyst contact, which occurred after the reporting period under review, was roundly welcomed in written comments. It was also suggested that more frequent access to senior management in the form of conference calls would be a good addition.

*USAir* ranked fifth, a significant improvement over its seventh place finish last year. The company lost some points in the area of detail in the financial statements. Also, the historical data in the annual report were not complete, particularly with regard to balance sheet items, and expense items, such as salaries and wages. Respondents also indicated that additional published materials, including more complete monthly traffic reports with domestic/international breakouts, would be useful. In the area of analyst relations, the company made significant progress, finishing fourth, up from seventh last year. The designated contact was cited as "most improved" and very "straightforward," and senior management's involvement was cited as a real plus.

## SUMMARY OF 1991 AIRLINE EVALUATIONS

| Maximum Points | Annual Reports & 10-Ks 40 | Rank | Quarterly & Other Published Material 30 | Rank | Investor Relations 30 | Rank | Total Points 1991 100 | Rank | 1990 Rank | 1989 Rank | 1988 Rank | 1987 Rank |
|---|---|---|---|---|---|---|---|---|---|---|---|---|
| Alaska Air Group, Inc. | 26.4 | 7 | 14.2 | 6 | 14.4 | 6 | 55.0 | 7 | 6 | 5 | 7 | 5 |
| AMR Corp. | 32.3 | 1 | 22.5 | 1 | 25.0 | 1 | 79.8 | 1 | 1 | 4 | 1 | 1 |
| British Airways PLC | 27.3 | 6 | 19.7 | 3 | 13.7 | 7 | 60.7 | 6 | 3 | 3 | 4 | — |
| Delta Air Lines, Inc. | 30.8 | 4 | 21.0 | 2T | 22.2 | 3 | 74.0 | 3 | 2 | 1 | 2 | 2 |
| Southwest Airlines Co. | 31.3 | 3 | 21.0 | 2T | 23.7 | 2 | 76.0 | 2 | 4 | 2 | 5 | 4 |
| KLM Royal Dutch Airlines | 22.2 | 8 | 9.8 | 7 | 7.8 | 8 | 39.8 | 8 | 8 | 9 | — | — |
| UAL Corp. | 31.7 | 2 | 16.0 | 5 | 17.0 | 5 | 64.7 | 4 | 5 | 11T | 3 | 3 |
| USAir Group, Inc. | 27.8 | 5 | 16.2 | 4 | 19.0 | 4 | 63.0 | 5 | 7 | 7 | 10 | 9 |

## AIRLINE SUBCOMMITTEE

Candace E. Browning, Chair, New York
Merrill Lynch & Company

Mark D. Ashton, CFA, Los Angeles
Capital Research and Management Co.

Paul P. Karos, New York
The First Boston Corporation

Helane Becker, New York
Shearson Lehman Brothers

Kevin Murphy, New York
Morgan Stanley & Co., Inc.

James M. Higgins, CFA, New York
The Bank of New York

Timothy Pettee, New York
Alliance Capital

# Apparel and Textiles

The Apparel and Textiles Subcommittee again recommended that awards be given in the two separate categories. The detailed ratings sheets included at the end of this report show that two companies below were ahead of the others surveyed in 1991.

| Apparel | Textiles |
| --- | --- |
| VF Corp. | Delta Woodside |

In Apparel, VF Corp. was again the leader, reflecting its excellent analyst communications, full sales and earnings divisional breakdowns in its reports, complete discussion of results in its quarterly reports, and in-depth information available on a day-to-day basis from management to analysts. Oxford again came in second, with special commendation for its quarterly letter to analysts. Close behind were Fruit of the Loom, Liz Claiborne and Phillips-Van Heusen.

In Textiles, Delta Woodside was the clear winner thanks to its detailed quarterly reports and conference calls. There is still considerable room for improvement in the textile and apparel industries for more detailed quarterly reports, as well as better financial relations. Many of the companies no longer offer 10-year histories. The absence of interim product line breakdowns again was cited as the area needing most improvement.

## Criteria For Companies Selected For Evaluation

The 18 companies selected for evaluation in the Apparel and Textile industry were rated on the basis of minimum standards set for company reports and the availability of management to analysts.

## Evaluation Procedures

Past suggestions of the committee and recommendations by the current members of the subcommittee were used in updating the scoring in the ratings sheets. Rating sheet scores were averaged.

## Comment

Most apparel and textile companies have been improving their overall financial relations programs over the years with better reporting in both annual and quarterly reports and more day-to-day availability of management to security analysts. For example, balance sheets have become standard for nearly all apparel and textile quarterly reports. On the other hand, any number of companies no longer provide segment sales. It is still hoped that these will be made available in the quarterly as well as annual reports.

## 1991 RANK (POINTS)

| APPAREL | TEXTILES |
| --- | --- |
| 1. VF Corp. (86) | 1. Delta Woodside (87) |
| 2. Oxford (78) | 2. Springs (76) |
| 3,4,5. Fruit of the Loom (70) | 3. Texfi (72) |
| 3,4,5. Liz Claiborne (70) | 4. Fieldcrest-Cannon (61) |
| 3,4,5. Phillips-Van Heusen (70) | 5. Guilford Mills (56) |
| 6,7,8. Kellwood (68) | 6. Unifi (53) |
| 6,7,8. Russell (68) | |
| 6,7,8. Tultex (68) | |
| 9. Leslie Fay (66) | |
| 10. Hartmarx (58) | |
| 11. Gitano (52) | |
| 12. Crystal Brands (48) | |

## SIX TEXTILE RATINGS FOR 1991 FISCAL YEAR

| | Maximum Scoring | DLW A | FLD B | GFD C | SMI D | TXF E | UFI F |
|---|---|---|---|---|---|---|---|
| **Annual and 10-K Reports (35)** | | | | | | | |
| • President's letter | 10 | 9 | 8 | 7 | 9 | 9 | 7 |
| • Product/geographic breakdown sales/earnings | 10 | 9 | 7 | 7 | 8 | 7 | 6 |
| • 10-year record | 5 | 2 | 2 | 2 | 2 | 2 | 5 |
| • Other (presentations, goals, footnotes, other financial information, etc.) | 10 | 8 | 8 | 7 | 9 | 8 | 7 |
| | 35 | 28 | 25 | 23 | 28 | 26 | 25 |
| **Quarterly and 10-Q Reports (15)** | | | | | | | |
| • President's letter | 10 | 9 | 7 | 7 | 8 | 8 | 6 |
| • Product/geographic breakdown sales/earnings, balance sheet and cash flow data | 5 | 5 | 4 | 1 | 3 | 3 | 2 |
| | 15 | 14 | 11 | 8 | 11 | 11 | 8 |
| **Financial Relations (50)** | | | | | | | |
| • Availability of management/analyst contact | 10 | 9 | 5 | 6 | 8 | 7 | 6 |
| • Depth of information communicated | 10 | 9 | 5 | 5 | 7 | 6 | 4 |
| • Meetings with analysts | 10 | 9 | 5 | 5 | 7 | 6 | 4 |
| • Timeliness & quality of press releases, conference calls, other | 20 | 18 | 10 | 9 | 15 | 16 | 6 |
| | 50 | 45 | 25 | 25 | 37 | 35 | 20 |
| Total | 100 | 87 | 61 | 56 | 76 | 72 | 53 |

A-Delta Woodside; B-Fieldcrest Cannon; C-Guilford Mills; D-Springs; E-Texfi; F-Unifi

## TWELVE APPAREL RATINGS FOR 1991 FISCAL YEAR

| | Maximum Scoring | CBR A | FTL B | GIT C | HMX D | KWD E | LES F | LIZ G | OXM H | PVH I | RML J | TTX K | VFC L |
|---|---|---|---|---|---|---|---|---|---|---|---|---|---|
| **Annual and 10-K Reports (35)** | | | | | | | | | | | | | |
| • President's letter | 10 | 5 | 7 | 7 | 8 | 8 | 8 | 8 | 8 | 8 | 7 | 7 | 9 |
| • Product/geographic breakdown sales/earnings | 10 | 2 | 7 | 5 | 6 | 7 | 7 | 8 | 8 | 7 | 7 | 7 | 9 |
| • 10-year record | 5 | 2 | 2 | 2 | 2 | 2 | 2 | 3 | 2 | 2 | 5 | 5 | 5 |
| • Other (presentations, goals, footnotes, other financial information, etc.) | 10 | 5 | 8 | 6 | 8 | 8 | 8 | 7 | 8 | 8 | 8 | 8 | 9 |
| | 35 | 14 | 24 | 20 | 24 | 25 | 25 | 26 | 26 | 25 | 27 | 27 | 32 |
| **Quarterly and 10-Q Reports (15)** | | | | | | | | | | | | | |
| • President's letter | 10 | 4 | 7 | 6 | 7 | 7 | 7 | 7 | 8 | 8 | 7 | 7 | 8 |
| • Product/geographic breakdown sales/earnings, balance sheet and cash flow data | 5 | 1 | 3 | 2 | 2 | 2 | 2 | 2 | 2 | 3 | 2 | 2 | 4 |
| | 15 | 5 | 10 | 8 | 9 | 9 | 9 | 9 | 10 | 11 | 9 | 9 | 12 |
| **Financial Relations (50)** | | | | | | | | | | | | | |
| • Availability of management/analyst contact | 10 | 1 | 7 | 6 | 3 | 4 | 5 | 8 | 9 | 9 | 8 | 8 | 9 |
| • Depth of information communicated | 10 | 1 | 7 | 5 | 7 | 8 | 6 | 6 | 9 | 9 | 7 | 6 | 8 |
| • Meetings with analysts | 10 | 1 | 8 | 6 | 5 | 7 | 7 | 7 | 6 | 5 | 5 | 5 | 8 |
| • Timeliness & quality of press releases, conference calls, other | 20 | 5 | 14 | 10 | 10 | 15 | 14 | 14 | 18 | 11 | 12 | 13 | 17 |
| | 50 | 8 | 36 | 27 | 25 | 34 | 32 | 35 | 42 | 34 | 32 | 32 | 42 |
| Total | 100 | 27 | 70 | 55 | 58 | 68 | 66 | 70 | 78 | 70 | 68 | 68 | 86 |

A-Crystal Brands; B-Fruit of the Loom; C-Gitano; D-Hartmarx; E-Kellwood; F-Leslie Fay; G-Liz Claiborne; H-Oxford; I-Phillips-Van Heusen; J-Russell; K-Tultex; L-VF Corp.

## APPAREL AND TEXTILES SUBCOMMITTEE

Jay J. Meltzer, CFA, Chair, New York
Goldman, Sachs & Co.

Deborah T. Bronston, CFA, New York
Prudential Securities, Inc.

Alan M. Silverman, CFA, New York
Ladenburg, Thalmann & Co., Inc.

Edward F. Johnson, New York
Johnson Redbook Service

Pamela Singleton, CFA, New York
Merrill Lynch

# Banking

## Recommendation for Award

The Banking Subcommittee reviewed the reporting and disclosure practices of the 75 largest publicly owned domestic bank holding companies. For 1991 reporting we have recommended that both First Chicago Corporation and Mellon Bank Corporation receive Awards for Excellence in Corporate Reporting. Each company was solidly in the first quintile in 1990, and each improved its performance in 1991. Each company stood out for segment reporting and enhanced disclosure of problem assets. Each company also provided complete details quarterly in a format consistent with its annual report.

## Summary

Bank reporting improved in 1991, with more companies (though still a *small* minority) adopting segment reporting, and further improvement in credit quality disclosure.

Segment reporting is critical to the evaluation of a company's franchises. The sum of the parts may be worth more than the whole company, but we'll never know unless major business lines or geographic segments are reported separately, with details of revenues, expenses, credit costs, and net income. A history and discussion of operating trends is necessary to the forecasting process.

The median score declined from 63.2% to 62.0%. However, the rating system was changed to allocate six points to enhanced disclosure of problem assets. Adjusted for this change, scores improved 2–3 points.

Very few companies adopted the regulators' recommended format for enhanced disclosure, but about half of the companies received some points for disclosing flows into and out of nonperforming status, accounting for cash received on nonperforming assets, and/or the carrying value of problem assets as a percent of the legal claim. Only one company, First Tennessee National, reports their internal risk ratings on their entire commercial loan portfolio. This practice provides an ideal early warning to investors, so that rises in nonperforming loans are less surprising.

Total scores of over 75% were achieved by First Chicago, Mellon Bank, Comerica, Signet Banking, First Union, First Tennessee Banking, Wells Fargo, SunTrust Banks, and First Interstate, a total of nine companies, up from only six last year.

## Changes for 1992

Reporting in 1992 presents some new challenges requiring revision of the rating system. Investor relations activity will be allocated only 15 points instead of 20. And as credit quality concerns subside, we will reallocate a few points to the new issues. Points will be allocated for the clarity of reporting the impact of FAS 106 (Retiree Health Care Benefits), FAS 109 (Deferred Taxes), and particularly FAS 107 (Fair Value Disclosure). Additional points will also be allocated to disclosure of the effect of interest rate changes and management of interest rate risk, including use of derivatives.

## Statistical Results

The survey was conducted by asking several analysts to evaluate each of the 75 companies in the survey. Scores were averaged for the final score, and reviewed for reasonableness. Because of the large number of companies reviewed, and the qualitative nature of some of the questions, the subcommittee would not recommend that these findings be used to determine compensation for investor relations professionals.

### First Quartile (85%–71%)

First Chicago
Mellon Bank
Comerica
Signet Banking
First Union
First Tennessee National
Wells Fargo
SunTrust Banks
First Interstate
Fleet Financial
Dominion Bankshares
Central Bancshares of the South
First Security
NationsBank
First of America
NBD Bancorp

Citicorp
Continental Bank
Meridian Bancorp

## Second Quartile (70%–62%)

Midlantic
First Bank System
National City
Bankers Trust New York
State Street Boston
Boatmen's Bancshares
Norwest
KeyCorp
Crestar
Mercantile Bancorp
PNC Financial
Riggs National
Bank of Boston
Shawmut National
Banc One
Michigan National
Firstar
Wachovia
Old Kent Financial

## Third Quartile (61.5%–53.5%)

UJB Financial
First Fidelity
Barnett Banks
BB&T Financial
Huntington Bancshares
BankAmerica
Republic New York
CoreStates Financial
Chase Manhattan
AmSouth
Mercantile Bankshares
First Alabama Bancshares
U.S. Bancorp
Hibernia
J.P. Morgan & Company
Society
West One Bancorp
MNC Financial
Chemical Banking

## Fourth Quartile

SouthTrust
Central Fidelity Banks
First Virginia Banks
Northern Trust

BayBanks
First Citizens BancShares
MBNA
Integra Financial
Bancorp Hawaii
First American Tennessee
First Empire State
Commerce Bancshares
BanPonce
Marshall and Ilsley
First Hawaiian
Bank of New York
Fifth Third Bancorp
Star Banc

## Findings By Section

### Annual Report (55 Points)

The average score this year was 63%, almost unchanged from last year. CEO letters and the strategic discussion and review sections at most companies still avoid clear statements of financial goals for which management should be held accountable.

Nearly 40% of companies received some points for line of business or geographical sector accounting, but the majority provided only minimal detail (e.g., net income only). This year ten companies, up from four last year, received more than half the points available. They were Citicorp, First Chicago, Fleet Financial, SunTrust Banks, Mellon Bank, First Bank System, Comerica, Signet Banking, Meridian, and First Security Corp.

The industry received 80% of the points available for credit quality reporting based on *prior* years' criteria, an excellent performance. However, the industry earned only 20% of the points for enhanced disclosure of problem assets in the first year these criteria were added to the scoring.

Interest rate risk and asset liability management were given a 5% weighting in 1991, but will be raised to 8–10% for 1992. The industry earned 70% of the points available for 1991. Given the dramatic improvements in net interest margins in 1992, and the complexity of the factors causing that increase, we will need to strive for more thorough and timely discussion of the impact of interest rate levels, interest rate spreads (e.g., prime vs. 6-month CD's), and off-balance sheet activities.

Capital and capital ratio disclosure is generally excellent, and non-interest revenue and expense reporting continues to improve.

Six companies received more than 80% of the points available for the annual report: Wells Fargo, First Chicago, First Union, Mellon Bank, Signet Banking, and Central Bancshares of the South.

### Quarterly Reporting (25 Points)

The average score in quarterly reporting was about 50%, down from 54% last year. The decline was due primarily to the assignment of 3 points to enhanced disclosure of problem asset flows and valuation.

Segment reporting is weaker in quarterly reports, but will likely improve as companies introduce segment reporting in an annual report, then follow up by including it in the next year's quarterlies.

Six companies received more than 75% of the points available, though none achieved more than 80%. They were Citicorp, First Chicago, SunTrust Banks, Mellon Bank, Continental Bank and Dominion Bankshares.

### Investor Relations

The average score for investor relations was 78%, up slightly from 76% a year ago. The following companies received scores of 90% or higher.

Chemical Banking
BankAmerica
NationsBank
Bankers Trust New York
First Interstate
First Union
Fleet Financial
PNC Financial
Norwest
Wachovia
Barnett Banks
NBD Bancorp
Mellon Bank
KeyCorp
First of America
Crestar Financial
Meridian Bancorp
Signet Banking
Central Bankshares of the South
MBNA

Once again, the subcommittee chairman greatly appreciates the help of all those listed below who served on this year's subcommittee.

## BANKING SUBCOMMITTEE

William J. Welsh, Chair, New York
J.P. Morgan Investment Management Inc.

Mark Alpert, CFA, New York
Alex. Brown & Sons, Inc.

Livia S. Asher, New York
Merrill Lynch Capital Markets

Frank J. Barkocy, New York
Advest, Inc.

Richmond S. Bates, CFA, New York
Metropolitan Life Insurance Co.

Carole Berger, New York
C.J. Lawrence, Morgan Grenfell, Inc.

Katherine H. Bissette, Atlanta
Sterne, Agee & Leach, Inc.

Nancy Avans Bush, CFA, New York
Brown Brothers Harriman & Co.

Matthew Byrnes, New York
Keefe Managers, Inc.

William Cohen, New York
Lord, Abbett & Co.

Sally Pope Davis, New York
Goldman, Sachs & Co.

Fred W. DeBussey, New York
Fitch Investors Service, Inc.

Marge DeMarrais, New York
Keefe Managers, Inc.

Henry C. Dickson, CFA, Chicago
Kemper Securities Group, Inc.

Joan Ellis, CFA, New York
U.S. Trust Co. of New York

Lawrence R. Fuller, Danbury
Benefit Capital Management Corp.

Felice M. Gelman, CFA, New York
Dillon Read & Co. Inc.

Diane B. Glossman, CFA, New York
Salomon Brothers Inc.

Mark Gross, New York
IBCA Inc.

James P. Hanbury, CFA, New York
Wertheim Schroder & Co. Inc.

Derek G. Hepworth, CFA, Minneapolis
Peregrine Capital Management, Inc.

Bruce T. Herring, CFA, Boston
Fidelity Management & Research Co.

Norman Jaffe, CFA, New York
Fox-Pitt, Kelton, Inc.

Norman Johnson, CFA, New York
Fitch Investors Service, Inc.

Chris Kotowski, New York
Oppenheimer & Co., Inc.

Michael Leit, New York
Bear, Stearns & Co. Inc.

Mark T. Lynch, CFA, New York
Lehman Brothers

Thomas D. McCandless, CFA, New York
Goldman, Sachs & Co.

Diane Meridian, Boston
Wellington Management Company

Michael A. Plodwick, New York
C.J. Lawrence, Morgan Grenfell, Inc.

Anthony Polini, St. Louis
A.G. Edwards & Sons, Inc.

Charles Rauch, New York
Standard & Poor's Corporation

James Rosenberg, New York
Lehman Brothers

Charles W. Rowe, Jr., CFA, Chicago
Sears Investment Management Co.

Mitchell C. Shafran, New York
Louis Nicoud & Associates

Dennis Shea, New York
Morgan Stanley & Co. Inc.

Jean I. Sievert, CFA, New York
Lehman Brothers

Harlan R. Sonderling, CFA, Boston
Putnam Management Co.

Cheryl A. Swaim, CFA, New York
Oppenheimer & Co. Inc.

Peter A. Taylor, New York
Scudder, Stevens & Clark, Inc.

Joseph M. Truta, CFA, Baltimore
The Adams Express Co.

Charles M. Vincent, Philadelphia
Provident National Bank

Andrew V. Vindigni, CFA, New York
General American Investors Co., Inc.

Lawrence R. Vitale, CFA, Chicago
Kemper Securities, Inc.

Andrew C. Whitelaw, CFA, San Francisco
RCM Capital Management

# Chemical

## Recommendation for Award

The Chemical Subcommittee recommended that Rohm & Haas receive an Award for Excellence in Corporate Reporting for 1991–92.

Rohm & Haas had the highest score. Its 88.6 total points were ahead of Monsanto's second place score (82.6) and Ethyl's (81.8). Olin Corporation had the lowest ranking in the survey, with 50.9 points.

## Criteria For Review

The subcommittee used a comprehensive questionnaire for this study. After two years' use of the initial document (1980 and 1981), a revised, more subjective questionnaire was developed in 1982. The questionnaire used in 1991–92 evaluations was an update of that revised document, which was designed by Theodore S. Semegran, CFA, of Shearson Lehman Brothers.

The 1991 review of 16 companies included large firms with chemicals as their major businesses as well as a number of large chemical conglomerates.

## Evaluation Criteria

Twenty analysts served on the subcommittee. Most of them evaluated two companies.

The evaluation criteria were divided into four major categories, which were assigned the following weights:

*45%-Annual Report*: Emphasis was on clear and useful breakout of sales and earnings and on segment reporting. Also critical was management's thorough discussion of corporate goals and review of operations. Selling price, volume, and mix data were also important elements.

*20%-Quarterly Reports*: Criteria were similar to those applied to the annual report, plus timely disclosure of relevant items.

*25%-Personal Contact*: Included a rating of the analyst contact(s), access to members of corporate management, and frequency of company meetings and trips.

*10%-Other Published Material*: Included non-solicited mailings of SEC material such as 10-Qs, 10-Ks, prospectuses, and proxies to security analysts. Mailings such as relevant company magazines, speeches by company officers, and the value of, or need for, a corporate fact book were also evaluated.

## Review Of Rating Results By Sector

A summary of the scores for each of the four sections in the questionnaire appears at the conclusion of this report. The annual report had the highest rating because it is the company's most important and most visible public document. The second most heavily weighted area was personal contact, since it is the most important source of information about the company after the annual report.

## Annual Report

Rohm & Haas achieved the highest score, while Monsanto was second. The major reasons firms did not score well in this category were that they omitted price/volume indices, useful segment data, meaningful discussion of company goals, and forecasts for the coming year. The subcommittee penalized companies that did not provide a table of contents if their annual reports had a considerable number of pages.

## Quarterly Reports

Usually the firms at the top of the annual report reviews also have excellent quarterlies. Rohm & Haas, Ethyl, and Monsanto were the highest ranked in this category. Detail and comparability between the annual and quarterly reports are keys to good scores. The inclusion of price and volume indices and detailed financial statements are also very important.

A number of firms received low scores because their quarterlies did not represent data comparable with that in their annual report. The omission of a cash flow statement also carried a penalty, as did the lack of a fourth quarter report.

## Other Material

Unsolicited mailings to chemical analysts of SEC documents such as 10-K's, 10-Q's, prospectuses, and proxies as well as company magazines and important press releases are becoming a more regular, welcome practice.

DuPont was rated first in this category followed by B.F. Goodrich and Lyondell.

## Personal Contact

No company received a perfect rating in this category; however, the overall scores were very high. This is a tribute to the investor relations departments and to the companies' senior management. Lyondell ranked first in this category followed closely by PPG Industries. A number of other companies also received high scores in this category, as companies have become more responsive to analysts' requests.

## Follow-Up Communications Program

The purpose of this review is to help corporate managements improve their financial communications. Copies of the results and a sample rating sheet are available to each company surveyed. In addition, each subcommittee member was given responsibility for answering requests for help in improving the company's overall communications programs from at least one firm.

### CHEMICAL INDUSTRY SECTOR EVALUATION AND SCORES-1991

| | Total | Annual Report | Quarterly Report | Other Material | Personal Contact | 1991 Rank | 1990 Rank | 1989 Rank | 1988 Rank | 1987 Rank |
|---|---|---|---|---|---|---|---|---|---|---|
| Rohm & Haas | 88.61 | 86.17 | 93.42 | 82.67 | 91.00 | 1 | 2 | 4 | 4 | 4 |
| Monsanto Company | 82.64 | 84.53 | 80.00 | 79.67 | 82.00 | 2 | 3 | 5 | 5 | 2 |
| Ethyl Corporation | 81.76 | 76.92 | 83.83 | 74.33 | 91.67 | 3 | 1 | 1 | 1 | 1 |
| DuPont | 81.74 | 78.50 | 74.67 | 90.33 | 90.33 | 4 | 4 | 2 | 2 | 5 |
| Lyondell Petrochemical Co. | 79.84 | 69.75 | 75.75 | 88.00 | 98.00 | 5 | 11 | NR | NR | NR |
| PPG Industries | 79.20 | 74.63 | 70.00 | 73.00 | 97.50 | 6 | 5 | 11 | 11 | 13 |
| Hercules Chemical | 77.20 | 75.50 | 78.75 | 68.50 | 82.50 | 7 | 9 | 3 | 3 | 11 |
| Imcera Corp. | 74.43 | 67.75 | 60.25 | 87.50 | 92.50 | 8 | 7 | 6 | 16 | 6 |
| B.F. Goodrich | 74.33 | 77.00 | 39.63 | 88.75 | 91.50 | 9 | 10 | 9 | 10 | NR |
| Dow Chemical | 67.85 | 63.10 | 61.25 | 49.50 | 89.00 | 10 | 6 | 10 | 10 | 8 |
| Georgia Gulf | 64.65 | 58.50 | 61.00 | 42.50 | 87.50 | 11 | 14 | 18 | 15 | NR |
| Imperial Chemical | 60.57 | 54.10 | 41.25 | 43.50 | 93.50 | 12 | 12 | 14 | 14 | NR |
| American Cyanamid | 58.93 | 57.75 | 45.25 | 67.00 | 67.50 | 13 | 16 | 13 | 9 | 10 |
| Quantum Chemical | 55.85 | 49.75 | 46.55 | 54.50 | 75.00 | 14 | 17 | 17 | 11 | 12 |
| Union Carbide | 51.80 | 45.53 | 37.75 | 52.50 | 58.00 | 15 | 8 | 8 | 7 | 8 |
| Olin Corporation | 50.90 | 52.33 | 66.50 | 60.00 | 32.50 | 16 | 13 | 16 | 6 | NR |

NR: No Report

# CHEMICAL SUBCOMMITTEE

Brian J. Corvese, Chair, New York
Chancellor Capital Management, Inc.

Leonard Bogner, New York
Prudential Securities

James T. Brown, CFA, New York
J.P. Morgan Investment Management, Inc.

Andrew Cash, New York
PaineWebber, Inc.

Jeff Cianci, New York
Bear, Stearns & Co., Inc.

Paul T. Lemming, CFA, New York
Kidder, Peabody & Co., Inc.

Charles LoCastro, New York
Donaldson, Lufkin & Jenrette, Inc.

Avi Nash, New York
Goldman, Sachs & Co.

Patricia O'Brien, New York
County NatWest Securities Corp.

Anantha K. S. Raman, New York
S.G. Warburg & Co., Inc.

Leslie C. Ravitz, CFA, New York
Morgan Stanley & Co., Inc.

Robert S. Reitzes, New York
C.J. Lawrence, Inc.

John Roberts, New York
Merrill Lynch Capital Markets

Andrea L. Schaefer, New York
UBS Securities Corporation

Theodore S. Semegran, CFA, New York
Shearson Lehman Brothers Inc.

Nick Spencer, New York
Sanford C. Bernstein & Co., Inc.

Harvey S. Stober, CFA, New York
Dean Witter Reynolds, Inc.

James H. Wilbur, New York
Smith Barney, Harris Upham & Co., Inc.

John R. Willard, New York
Salomon Brothers, Inc.

William R. Young, PhD, New York
Donaldson, Lufkin & Jenrette, Inc.

# Computer and Electronics

## Summary and Recommendation for Award

The Computer and Electronics Subcommittee continued its good work this year, as we added three new members and evaluated new companies in our industry. We added two new members from the institutional side and one from a brokerage firm. We also changed the group of companies we evaluated, dropping one company and adding one other. We again refined our criteria for evaluating the companies, with much more detailed emphasis on quarterly information, interim reporting, and the management of expectations. These factors are becoming even more important in the fast-changing industry we evaluate and in the uncertain economic environment we must deal with. We evaluated fifteen leading companies in our industry. After extensive preliminary screening and subsequent deliberation, we have chosen IBM to receive an Award for Excellence in Corporate Reporting.

### Overall Comments

The development we highlighted over the last several years continues: the emergence of electronic communication as a critical and timely way of communicating with investors. In our industry we are continually confronted with information, and the most critical part of this communication is the quarterly conference call. There have been continued improvements in these calls, so they often include prepared statements by management on the state of their business, selective polling of only those with questions, and improved dissemination of critical income statement and balance sheet information by the time of the call. The coordination of the call and the interim information is usually done by the investor relations group, and we continue to weight as the most important functions for our industry the job done by the investor relations staff and the quality of the quarterly and interim information they distribute. We should emphasize that both are important: good interim information on general business and product trends and solid quantifiable quarterly figures, or quite specific commentary, so that a model for the business can be maintained. Again, the excellent companies do both, but there is room for improvement among all of the companies we evaluated.

We mentioned our concern last year about the growing threat of litigation against many companies in our industry. This threat seems to be easing somewhat as some companies have fought and won lawsuits claiming deception. We continue to advocate a safe-harbor rule of acceptable disclosure practices. The two methods we prefer are as follows: Some companies establish a band of expectations, and as soon as it is apparent that the band will be broken, they will issue a press release and discuss the change. Other companies discuss interim results on a continual basis, so that any changes are communicated in a gradual way. We think these are the best ways to deal with interim changes. We do encourage companies to talk about interim results and not to impose a blackout period during which they will not even comment on results. This silence creates a period when rumors can be started and not denied, causing excessive volatility in the stock prices of these companies.

In our industry, results are volatile, with many companies making or missing their expectations in the last few weeks of the quarter. The "stop-go" economy and expectations have reinforced this psychology. If companies have discussed a positive trend and that trend changes, their stocks usually decline when that information becomes public. To help deal with these issues, we established several new evaluation categories for management candor. What we are advocating is that it is part of management's job to manage expectations so they do not get overly enthusiastic and unrealistic. We understand that it is easy to stand back and enjoy the enthusiasm and increase in expectations that often follow good results in this industry, but we feel strongly that a responsible management and investor relations program will try hard to anchor future estimates to their view of reality. Therefore, we added a category for "Candidness of Investor Relations," with criteria such as presenting a realistic outlook; mentioning potential negatives as well as potential positives; and guiding expectation both up and down. We also added similar categories in the annual and quarterly disclosure practices. We think that companies will lessen the volatility of their stocks, increase their credibility, and enable themselves to rebound from adversity faster if they follow these guidelines.

### Summary of Results

The general evaluation scheme and ratings we chose are: annual report and 10-K, 30 percent; quarterly reports, press releases, conference calls, 10-Qs and other interim information, 30 percent; other publications, 5 percent; and the investor relations effort, 35 percent.

The individual ratings of the different companies are summarized in the table at the end of this report. We nominated IBM for the award because it was good in all categories, but particularly improved in its annual report and investor relations. This is a company that talked extensively with members of the committee in a genuine effort to improve its communications and disclosure policies. During a difficult period for the company, it increased its disclosure, held more frequent and informative meetings about its operations, and was painfully candid about its prospects. We certainly commend this company and its management and investor relations people. We also encourage all companies in this industry to contact members of this committee at any time for guidance or suggestions on how they might improve their programs and policies.

## Company Comments

In these cases, we have tried to indicate what each company did well in the past year and where there is room for improvement in its reporting and investor communication efforts. It is indeed interesting that almost every company has an attribute that could benefit its peers. (The following section is in alphabetical order.)

*Amdahl*: Overall, we felt Amdahl did the following things well:

- Senior management readily available for in-depth discussions.
- Good discussion of pricing trends in annual report.
- Revenue breakout is good—could use quarterly.
- Sending analysts packets of articles is helpful.

The areas where we think there can be improvement are:

- Conference call is weeks after earnings announcement. Should have more balance sheet and product revenue detail when announcing earnings.
- Would like to see engineering change reserves disclosed quarterly.
- Guidance tends to be optimistic.

*AMP*: Overall, we felt AMP did the following things well:

- Great summary discussion of costs and prices by geography.
- Great summary of currency effects on sales.
- 10-year statistics page.
- Forecast of earnings with assumptions by geographic markets.

The areas where we think there can be improvement are:

- Currency effect on earnings.
- Breakout by customer.
- Size of market served, share of those markets.

*Apple Computer*: Overall, we felt Apple Computer did the following things well:

- Distributes electronic information well.
- Conference calls informative.
- Meetings helpful.

The areas where we think there can be improvement are:

- Visit with investors more often individually.
- Top management availability at company.
- Need more segment data.
- Need to be a lot more specific on breakdowns and financial data.

*Compaq Computer Corporation*: Overall, we felt Compaq did the following things well:

- Good disclosure of currency, hedging policy, etc.
- Excellent analyst meetings with industry data and commentary.
- Product announcements with analysts invited.

The areas where we think there can be improvement are:

- Annual report really needs work—tables and presentation could be much better.
- You really have to search to find some relevant information such as employees, costs and there is little commentary about future spending plans.
- Although much of the data is available, you really have to work to isolate the magnitude of the factors affecting EPS changes. Why not make it easier with a summary paragraph detailing prices, currency, units, mix and the effects on earnings.
- Better disclosure of product lines/divisional data.

- Need to reestablish Investor Relations credibility and image.

What has this company done to improve its past practices:

- We're very impressed that during its austerity period, the company has continued to hold analyst meetings and product announcements to which the financial community is invited.
- Also, despite the lawsuits against it, the company has been quick to issue press releases which help manage expectations.
- The company appears to be moving to more disclosure about its different business lines.

*Cray*: Overall, we felt Cray did the following things well:

- CEO and/or President and CFO always on conference call.
- Always updates forecast guidance on call.
- When outlook changes, quick to signal and use conference call.

The areas where we think there can be improvement are:

- Long quiet period translates to protracted periods of stale information and absence from industry conferences.

*Digital Equipment*: Overall, we felt Digital Equipment did the following things well:

- Very open.
- Good conference calls.
- Management accessible.
- Several meetings.

The areas where we think there can be improvement are:

- Product segment data needs improvement.
- Currency analysis breakdown.
- Improved accuracy in sales forecasts (overly optimistic).
- Disclosure on tracking product segment data.

*Hewlett-Packard*: Overall, we felt Hewlett-Packard did the following things well:

- Product segment breakout.
- Balance sheet reporting.
- Quarterly reports.
- Biannual analysts meeting.

The areas where we think there can be improvement are:

- Quarterly cost of revenue.
- Accessibility of senior management.

What has this company done to improve its past practices (optional comment)?

- Split computers into segment categories.

*IBM*: Overall, we felt IBM did the following things well:

- When there is a material event or change in outlook, a conference call is done immediately to disseminate the information.
- Meetings to discuss business units are excellent. More financial data are available and senior executives are accessible.
- Guidance has been handled well—accurate and timely.
- Company discussion of industry trends and IBM's position has improved markedly.
- Disclosure of business unit financial results for Federal Systems and ICC was helpful and we look forward to seeing more units detailed.

The areas where we think there can be improvement are:

- Full income statement and balance sheet at time of earnings announcement would be helpful.
- IBM's presentations at technology conferences sometimes bland.
- Would like IBM to go back to disclosure of currency impact.

What has this company done to improve its past practices?

- IBM has worked hard over the past five years to improve its investors relations program and it shows. The company is more frank and open. It is readily discussing industry trends. The number of analyst meetings has been increased. IBM is one of the most improved companies.

*Intel*: Overall, we felt Intel did the following things well:

- Well organized, well run conference calls.
- Good exposure at conferences.
- Willing to discuss tone of business during quarter.

The areas where we think there can be improvement are:

- More product segment breakdown needed.
- Should put out more informational press releases.
- No earnings guidance given.

*Motorola*: Overall, we felt Motorola did the following things well:

- Very detailed quarterly earnings releases.
- Releases news regularly.
- Willing to act on suggestions for improving investor relations.

The areas where we think there can be improvement are:

- Earnings information by division would be helpful on quarterly basis.
- No earnings guidance provided.

What has this company done to improve its past practices (optional comment)?

- Too many items to detail. Vast improvement over past two years.

*Stratus Computers*: Overall, we felt Stratus Computers did the following things well:

- Excellent breakout of channel sales.
- Up-front, detailed guidance given on conference call following earnings release.
- Timely informative releases (i.e., product updates, contract awards).

The areas where we think there can be improvement are:

- More "road show" opportunities with top management.

*SUN Microsystems*: Overall, we felt SUN did the following things well:

- Communicate its mission/strategy clearly.

The areas where we think there can be improvement are:

- Little detail of product line breakdown, and details regarding maintenance, software.

What has this company done to improve its past practices (optional comment)?

- The company's investor relations effort regressed during FY 1991. For the bulk of the year the company was reluctant to discuss current business conditions and refused to discuss business outlook.

*Tandem*: Overall, we felt Tandem did the following things well:

- Revenue by product line breakdowns.
- More detail on bookings by product line and by geography.
- More commentary on revenue performance vs. plan.
- Improved information flow during quarter.

The areas where we think there can be improvement are:

- No product sector breakdowns.
- No profitability by product.
- No breakdown of division/unit performance.

*Texas Instruments Incorporated*: Overall, we felt Texas Instruments did the following things well:

- Annual meeting which adjourns two times for discussions with top management and board members.

The areas where we think there can be improvement are:

- Management only accessible if you visit them; should try to visit investors.
- Not tolerant of cautionary views, too optimistic.
- Need disclosure program dealing with divestitures.

*Xerox*: Overall, we felt Xerox did the following things well:

- Proactive in visiting existing/potential investors.
- CEO gives his "state of the company" view at conference call after Q4 release.
- Very detailed rundown of analytics at time of quarterly releases/full data available immediately.
- Excruciatingly detailed footnotes in annual report.

The areas where we think there can be improvement are:

- Open up more fully on trends/influences in financial services.

- Top management (CEO) could be more visible re state of business throughout year.

What has this company done to improve its past practices?

- Took our suggestion to work through analytical presentation of document processing cash flows.
- Initiated quarterly conference call.
- Expanded analytical data in quarterly release.
- Very quick to release and fax out info on corporate developments both good and bad.

## COMPUTER AND ELECTRONICS EVALUATION SUMMARY

| Company | Annual Report and 10-K | Quarterly Reports | Other Publications | Investor Relations |
|---|---|---|---|---|
| Amdahl | Above Average | Below Average | Average | Average |
| AMP | Above Average | Average | Average | Above Average |
| Apple Computer | Below Average | Average | Average | Above Average |
| Compaq Computer | Below Average | Average | Average | Below Average |
| Cray Research | Above Average | Above Average | Average | Above Average |
| Digital Equipment | Below Average | Below Average | Average | Above Average |
| Hewlett-Packard | Above Average | Above Average | Average | Average |
| IBM | Above Average | Average | Average | Above Average |
| Intel | Average | Below Average | Average | Average |
| Motorola | Average | Average | Below Average | Average |
| Stratus Computer | Above Average | Above Average | Average | Average |
| SUN Micro Systems | Above Average | Average | Average | Below Average |
| Tandem Computer | Average | Below Average | Average | Average |
| Texas Instruments | Average | Below Average | Below Average | Below Average |
| Xerox | Average | Average | Average | Above Average |

## COMPUTER AND ELECTRONICS SUBCOMMITTEE

Walter C. Price, Jr., CFA, Chair, San Francisco
RCM Capital Management

Tim Allen, Los Angeles
Bank of America

Paul E. Haagensen, CFA, Boston
The Putnam Companies

Steven M. Milunovich, CFA, New York
Morgan Stanley & Co., Inc.

Mark A. Morris, Los Angeles
Trust Company of the West

Jay P. Stevens, CFA, New York
Dean Witter Reynolds, Inc.

Stephen R. Weber, CFA, Boston
Cowen & Company

Don Young, New York
Shearson Lehman Brothers

# Container & Packaging

## Recommendation for Award

Sonoco Products Company earned the #1 slot for the 3rd year in a row. Except for the quarterly review, the company received the best scores in all of the categories for the companies we evaluated. The layout of the annual report was not only easy to read but informative; the data were where one would expect to find it. The company had an informative President's Letter, a detailed profit/loss statement and a segmented breakout for both sales and operating profits. What's more, one analyst indicated that Sonoco's annual analyst and shareholders meeting made it a pleasure to follow the company. Given the above performance, we believe that Sonoco should be given an Award for Excellence for notable efforts towards effective communication to its shareholders in the financial community.

Although it was a close race, Bemis beat out Sealed Air for the #2 spot. Bemis's informative annual report and breakout of sales and profits by operating segments were a big hit with analysts. The only criticism of Bemis is that it did not provide industry trends and the company has been reluctant to discuss problems.

## Objectives and Suggestions

For the fourth consecutive year, this subcommittee has attempted to provide feedback to packaging companies on the strengths and weaknesses of their corporate information programs. Our objective is to get the companies to clearly communicate their corporate strategies, the factors that affected their operations and their financial results. We encourage these companies to provide more information on price, cost and volume trends, segment/division operating data, analysis of year-to-year changes in earnings per share and fourth quarter results. Complete information and financials are essential for making good investment decisions.

## Evaluation Procedures

Each of the 11 companies in this packaging/containers universe was evaluated by at least three of our team of seven analysts. The annual report carried the heaviest weighting, accounting for 45% of total points. The remaining score was divided among Quarterly Reports (20%), Investor Relations Effort (25%) and Other Publications (10%). The criteria for evaluation, unchanged from last year, included the following:

*Annual Report*: Reviewed for thoroughness and clarity in presentation. The Chief Executive's letter was expected to discuss the year's highlights, both positive and negative, and the company's objectives. Detailed operating and divisional data and a ten-year financial history were emphasized.

*Quarterly Reports*: Evaluated for commentary on operating results and segmented operating data. Benchmarks included a detailed income statement, balance sheet and cash flow data.

*Investor Relations Effort*: Focused on a well-informed analyst contact, the availability of senior officers, periodic analyst presentations and the timeliness of information dissemination.

*Other Publications*: Included 10-Qs, 10-Ks, prospectuses, proxies, company factbook and other relevant material. Emphasis was placed on unsolicited mailings of pertinent information.

## Company Comments

*Ball Corporation*: The Company was cited for its quality Investor Relations program, professionally orchestrated analysts meetings, regular field trips, and opportunities to meet top management and visit plants. Analysts note, however, that Ball Corporation falls short on providing a segmented breakdown of sales and operating income on a quarterly basis. In addition, the Company has significantly reorganized its various business units to the detriment of a clear historical perspective.

*Bemis Company, Inc.*: By a narrow margin, Bemis, once again, captured the #2 position based on its excellent annual and quarterly reports. In addition, the company gets high marks for the segmented reporting of its line of businesses and its exceptional cash flow statement. Improvement in Bemis's overall ranking would require a more thorough discussion of future goals in the Chief Executive's Letter, a ten-year financial summary and inclusion of price, cost and volume indices.

*Constar International, Inc.*: The Interview With Management portion of the annual report was innovative, informative and provided unique and in-depth insight into the operations of this packaging company. A shortfall in Constar's reporting practices includes lack of summarized quarterly reports and minimal industry data. However, we carry on our praise of the candid discussion in the Chief Executive's letter in the annual report. The annual was well structured and contained adequate statistical data.

*Crown Cork and Seal Co., Inc.*: In spite of receiving the lowest score in our survey, Crown has exhibited the most dramatic improvement of the 11 companies that we critique. Current management has been more responsive and forthcoming in providing in-depth financial data and more access to key decision makers. We look forward to further information from Crown including analysis of its worldwide markets and more discussion of its various domestic packaging businesses.

*Engraph*: Engraph's annual report was particularly helpful in providing an informative "financial highlights" page, a comprehensive eleven-year financial summary, and a very complete statement of cash flow. The company also received high marks for stating its financial objectives, its investor relations effort, and its colorful graphics portraying the company's exceptional printing capability. The annual report could be improved by expanding the Chairman's Letter to cover important topics more thoroughly and by including more detail in the notes to the financial statements and the segment information.

*Heekin Can, Inc.*: The Company fell from fifth to tenth place in our overall rankings. It is possible that Heekin's poor financial showing in 1991 contributed to its less than stellar performance. The failure to sufficiently address reasons for the earnings shortfall provided little guidance toward future results, precipitating Heekin's receiving low marks. One analyst quipped that, as results deteriorated, his contact became more difficult to reach.

*Owens-Illinois*: Owens-Illinois was not a public company for most of 1991, hence its score does not reflect the true measure of its corporate information program. Its annual report was noted for well-documented segment data, while the company's investor relations "team" effort scored high for accessibility and information flow. Overall, Owens-Illinois's rating is sure to climb in the 1992 poll.

*Sealed Air Corporation*: Sealed Air rose from ninth to third position. A change in discussion from a single theme to a focus on the company's basic businesses was a major contributor to its overall improvement. The company's strategy of growth through technology is interesting and serves to highlight its packaging capabilities. However, the company's "high-tech" charts were unnecessarily complex and confusing.

*Sealright Co., Inc.*: For the third year in a row Sealright scored in the lower quartile of the survey. The absence of a discussion of company goals, corporate philosophy and a detailed plan for the future contributed to Sealright's lackluster performance. Also, the failure to provide a ten-year financial history and segmented sales and earnings by division was highlighted by several analysts.

*Van Dorn Company*: Although financial reporting efforts were improved last year, Van Dorn failed to better its seventh place ranking. The Chairman's Letter was a commendable attempt at communicating the company's financial goals and operating philosophies. Reviewers also gave the company high marks for its eleven-year historical review and detailed sales and earnings breakdown by division. The downside was management's inability to achieve its overly optimistic profit forecast.

## 1991 CONTAINER & PACKAGING EVALUATION

| Company | Annual | Quarterly | Other | Investor Relations | Total | Weighted Total | 1991 Rank | 1990 Rank | 1989 Rank | 1988 Rank |
|---|---|---|---|---|---|---|---|---|---|---|
| Sonoco Products Company | 83.8 | 57.5 | 10.0 | 23.0 | 174.3 | 82.2 | 1 | 1 | 1 | 3 |
| Bemis Company, Inc. | 67.8 | 64.9 | 8.0 | 19.9 | 160.6 | 71.4 | 2 | 2 | 6 | 1 |
| Sealed Air Corporation | 57.6 | 68.0 | 8.3 | 22.9 | 156.8 | 70.8 | 3 | 9 | 8 | 2 |
| Ball Corporation | 61.1 | 53.3 | 9.0 | 22.3 | 145.7 | 69.5 | 4 | 4 | 4 | 8 |
| Constar International Inc. | 63.3 | 61.3 | 6.0 | 20.2 | 150.8 | 66.9 | 5 | 6 | 3 | 5 |
| Owens-Illinois | 62.9 | 54.7 | 7.6 | 19.9 | 145.1 | 66.7 | 6 | NA | NA | NA |
| Van Dorn Company | 65.7 | 40.7 | 7.3 | 15.0 | 128.7 | 60.0 | 7 | 7 | 10 | 6 |
| Engraph | 52.9 | 56.7 | 6.8 | 16.7 | 133.1 | 58.6 | 8 | 3 | 5 | NA |
| Sealright Co., Inc. | 49.9 | 48.9 | 7.5 | 18.3 | 124.6 | 58.0 | 9 | 8 | 7 | 7 |
| Heekin Can, Inc. | 52.8 | 46.0 | 7.3 | 12.8 | 118.9 | 53.1 | 10 | 5 | 2 | 9 |
| Crown Cork & Seal Co. Inc. | 47.6 | 38.5 | 5.5 | 18.0 | 109.6 | 52.6 | 11 | 10 | 9 | 10 |

## CONTAINER AND PACKAGING SUBCOMMITTEE

Cornelius W. Thornton, Chair, New York
Goldman, Sachs & Co.

Robert J. Bishop, New York
Tiger Management

Stephen C. Orr, CFA, Boston
State Street Research & Management Co.

Timothy P. Burns, Cleveland
The First Boston Corporation

Richard S. Palm, CFA, New York
Merrill Lynch

Jerry Melin, New York
Rothschild, Inc.

Tom Sprague, Boston
Fidelity Management & Research Co.

# Diversified Companies

## Recommendation for Award

The Diversified Companies Subcommittee unanimously agreed that the Award for Excellence in Corporate Reporting should be given to *Harsco Corporation* this year. The subcommittee also unanimously agreed that a Letter of Commendation should be sent to Allied-Signal, Inc.

Although *HSC* by no means ran away from the pack on a purely mathematical basis, it did achieve the highest score overall and was ranked first, second, or third in ten of the fourteen categories the Diversified Subcommittee rates. This impressive performance included four gold medal performances in categories that related to *HSC's* annual report.

*ALD* was the hands down winner in the "most improved" category, as it vaulted eight places in the overall results this year. Its efforts were ranked third or better in eight of the fourteen categories graded.

## General Comments

The Diversified Companies Subcommittee's universe contracted to 12 companies this year with the deletion of Eastman Kodak. The subcommittee roster also shrank by one member.

## Methodology

All five subcommittee members graded each company on a 1–100 basis in the first nine categories shown in the table at the conclusion of this report. Each company's average score, which was defined as total score divided by five evaluators, was multiplied by a weighting factor assigned to each category. (The weighting factor appears as "category weighting" on the accompanying table.) Because analyst coverage in the diversified companies "industry" is not as homogeneous as it is in other industries, the subcommittee averaged the scores in the last five categories by the number of evaluators who felt familiar enough with the companies to grade them. The average weighted points were totaled for each company's final score.

## Individual Comments

Every year since its reconstitution in 1988, the subcommittee has devoted a paragraph of good news/bad news to each company, but this year the subcommittee decided to take Bing Crosby's advice in the 1944 film, "Here Come the Waves," and just "Accentuate the positive..." Therefore, we have remodeled this section of our report and have commented here not on a company-by-company, paragraph-by-paragraph, good news/bad news basis but rather on a ratings category-by-ratings category basis. Although a few companies dominate our report with this approach, they deserve to! We hope that where it is appropriate the other companies examined by the subcommittee in this report follow the leads of these companies. And, quite frankly, the subcommittee is weary of saying the same negative things (even in a polite way) year after year about companies in our universe. Lastly, anyone interested just in statistics should turn to the final page of our report, a compilation the subcommittee views as secondary in importance to the lessons that may be learned from our commentary on the best performances within each category.

## Financial Highlights (2%)

This is a minor category whose importance is greater than its weighting. When one opens an annual report, one expects to see financial highlights much the same as a prospective car buyer, upon lifting the hood, expects to see an engine. *HSC*, *MMM*, and *ALD* displayed V-8 highlights: a lot of them, all of them relevant, in easy to read formats.

## Chairman's Letter (8%)

The subcommittee looked for candor and details and found both elements in *HSC's* and *ALD's* presentations. *HSC's* letter was particularly notable for its complete "Outlook" section, *ALD's* for the detail provided about their restructuring, and *MMM's* for its traditional honesty in dealing with success or failure to achieve corporate goals. (P.S. *MMM* usually achieves them, and they aren't lay-ups.)

## Officers and Directors (4%)

If you're going into the hospital, you want to know who's going to operate on you. Similarly, shareholders and analysts want to know who operates the companies they own or follow and who represents the shareholders. Kudos to *HSC* for providing brief biographies of directors (including ages and years of service) and a listing of officers and division presidents (also with ages and years of service). *MMM* listed only years of service for directors and corporate officers, but this was more information than the rest of the mastheads of the diversified companies provided. *TXT* was also noted for its listing of divisions, their addresses, and their presidents.

### Statement of Corporate Goals (6%)

*MMM* continued to shine in this category. They are, in a phrase, to the point. Year after year, *ALD* was not far behind. Neither was afraid to use the "g" word ("goals").

### Discussion of Segment Operations (9%)

The subcommittee was unanimous in citing *HSC* for its well-written, interesting, and complete discussions of its segments and operating divisions within those segments.

### Financial Summary/Footnotes (12%)

You can't beat *MMM*'s 11-year financial summary, although *HSC*'s and *ALD*'s presentations of historical data were also first-rate. The subcommittee also wished to cite *HSC*'s footnotes for their completeness and clarity.

### 10-Ks, 10-Qs, Other Required Information (4%)

The dispersion here was minimal. Congratulations to all companies for jobs well done.

### Quarterly Reports (20%)

This is, pretty unarguably, the most important category, not because it carries the most weight but because analysts expect complete reporting here. Our collective hat is off to *TXT*, which, for the second year in a row provided a model quarterly report. *TRW*, a perennial heavyweight in this category, did not disappoint either. And as proved typical this year, anytime the watchwords were "completeness in reporting," *HSC* and *ALD* were not far behind in the rankings. What made these four fine efforts stand out were their inclusions of the big three financial statements (income statement, balance sheet, and cash flow statement), segment results, and commentary. *HSC* even provided information about operating divisions within segments in their quarterlies. (The subcommittee asked itself more than once in reviewing other companies' quarterly reports: What is so difficult about including the basic financial statements? Is it we who "don't get it" or is it the companies? If banged up heads and walls on our part indicate anything—we've been prodding, arguing, and haranguing for full disclosure for years—then it's the companies who still haven't got it.)

### Other Published Information (10%)

*TRW*'s "Data Book" garnered top honors again (although one nitpicker on the subcommittee wished that *TRW* had carried its calculations to at least one decimal point). We welcomed *ALD*'s effort in this area, really enjoyed *TXT*'s "Textron in Print" (a cut, pasted, and photocopied compendium of articles about the company mailed monthly), and liked *ITT*'s factbook as well. *DL* received very favorable comments on its readable and attractive "Dial at a Glance" and for its watchable and interesting video. We hope that other companies will take the data book lead of *TRW*, *ALD*, and *ITT*, and that other companies might consider publishing something akin to *TXT*'s "Textron in Print."

### Designated Contact (2%)

In this category we looked for the name and address of I/R contacts in the annual report. If they appeared, credit was given. If they didn't, (less) credit was given anyway because their names appeared on S&P tear sheets.

### Investor Relations Staff (12%)

*TXT* and *TRW* maintained their top on the heap, A-#1 positions with solid performances. Also singled out for high praise were the staffs at *ALD*, *MMM*, and *ROK*.

### Presentations (5%)

The subcommittee thought that, at a minimum, companies should either host quarterly meetings or have quarterly conference calls. *ROK* and *DL* leaped into the limelight here with *ROK* garnering top honors for their sincere and diligent efforts to bring operational managers before analysts every quarter. *MMM* was cited for their travelling quarterly meetings/conference call combos, as was *HSC* for their regular appearances before analysts. *ITT* also continued its tradition of excellent quarterly meetings. Additionally, the subcommittee wished to commend *MMM* and *ITT* for providing transcripts of their quarterly meetings and *TRW* for a transcript of its annual meeting for analysts.

## Field Trips (5%)

The top ranked *DL* annual field trip remained top ranked. ("Aren't you glad you follow Dial?" the jingle could be rewritten.) *HSC* has taken advantage of its far-flung empire and taken analysts from soup to nuts (5-ton trucks to metal reclamation), and *TRW* did another great job last spring at its annual meeting for analysts.

## Annual Meeting (1%)

There was little dispersion of results here.

## Summary Comments

All diversified companies should provide the following information in their publications efforts:

1. *A statement of corporate goals.* (See 3M's annual report, page 3 and Allied-Signal's annual report, page 2.)

2. *A fact book.* (Write to TRW, if you want a model.)

3. *A "Textron in Print" for your company.*

4. *Ages and length of service of directors and executive officers.* (See Harsco's annual report, pages 52 and 54.)

5. *More complete financial highlights.* (Just open the Harsco, 3M, and Allied-Signal annuals.)

6. *A ten-year financial summary.* (See 3M's annual report, page 48.)

7. *Transcripts of question and answer periods at meetings, particularly meetings for financial analysts.*

8. *Detailed breakdowns of segment operations in quarterly shareholder reports.* (See Textron's, Harsco's, and TRW's quarterlies. These reports are superb and deserve to be emulated by any company.)

The subcommittee also wished to note that next year it plans to look at the proxy statements of the companies in the Diversified Companies universe. Full and understandable disclosure will be the standard for successful reporting here.

**DIVERSIFIED COMPANIES SUBCOMMITTEE**

Anthony M. Maramarco, CFA, Chair, Springfield
Massachusetts Mutual Life Insurance Company

Eric B. Anderson, CFA, Hartford
Shawmut National Corp.

John L. Kelly, CFA, New York
Goldman, Sachs & Co.

John A. Modzelewski, CFA, New York
PaineWebber, Inc.

David S. Moore, New York
Donaldson, Lufkin & Jenrette

## DIVERSIFIED COMPANIES 1991

| | Category Weighting | ALD | DL | FIGI | HSC | ITT | MMM | PC | ROK | TDY | TXT | TRW | TYC |
|---|---|---|---|---|---|---|---|---|---|---|---|---|---|
| **ANNUAL & REQUIRED PUBLISHED INFORMATION** | | | | | | | | | | | | | |
| Annual Report | | | | | | | | | | | | | |
| 1. Financial Highlights | 2% | 1.76 (2) | 1.66 (4) | 1.54 (8) | 1.84 (1) | 1.56 (6) | 1.76 (2) | 1.56 (6) | 1.50 (10) | 1.35 (12) | 1.58 (5) | 1.51 (9) | 1.42 (11) |
| 2. President's Letter/Review | 8% | 6.96 (2) | 6.64 (4) | 6.24 (9) | 7.12 (1) | 6.48 (6) | 6.93 (3) | 6.24 (9) | 6.56 (5) | 5.50 (12) | 6.32 (8) | 6.40 (7) | 6.08 (11) |
| 3. Officers and Directors | 4% | 3.42 (5) | 3.35 (8) | 3.30 (10) | 3.65 (1) | 3.40 (6) | 3.55 (2) | 3.35 (8) | 3.50 (4) | 3.00 (12) | 3.55 (2) | 3.40 (6) | 3.20 (11) |
| 4. Corporate Goals | 6% | 5.30 (2) | 4.58 (7) | 4.28 (11) | 5.28 (3) | 4.73 (6) | 5.78 (1) | 4.35 (10) | 4.58 (7) | 4.05 (12) | 4.80 (5) | 5.10 (4) | 4.50 (9) |
| 5. Discussion of Divisions | 9% | 7.70 (3) | 7.74 (2) | 6.21 (12) | 8.10 (1) | 7.38 (7) | 7.47 (4) | 7.47 (4) | 7.38 (7) | 6.86 (11) | 7.47 (4) | 6.93 (10) | 7.11 (9) |
| 6. Financial Summary/Footnotes | 12% | 10.56 (3) | 9.72 (7) | 8.76 (12) | 10.68 (2) | 9.48 (8) | 10.92 (1) | 9.48 (6) | 9.96 (6) | 9.45 (10) | 10.08 (5) | 10.20 (4) | 9.00 (11) |
| 7. 10-Ks, 10-Qs, Other Required Info. | 4% | 3.48 (6) | 3.52 (2) | 3.40 (7) | 3.52 (2) | 3.40 (7) | 3.50 (5) | 3.32 (12) | 3.40 (7) | 3.35 (11) | 3.56 (1) | 3.52 (2) | 3.40 (7) |
| **QUARTERLY & OTHER PUBLISHED INFORMATION NOT REQUIRED** | | | | | | | | | | | | | |
| 8. Quarterly Reports | 20% | 17.40 (4) | 15.20 (9) | 15.00 (10) | 17.80 (3) | 15.80 (6) | 17.32 (5) | 14.72 (11) | 15.80 (6) | 15.50 (8) | 18.48 (1) | 18.20 (2) | 14.40 (12) |
| 9. Other Published Information | 10% | 9.48 (3) | 9.40 (5) | 7.88 (12) | 8.80 (6) | 9.44 (4) | 8.70 (7) | 8.50 (9) | 8.38 (10) | 8.63 (8) | 9.50 (2) | 9.64 (1) | 8.13 (11) |
| **OTHER ASPECTS** | | | | | | | | | | | | | |
| 10. Designated Contact | 2% | 1.83 (4) | 1.90 (3) | 1.65 (11) | 1.82 (6) | 1.78 (8) | 1.93 (2) | 1.70 (10) | 1.80 (7) | 1.58 (12) | 1.94 (1) | 1.83 (4) | 1.73 (9) |
| 11. Investor Relations Staff | 12% | 10.89 (3) | 10.60 (7) | 10.00 (10) | 10.65 (6) | 10.20 (8) | 10.71 (4) | 10.00 (10) | 10.71 (4) | 8.60 (12) | 11.60 (1) | 11.04 (2) | 10.20 (8) |
| 12. Presentations | 5% | 4.16 (6) | 4.33 (2) | 3.50 (12) | 4.31 (3) | 3.92 (8) | 4.31 (3) | 3.67 (11) | 4.56 (1) | 3.75 (10) | 4.08 (7) | 4.25 (5) | 3.92 (8) |
| 13. Field Trips | 5% | 3.58 (7) | 4.70 (1) | 3.33 (8) | 4.38 (2) | 3.33 (8) | 4.13 (4) | 3.08 (12) | 4.13 (4) | 3.17 (11) | 3.92 (6) | 4.38 (2) | 3.33 (8) |
| 14. Annual Meeting | 1% | 0.75 (1) | 0.73 (2) | 0.70 (8) | 0.70 (8) | 0.68 (10) | 0.68 (10) | 0.67 (12) | 0.72 (6) | 0.73 (2) | 0.73 (2) | 0.72 (6) | 0.73 (2) |
| | 100% | 87.28 | 84.07 | 75.78 | 88.65 | 81.58 | 87.67 | 78.11 | 82.96 | 75.51 | 87.61 | 87.11 | 77.14 |
| **OVERALL 1991 RANK** | | 4 | 6 | 11 | 1 | 8 | 2 | 9 | 7 | 12 | 3 | 5 | 10 |
| **OVERALL 1990 RANK** | | 12 | 7 | 11 | 4 | 6 | 3 | 9 | 8 | 13 | 2 | 1 | 10 |
| **OVERALL 1989 RANK** | | 7 | 5 | 9 | — | 4 | 2 | 8 | 6 | 11 | 10 | 1 | — |
| **OVERALL 1988 RANK** | | 6 | 3 | 10 | — | 7 | 4 | 8 | 5 | 11 | 9 | 2 | — |
| **OVERALL 1987 RANK** | | 6 | | | | 7 | 5 | | 3 | 8 | | 4 | |

ALD-Allied-Signal; DL-Dial Corp; FIGI-Figgie International; HSC-Harsco Corp; ITT-ITT Corp; MMM-Minnesota Mining; PC-Penn Central; ROK-Rockwell International; TDY-Teledyne; TXT-Textron; TRW-TRW Inc; TYC-Tyco Laboratories Inc.

# Electrical Equipment

## Recommendation

The Electrical Equipment subcommittee has set high standards for its award and none of the companies rated here met them. We would note that two companies, Honeywell and Cooper, came close to meeting the requirements in each segment while General Electric exceeded them in two but continues to fall short in quarterly segment reporting.

We'd make one final note. This is the first year for Honeywell in this category. It is also the first time in the last twenty years that a newcomer ranked at the top of its peer class. The subcommittee would like to urge both Honeywell and Cooper to continue their fine efforts in investor reporting as we believe they are both close to achieving an Award for Excellence which has not been recommended by this group for many years.

## Evaluation Procedures and Criteria

This subcommittee wants to thank Paul Blaustein for all of his years of diligent effort on this group. In his place, we would like to welcome Julie Bowman of Ohio State Teachers and David Altman of Goldman Sachs. It was with their effort that we could maintain our fine coverage of the appliance manufacturers as well as to introduce two new companies for subcommittee rating.

After several years in which there was little change in the rating format, this subcommittee undertook a complete review of each of the questions. Because of the broad corporate diversity in the group, questions had gotten wordy and unclear. Changes in the Annual Report and Interim Release sections were made. In some sectors questions that had incorporated several different criteria were separated, while in others where the subject matter was essentially the same (such as in the case of 5/10 year reporting), the questions were consolidated. In doing so, the subcommittee found that it was necessary to slightly alter the segment point count. We'd note on detail, that a question related to proxy material was added but the committee's strong stance on quarterly segment reporting was maintained. Thus, this latter question, (1 of 37), still accounted for 9% of all the rating points. Listed below is the breakout of the three segments in this report:

|  | 1991 | 1990 | 1989 |
|---|---|---|---|
| Annual Report | 41 | 40 | 40 |
| Interim Releases | 29 | 30 | 30 |
| Programs directed to professional investors | 30 | 30 | 30 |

The committee was totally satisfied with its questions on Section III (programs directed to professional investors). It was the thought of several, in fact, that this section was the most important of the three; cooler heads prevailed however, since many investors do not have access to this source and so in a more balanced sense, the information imparted in the Annual and Interim Release format was considered of greater importance in that it reaches a much broader investor audience.

## General Comments

On the negative side, quarterly segment reporting continues to be uneven. We'd note here again that Cooper, General Signal and Honeywell do an especially fine job in this matter. A recent line of business breakout by Magne Tek, whom we hope to include next year, is the best we've ever seen in this industry. The latter was done for the year but is an extraordinary model of clarity in the performance of that company's major business units. Verbal breakouts of line-of-business reporting are improving all the time and we will make another effort to get GE to report quarterly segment information; if it does, we believe all the remainder will fall in line. On a positive note here, we'd reiterate that GE scored highest on its Annual Report format as its Chairman's message is consistently the strongest in the industry. Its investor relations effort is even better as three separate subcommittee members accorded this company 30-of-30 points.

We've made a point of requesting our subcommittee members to give a brief highlight review of the companies they rated. While not all members participated we thought we would try and synopsize some of their comments:

> Baldor: Could do more to flesh out their annual and quarterly report presentations. Direct contact with top management and meeting attendance excellent.

> Cooper: Provides a comprehensive array of

written material including an excellent statistical supplement. Investor relations work very good but could use more access to business operators.

Emerson: Chairman's presentation in annual report the last several years has been excellent but would like to read more specifics about remaining industrial operations. Quarterly report segment presentation poor but analyst meetings on major topics especially good.

General Electric: Does it all well in the annual report and professional investor segments. Written quarterly briefs on group performance is a right step, now need the numbers with the words. Occasional meetings with business operators a highlight.

General Signal: Provides comprehensive financial information as well as excellent detail of individual units. Would like to see a fourth quarter report.

W.W. Grainger: Direct investor relations contact has improved considerably. Company still has a long way to go in terms of providing meaningful investment information as well as management access and attending public investor presentations; one held by the company could help bridge that gap.

Honeywell: A fine all around job; needs a little more familiarity with the subcommittee and industry members.

Maytag: Top job with annual report and fact book. Little information relative to specific appliance brands and greater analyst contact desired.

Reliance Electric: Good beginning investor information program. Needs more seasoning among subcommittee members and investors and could do a better job in breaking out information of its industrial group (quarterly & annuals).

Westinghouse: Excellent 10-Q disclosures and praised for early release of orders and earnings. Major shortfall in results tends to distort other comments.

Whirlpool: Seems to do an average all around job. Would like more individual business unit information particularly on finance subsidiary. Consistent, steady improvement in information flow.

Zenith: Company's annual report given high marks but interim releases a weak point, with good solid results provided in their professional investor program.

As a final point the subcommittee members would like to see much more industry information including size, prospects, major drivers and market share.

## Communications

The subcommittee chairman plans to send the appropriate amount of copies of the 1991–1992 Corporate Information Committee report to each member. It will be their responsibility to send out, with an accompanying letter for subsequent discussion, copies to the companies they rated.

## ELECTRICAL EQUIPMENT INDUSTRY—1991

| Company | Annual Report | Interim Releases | Mgmt/Anly Relations | 1991 Total | 1990 Total | 1989 Total | 1988 Total | 1987 Total |
|---|---|---|---|---|---|---|---|---|
| Honeywell Inc. | 36.0 | 25.7 | 27.0 | 88.7 | — | — | — | — |
| General Electric | 37.0 | 20.3 | 30.0 | 87.3 | 88.4 | 83.9 | 85.3 | 83.7 |
| Cooper Industries | 37.0 | 23.7 | 26.3 | 87.0 | 83.0 | 82.5 | 77.3 | 79.7 |
| Maytag | 34.7 | 22.3 | 24.6 | 81.6 | 80.2 | 80.4 | 83.1 | 78.6 |
| General Signal | 33.3 | 22.5 | 25.5 | 81.3 | 78.8 | 76.4 | 78.3 | 77.5 |
| Zenith | 36.0 | 19.0 | 24.5 | 79.5 | 75.0 | 77.1 | 71.3 | 75.7 |
| Whirlpool | 35.3 | 20.0 | 22.7 | 78.0 | 83.7 | 86.2 | 82.8 | 83.3 |
| Baldor Electric | 32.0 | 19.7 | 26.0 | 77.7 | 72.6 | — | — | — |
| Reliance Electric Co. | 31.7 | 17.7 | 26.3 | 75.7 | — | — | — | — |
| Emerson Electric | 30.7 | 15.3 | 26.7 | 72.7 | 70.0 | 78.3 | 80.0 | 75.2 |
| Westinghouse | 27.0 | 19.0 | 21.0 | 67.0 | 78.0 | 79.5 | 83.0 | 77.0 |
| W. W. Grainger | 29.7 | 19.7 | 16.3 | 65.7 | 67.1 | 64.8 | 62.3 | 70.7 |

## ELECTRICAL EQUIPMENT SUBCOMMITTEE

Stanley L. Rubin, CFA, Chair, New York
Merrill Lynch & Company

David A. Altman, CFA, New York
Goldman, Sachs & Co.

Julie Bowman, CFA, Columbus
The State Teachers Retirement
System of Ohio

Mark Hassenberg, New York
Donaldson, Lufkin & Jenrette

James G. King, CFA, Boston
Pioneering Management Corp.

Gary A. Langbaum, CFA, Chicago
Kemper Financial Services, Inc.

Russell L. Leavitt, New York
Salomon Brothers, Inc.

Robert Sharpe, New York
Capital Research Company

Samuel A. Yee, CFA, Chicago
The First National Bank of Chicago

# Environmental Control

## Overview

The Environmental Control Subcommittee included an expanded number of companies in the 1991 survey of corporate reporting practices. Reflecting the increased number of sectors and diversity of companies in the group, we included twenty-seven in this year's evaluation compared to twenty-one on last year's survey. Of import, the companies, in general, continued to make progress in meeting most of the verbal information needs of the investment community. However, in noting continued areas where improvement is needed, the subcommittee focused on financial statement disclosure as the accounting practices of some of the waste services companies have been questioned in the last year. Nevertheless, the direction of the last year was a positive one in movement towards more accessibility of investor/management contacts, which allowed for improved qualitative input from the members of the subcommittee.

As the environmental services industry has continued to evolve over the past year, the many changes taking place within the context of a difficult external economy led to greater responsiveness to analysts by many of the management's in the group. To provide an enhanced perspective on the efforts, the subcommittee included several buy-side analysts to round out the traditional sell-side views. Even with the continued underperformance by the broad group of stocks, the commentary reflected progress in addressing the verbal aspects of a corporate reporting program, which has become increasingly important in gaining an understanding of the near and long-term dynamics facing the environmental services companies. To reflect this fact, the subcommittee adjusted the format of the 1991 survey to account for what we believe should be the greater emphasis placed on the investor relations/management contact area of a company's communication efforts. In other areas, following the release of 1991 annual reports, many companies have shown progress thus far in some of the financial reporting/accounting areas which have received a substantial amount of attention during 1992. More segment information and accounting openness has been evident this year, but it does not appear these efforts will be fully appreciated by the subcommittee until the 1992 annual reports are released and the resulting survey is compiled next year. This came to light particularly given the subsequent Chambers Development situation which has caused a reevaluation of all companies' accounting practices.

## Evaluation Categories

With the changes in the group over the past two years, the subcommittee thought that a change in the evaluation categories would provide a more accurate assessment of the 1991 corporate communications efforts undertaken by the waste services firms. This year's survey sections and weightings were as follows:

(1) Investor relations/management contact now receives the highest weighting from the subcommittee reflecting the increased importance of this interaction as opposed to the traditional annual report information and other printed material. The five categories totaling 45 points covered accessibility and responsiveness of company contacts and managements.

(2) Quality of annual report, including both the narrative and financial sections, held a total of 30 points contained within seven questions. This category held less prominence in the survey than in previous years as the subcommittee has found most of the material contained in the annual has become relatively standardized, except for the occasional new glimpses a company may give at disclosing segment operating results or in terms of management discussion and analysis.

(3) Other printed material comprised the final category of this year's evaluation. This included questions related to 10-Qs, 10-Ks, and other company materials. The weighting was 25 points covered in four questions.

(4) Additional qualitative comments were included for a swing factor in which plus or minus up to five points were allocated for companies either showing exemplary or disappointing performance in any particular survey area.

## Survey Results

In the end, the subcommittee survey results showed a very tightly packed field with three companies tied for first place. Given the deadlock between Waste Management, Chemical Waste Management and Browning-Ferris, the subcommittee will not recommend a company receive this year's Award for Excellence in Corporate Reporting in the hope that all the companies strive for continued improvement in their overall programs to deliver information to the investment community in a timely and accurate manner.

## Company Comments

Waste Management was again at the top of the list, along with Chemical Waste Management, which tied its parent company. But the most visible changes in the results of the 1991 survey were the impressive rebound of Browning-Ferris into a tie for the highest score (after falling to thirteenth in last year's survey), and the dramatic fall of Chambers Development, which given its lack of 1991 audited financial results due to an accounting change, made it difficult for the subcommittee members to complete much of the evaluation.

With three evaluations needed to be included in the survey, only one additional company was ranked in this year's results despite the fact that there were six more companies on the overall list. The exclusion of seven companies from the rankings showed the narrowing list of companies being focused on at this time by the members of the subcommittee as the investment environment for the industry continues to remain difficult. In this year's survey, fourteen of the twenty ranked companies received 70% of the total possible points or better. In terms of improvements, of the companies included and ranked in last year's survey seven had higher scores, while nine had lower averages.

*Waste Management*, despite not being recommended for the Award for Excellence, still received the highest ranking from the subcommittee. In response to the scrutiny of accounting procedures in the waste services industry during 1992, the company has begun to provide further financial disclosure, which although not covered in the 1991 survey, received positive commentary from the subcommittee members. The company's recently commenced quarterly conference calls for the parent and subsidiary companies' earnings releases also has gained mention. The company's presentations and availability received commendation as reflected in its top average score in the investor relations/management contact segment of the survey.

*Chemical Waste Management's* investor relations program also received the highest average marks. With the start of its quarterly conference calls in 1992 and the continued accessibility of the company's contact with the investment community, the subcommittee recognized the corporate reporting practices as tied for first place overall. The company's management commentary in its annual report also received positive mention from the subcommittee. Some members expressed the desire to meet new members of the senior management team, which was accomplished at the company's 1992 analysts meeting and should be reflected positively in next year's survey.

*Browning-Ferris* made significant improvement following last year's survey in which the subcommittee believed the stock's difficult performance, rather than a diminished corporate reporting effort, led to the lower ranking. The sharp improvement into a first place tie for 1991, in the subcommittee's opinion, was a culmination of the more than dozen-year effort put forth by the company's recently departed director of investor relations. These results were highlighted in the company's highest average ranking in the investor relations/management contact portion of the 1991 survey as the responsiveness and insight of Browning-Ferris' investment contact was unmatched. The company-sponsored analyst meeting, its first in several years, was cited as very helpful in gaining a more complete understanding of the company. Several members also mentioned the improved context and detail in presentations to analysts. The subcommittee looks forward to a continuing positive relationship with the investment community from the company's new contact, as has been the case for more than the past dozen years.

*Clean Harbors* moved up dramatically into a fourth place tie from its position at the bottom of last year's survey rankings. The increased weighting of the communications aspect in this year's survey helped the company as the subcommittee recognized the accessibility of both the investor relations contact as well as members of senior management. Commentary from the annual report and the company's annual analysts meeting also showed up as qualitative positives.

*Mid-American Waste*, in its first year in the survey, tied for fourth place. The company's responsiveness to the investment community was noted by the subcommittee as well as the candid commentary on investment-relevant issues. The first-year results, which came from five respondents, were impressive as the company has been public for less than three years.

Overall, the subcommittee feels this year's survey more accurately reflects the relative importance of the communications efforts by the waste services companies in meeting the needs of the investment community in the rapidly-changing environmental services industry. Although a great deal of attention in the group has been paid to accounting issues in the last year, many of the company's are today responding by providing further disclosure and discussion.

The subcommittee was somewhat disappointed with the large number of companies not evaluated by the requisite three members to receive rankings in this year's survey, but suspect that this will change should the group come more into favor with investors over the next year.

## Communication with Companies and Subcommittee Members

The subcommittee plans to send a copy of this report to each of the companies reviewed and to make itself available to discuss the evaluation procedures.

### 1991 ENVIRONMENTAL CONTROL SUMMARY EVALUATION TABLE

| 1991 Rank | Company | No. of Responses | Score Range | Average Score | 1990 | 1989 | 1988 | 1987 |
|---|---|---|---|---|---|---|---|---|
| 1T | Browning-Ferris Industries | 9 | 99–68 | 82 | 13 | 3 | 3 | 2 |
| 1T | Chemical Waste Management | 9 | 100–72 | 82 | 3T | 2 | 2 | 3 |
| 1T | Waste Management | 9 | 100–64 | 82 | 1 | 1 | 1 | 1 |
| 4T | Clean Harbors | 3 | 81–69 | 76 | 20 | NR | NR | NR |
| 4T | Mid-American Waste Systems, Inc. | 5 | 98–60 | 76 | — | — | — | — |
| 6 | International Technology Corp. | 3 | 77–74 | 75 | 7 | 11 | 10 | 10 |
| 7 | TRC Companies | 4 | 82–72 | 73 | 2 | 9 | 7 | 8 |
| 8 | EMCON Associates | 3 | 75–70 | 72 | 5 | NR | — | — |
| 9T | The Brand Companies, Inc. | 5 | 78–65 | 71 | — | — | — | — |
| 9T | Environmental Elements Corporation | 3 | 76–66 | 71 | — | — | — | — |
| 9T | Harding Associates | 4 | 72–68 | 71 | 9T | 7T | — | — |
| 12T | Laidlaw Industries | 6 | 74–50 | 70 | 19 | 4 | 4 | — |
| 12T | Rollins Environmental Services | 8 | 82–61 | 70 | 15 | 14 | 15 | 11 |
| 12T | Wheelabrator Technology | 6 | 100–52 | 70 | 16 | 12 | — | — |
| 15T | Attwoods plc | 4 | 70–60 | 67 | 9T | NR | 14 | NR |
| 15T | Sanifill, Inc. | 3 | 79–57 | 67 | — | — | — | — |
| 17 | Groundwater Technology | 4 | 72–52 | 66 | 8 | 5T | 5 | NR |
| 18 | Roy F. Weston | 3 | 68–51 | 60 | 17 | 16 | 9 | 5 |
| 19 | Western Waste Industries | 3 | 59–53 | 55 | 9T | NR | NR | NR |
| 20 | Chambers Development | 9 | 66–21 | 36 | 3T | 7T | 8 | 7 |
| | NR Companies | | | | | | | |
| | Air & Water Technologies Corp. | | | | NR | NR | | |
| | Canonie Environmental | | | | 9T | 10 | | |
| | Geraghty & Miller | | | | 6 | 5T | | |
| | Horsehead Resource Development Co. Inc. | | | | NR | NR | | |
| | ICF International, Inc. | | | | NR | NR | | |
| | OHM Corporation | | | | 14 | 13 | | |
| | Ogden Projects | | | | NR | NR | | |

Note: Scores have been rounded to the nearest whole number.
NR No rank because less than three analysts evaluated the company.
T Tie
— Not included in evaluation.

## ENVIRONMENTAL CONTROL SUBCOMMITTEE

Marc H. Sulam, Chair, New York
Kidder, Peabody & Company Inc.

William J. Genco, New York
Merrill Lynch

Tracy Hamill, New York
J.P. Morgan & Co., Inc.

Elaine A. Kassanos, CFA,
San Francisco
RCM Capital Management

Jim McDonald, Chicago
The Chicago Corporation

Stephen L. Schweich, Baltimore
Alex. Brown & Sons, Inc.

Brian Stansky, Baltimore
T. Rowe Price Associates

Vishnu Swarup, New York
Prudential Securities, Inc.

Leone Young, New York
Smith Barney, Harris Upham & Co.

# Financial Services

### 1991–92 Results

The Diversified Financial Services Subcommittee reviewed the corporate reporting practices of thirteen companies, with the addition of one company, Alliance Capital, and with two companies, Federal National Mortgage Association and Student Loan Marketing Association, transferred to the thrift & mortgage markets subcommittee. The Subcommittee included twenty-one members, an increase of five from last year. The scoring process again was based on a standardized scoresheet, which was slightly modified this year to add emphasis to foreign operations, segment reporting, and supplemental financial data.

Again this year, no company scored in the 90th percentile, although two companies, T. Rowe Price and Household International, tied for first place for the second year. Similarly, Transamerica and Primerica tied for second place, a very close second place at that, and also for the second year in a row. PaineWebber and Alliance Capital L.P. tied for third place.

The Subcommittee is disappointed that no company has met the criteria for excellence in reporting, although we are pleased to find that many companies have shown significant improvement in their reporting practices. Furthermore, companies are increasingly seeking our perspective on their reporting practices. We also realize that financial services is an emerging industry with few fixed reference points for reporting, and that we are all seeking an appropriate, cost-effective forum for companies to better communicate their results to the investment community.

Overall, the average percentile score fell modestly to 74.0% in this year's survey from 77.2% last year. The bulk of the decline was due to disappointment with the discussions of the results of operations, particularly related to the balance sheet (scores declined from an average of 74.5% to an average of 68.6%) and off-balance sheet factors (scores declined from an average of 74.4% to 68.7%). In view of general market concerns about leverage, and financial companies' generally high leverage, it is perhaps not surprising that analysts are scrutinizing these areas more closely. In addition, average scores declined for miscellaneous published information (to 81.8% from 88.7%), largely due to a slightly higher weighting for published financial supplements.

While the average score on supplemental financial data increased to 81.4% from 74.5%, a trend that the Subcommittee is happy to see, this score is still below the average for quarterly reporting, the other major component of this section.

### Trends in Reporting Practices

Five companies showed increases in their average scores this year: PaineWebber, Merrill Lynch, Morgan Stanley, Salomon Brothers and Dreyfus. Significant improvement in management accessibility and the investor relations effort was the common theme in the results of all of these companies, while the first three companies showed improvement in some fashion on most sections of the survey. Seven companies showed deteriorating scores, although some portion of the deterioration can be traced to the modest changes in weightings on foreign operations, segment reporting and the financial supplement. Nonetheless, Subcommittee members were generally much tougher in scoring the management discussion and analysis sections, which explains another substantial portion of the decline in scores.

### Criteria for Inclusion and Methodology

The thirteen companies' reporting practices were evaluated using size, general investment interest, capitalization and float as requirements for inclusion. One company was added to the survey (Alliance Capital, L.P.), and two companies were transferred to another subcommittee (Fannie Mae and Sallie Mae).

Each company was reviewed by at least three analysts using a standardized scoresheet incorporating basic required information as well as specific industry-related criteria. The points assigned by reviewers were added to generate a raw score for each category, which was then converted into standardized percentage scores. The scoring was adjusted this year to emphasize foreign operations, segment reporting and supplemental financial data.

Due to the diversified nature of the industry, several sections of the scoresheet, such as foreign operations or segment reporting, do not apply to all companies. As a result, the raw scores are not meaningful. The percentile rankings, using the standardized percentage scores, were used for the committee's final assessment.

## General Comments by Scoresheet Sections

Overall, scores were generally down in most categories, with the exceptions being the Chairman's letter and segment reporting, where scores were flat to last year's Survey. The following comments are general observations of the Subcommittee, while the results of this year's survey and the historical trend in scores are shown on separate tables.

*Part I. Management Integrity.* While reviewers took note of the Salomon Brothers Treasury affair, it has been determined that the current management should not be penalized for the former management's deeds with regard to the Treasury auction issue. Indeed, several reviewers noted that Salomon went to extra lengths in their annual report to try to explain what went wrong and the steps that had been taken to rectify the situation.

Also, a few reviewers expressed concern about certain companies where top management had apparently been misled by lower-level management about important business situations. We do not believe that it is appropriate at this time to cite these situations in this report, although we are concerned about the seeming lack of controls in those financial businesses. These situations raise the issue of senior management's real knowledge of the problem situations and their willingness to disclose those issues to the owners of any company, the shareholders. This is a thorny issue that is of grave concern to all analysts and shareholders.

*Part II. Letters to Shareholders* would be more meaningful with more precise discussion of factors that affected the current year's results, as well as more emphasis on the critical variables that could affect the upcoming year. Only one company, T. Rowe Price, scored in the 90th percentile. Nearly every company showed weakness in describing the upcoming year's outlook within the context of the business and economic environment.

*Part III. Results of Operations* declined to the 72nd percentile from the 81st percentile last year. No company scored above 90%. Managements' discussions of the balance sheet, especially off-balance sheet factors, remained the downfall of most companies. In view of the many negative earnings surprises that have been emanating from excesses in lending and related businesses, as well as ongoing concerns about the emerging markets for swaps and derivatives, reviewers are more critical of disclosure in this area.

In addition, many analysts would find more data concerning investments in technology, acquisition or other business expansions to be quite useful.

*Part IV. Segment Reporting* showed a modest decline to the 74th percentile from the 76th percentile last year. No company scored above 90%. While half of the companies with segments scored over 90% on required basic information on each segment (revenues, net income and total assets), only Household International scored over 80% on disclosing key *details* on each segment, such as loan losses and reserves for lending businesses. Furthermore, many companies provide a confusing medley of information, with the discussion of key businesses sometimes bearing little relationship to reported data.

Two companies were cited for inconsistencies between the verbal descriptions of their key business segments and their financial disclosure of those segments. Securities brokerage firms are particularly guilty in this respect. These firms will often emphasize their asset management operations in the text but provide very little or no data to support that discussion. In addition, some companies are deemed by reviewers to have segments one year, but those segments seem to disappear the next year. It would appear that such companies might benefit from a more consistent presentation.

In general, companies with wide-ranging financial operations that publish statistical supplements tend to show better results in this category. Supplements give companies more discretion than SEC reporting requirements to address each business line within the context of its related industry. For example, many companies will provide surprisingly complete income statements, balance sheets and associated data (such as problem loans for lending operations or combined ratio details for property-casualty insurance operations) in their financial supplements.

*Part V. Foreign Operations* disclosure showed a modest decline to the 57th percentile from the 61st percentile. The highest rank achieved by any company on this section was Alliance Capital. Three of eight companies deemed to have significant foreign operations scored below the 50th percentile, compared to two of seven companies last year. Modestly rising scores on disclosure regarding foreign taxes were offset by modest deterioration in the general discussion of the financial impact of foreign operations, while discussions regarding the impact of currency fluctuations remained flat to last year.

One new question was added to this section this year concerning the products and services that companies offer overseas and their general impact on the companies' results. The average score on this question was in the 52nd percentile, suggesting that companies in the financial services industry generally disclose very little to shareholders about the nature and impact of their overseas business. In an increasingly global world, such disclosure might be helpful to shareholders in assessing potential investments.

*Part VI. Quarterly Reports & Other Published Information* showed modest deterioration to the 82nd percentile from the 89th percentile. Merrill Lynch and Transamerica scored over 90% on this section. It appears that about half of this decline can be traced to a modest increase in the weight given to supplemental reporting, where scores have tended to average below the scores on quarterly reporting.

Nonetheless, the subcommittee is pleased to note that scores on financial supplements rose to the 81st percentile from the 75th percentile last year, and reviewers generally expressed a lively appreciation for such reporting. Seven companies were acknowledged as providing supplements, an increase of one from last year.

*Part VII. Other Aspects of Corporate Reporting*, which includes basic information on officers and directors as well as management accessibility and investor relations efforts continued to show an improving trend. In particular, scores for management accessibility rose to the 88th percentile from the 81st percentile last year, a meaningful and welcome increase. Surprisingly few companies include the key responsibilities of senior management along with their titles.

## Company Comments

*Alliance Capital, L.P. (AC)* appearing for the first time in this year's survey, achieved a slightly higher than average score at 75.8%. Overall, reviewers found the Chairman's letter to be excellent, even though the discussion of the outlook for the coming year was considered to be overly optimistic and short on substance. The discussion concerning foreign operations achieved the best score in the group, possibly because Alliance Capital operates in a much simpler business than most of the companies that we reviewed. The company could do a better job of disclosing miscellaneous financial information, such as the age and general responsibilities of key officers. The investor relations effort as well as management's accessibility were given high marks. Finally, while the company was lauded for its breakdown of revenues and assets managed, reviewers raised a number of company specific issues relating generally to disclosure of alternative sources of liquidity and potential contingent liabilities that might need more attention in future reports.

*American Express (AXP)* declined significantly in its results this year (74.3%) compared to last year (82.6%). Declining scores on the Chairman's letter, discussions of the income statement and balance sheet, and discussions of foreign operations all showed declines relative to last year. Reviewers again sought more balance in the Chairman's letter regarding positive and negative developments, as well as desiring more specific financial goals within the context of well-discussed strategic goals.

Comments on the discussions of the income statement and balance sheet tended to focus on prior lack of disclosure, such as loans in the Optima unit and their attendant risks, as well as an appropriate and reasonably complete breakout of segment income statements. One analyst also noted that the company's discussions of interest rate risk seemed inadequate given AXP's exposure in nearly all of its businesses. Furthermore, the company received low marks on its discussion of foreign operations, with reviewers assigning particularly low scores to explanations of the impact of currency fluctuations and the key economic and operational factors that affect the foreign business.

Despite these concerns, reviewers focused on the company's financial supplement, which generally received high marks and was mentioned as being critical to any in-depth analysis of the company. Furthermore, management accessibility improved dramatically along with the investor relations effort.

*Beneficial Finance (BNL)* scored 72.1% compared to 81.2% last year. It appears that a portion of this decline was due to the change in scoring for segments and foreign operations. Reviewers generally were interested in more discussion of revenue projects like the refund anticipation loan, as well as the company's technology investment in BenCom III. There was also great interest in more information on asset/liability sensitivity and net interest margin.

The company continued its improving trend in other aspects of reporting practices, mainly management accessibility and the investor relations effort, where the score improved to 88.3% from 83.2% last year and 55.0% in the prior year.

*Bear Stearns (BSC)* again showed overall flat results (71.2% vs. 72.2%). The Chairman's letter showed substantial improvement with a score of 72.2% vs. 50.0% last year. While reviewers generally noted an improved discussion of goals and strategies, they continue to note that this company could provide a better sense of the Chairman's outlook for the coming year. The company also showed a dramatic improvement in management's accessibility to analysts.

Once again, analysts noted that the text of Bear Stearns' reporting discusses two segments (clearing and securities brokerage), but provides no separate financial details on these two areas.

Bear Stearns was again lauded for its discussion of the balance sheet, an area that is generally weak throughout the financial services group but of growing concern to analysts.

*Dreyfus Corporation (DRY)* showed modest gains this year, scoring 65.3% overall vs. 61.5%, and the company once again occupied last place in our survey. Results were flat to down in every area except management accessibility and investor relations.

Dreyfus has consistently scored at the bottom of the financial services group. The company's scores have remained in a narrow range, and reviewers remain dismayed with the company's disclosure. However, the company's new investor contact appears to be making some headway, and we remain hopeful of better performance in the future.

*Household International (HI)* scored 80.2% this year, down from 88.4% last year but up from 78.1% the prior year, placing it again in a tie for first place. While Household suffered from the modest change in scoring, the primary reason for the lower score this year centered on the Chairman's letter, where reviewers would have liked to have seen a better discussion of corporate goals and strategies, and lower scores on segment reporting. Reviewers consistently commented that Household's reporting format tends to be inconsistent from year to year, and that it is difficult to find all of the important pieces of information: they are all there but difficult to find and put together.

Overall, the company received high marks for its financial supplement, and the investor relations effort continues to score over 90%, although reviewers were somewhat disappointed with the candor and accessibility of management.

*Merrill Lynch (MER)* showed a modest improvement in its overall score to 68.7% from 66.8% last year. Improving areas were partially offset by declines elsewhere. The Chairman's letter again improved to 68.9% from 63.9%, with most of the improvement in the discussion of corporate goals and strategies as well as the outlook for the coming year. Other improvements included quarterly reporting and very positive comments on the financial supplement, along with a noted improvement in the accessibility of management as well as the investor relations effort. Several reviewers noted that Merrill Lynch is making clear progress in its reporting practices.

Merrill Lynch's results on the survey continue to suffer from some confusion with regard to segment reporting and the extent of international operations. Some analysts felt that the segment disclosure needs to be improved, while others felt that the company operates in only one segment. In the same vein, some analysts felt that the disclosure of international operations could be more complete, while others skipped the section, citing the integration of the company's operations that does not lend itself to such reporting. Such dichotomies are not uncommon, and usually suggest a need for greater clarity.

*Morgan Stanley (MS)* overall receives great respect for its reporting, even though the overall score is a below-average 66.0% up this year from 62.7% last year. The basic issue with this company is that it tends to provide insight in conversations with management and investor relations, but its disclosure of financial data overall falls short of the mark. As other companies in the survey continue to improve their financial reporting, Morgan Stanley continues to fall in the overall rankings despite ongoing increases in their overall score.

In particular, the Chairman's letter and other text discuss the company's processing operations and money management activities, but the related financial data are scarce to nonexistent. This issue is not unique to Morgan Stanley: it concerns nearly all securities firms. However, given the overall high regard for MS, the issue is of particular relevance to this company.

In addition, the company's disclosure of foreign operations is controversial. Some reviewers note that due to the integration of the company's operations, foreign data are not meaningful, while others contend that a material percentage of pre-tax profit is generated by those operations, resulting in a need for greater disclosure.

As a general note, public securities firms have historically been reluctant to disclose detailed information, which might in part account for the perceived unreliability of their earnings.

Morgan Stanley again received good marks for management availability and candor, and investor relations scored over 90.0%. The Chairman's letter was generally well-regarded, although it would be helpful if the letter would share more of the Chairman's insights as to the factors that might affect the upcoming year.

*PaineWebber Group (PWJ)* showed improved scores across the board, even with the slight negative of the scoring change, resulting in an overall score of 76.1% compared to 59.4% last year and an improvement from the 64.5% overall score of the year before. The Chairman's letter improved substantially, and management accessibility as well as the investor relations effort scored over 90%. The Subcommittee is pleased to see this company make strides in its corporate reporting efforts.

Nonetheless, PaineWebber seems to continue to suffer from a lack of clarity as to the scope and nature of its business, particularly as reflected in segment reporting. One analyst noted that asset management is now over 10% of revenues (probably revenues net of interest expense) and hence is large enough to be disclosed as a separate segment. This statement is true for many securities firms. We would note that over the last several years, segment reporting, along with international operations, seem to appear and disappear as important areas for this company, suggesting that more consistency in the disclosure and discussions in these areas may be needed.

*Primerica (PA)* scored 79.5% overall this year, down from 87.0% last year, with about half of the decline due to the changes in scoring this year. Overall, reviewers remain enthusiastic about the company's reporting practices, noting the relative balance between qualitative and quantitative factors.

A frequent comment, however, noted that Primerica's reporting would benefit from a more detailed break-down of revenues from Smith Barney (the securities brokerage subsidiary), as well as breaking out the two asset management subsidiaries from other operations. Analysts also felt that certain statutory data for the insurance operations would be helpful.

Primerica continues to excel in management accessibility and candor, as well as investor relations, where the scores exceeded 90%.

*Salomon Inc. (SB)* sustained the significant strides of last year with an overall rating of 72.8% compared to 71.2%, which was up from 63.8%. Scores improved in most categories except foreign operations and segment reporting. We are particularly pleased to see Salomon score above 90% on accessibility of management, while the investor relations effort showed a substantial increase. This company, which has historically been regarded as a very poor reporter, has made meaningful progress in its reporting efforts, which seems to have been accelerated by the Treasury bidding scandal.

Specific analyst comments noted improvements like the discussion of balance sheet items (liquidity management, fair value of assets, and discussion of risks). Furthermore, the management letters (there were three) showed significant gains, particularly for the review of the prior year which scored 97.2%—certainly among the highest scores ever for this section.

Salomon, however, has plenty of room for improvement. The company scored 46.7% on its disclosure of international operations, even though, as one reviewer noted, nearly a third of revenues are derived from foreign sources. In addition, segment disclosure would benefit from greater detail with regard to Phibro, as well as more information regarding Salomon Brothers net interest spreads.

*Transamerica (TA)* continued its tradition of above-average reporting, despite the adverse effect of the scoring changes, with a score of 79.5%, putting it among the four best companies in this year's review. For three years in a row, Transamerica has scored over 90% for its overall investor program (including management accessibility and candor) and in its miscellaneous reporting (including the quality and consistency of quarterly reports as well as the company's highly regarded financial supplement).

Transamerica continues to suffer from some confusion regarding its international operations. One reviewer commented that if the company is indeed a domestic company with a minority interest in an overseas operation, they should state this fact up front to present a clear picture to the reader.

Some reviewers were also disappointed in the discussion of the balance sheet and off-balance sheet factors. Asset/liability management discussion was frequently mentioned for this company as an area where analysts would like to see more information. Also, concern about derivatives and their potential risks has grown, and more forthright disclosure concerning whether and how such instruments are used by the company would be useful.

*T. Rowe Price (TROW)* scored 80.4% this year compared to 88.0% last year, with most of the decline due to low evaluations of its discussion of the balance sheet and off-balance sheet factors. In view of the growing concern among analysts regarding asset/liability management (which in some ways is not as critical for T. Rowe as for others) and the use of swaps and derivatives, reviewers would have appreciated any comments that could put these industry-wide concerns into perspective.

Overall, the consensus view of T. Rowe Price is that the company is not exceptional in its reporting practices, although the company solidly addresses the important factors.

## Conclusion

The financial services industry is an emerging industry in which both analysts and companies continue to strive for more appropriate reporting practices. The scoring process has undergone dramatic change over the years, reflecting trends in the industry, although we are pleased to have established more stability in this process since 1988. The subcommittee is pleased that companies are increasingly seeking and heeding our views about their reporting practices and that the average performance on the survey is improving with time. We hold out hope that future years will unveil a company that deserves an Award for Excellence.

### 1991–1992 SURVEY

|  | Total | Rank | Chairman's Letter II. | Results of Operations III. | Segment Reporting IV. | Foreign Operations V. | Other Publ. Information VI. | Other Aspects VII. |
|---|---|---|---|---|---|---|---|---|
| AVERAGE | 74.0% |  | 72.3% | 72.3% | 74.2% | 57.4% | 81.8% | 81.9% |
| LAST YEAR | 77.2% |  | 73.0% | 80.6% | 75.6% | 60.6% | 88.7% | 80.8% |
| PRIOR YEAR | 73.4% |  | 69.4% | 77.3% | 76.0% | 53.6% | 80.6% | 76.4% |
| TROW | 80.4% | 1* | 92.6% | 69.0% | — | — | 81.5% | 77.7% |
| HI | 80.2% | 1* | 77.8% | 81.6% | 83.8% | 61.3% | 89.3% | 86.8% |
| PA | 79.5% | 2* | 77.8% | 76.6% | 79.7% | — | 80.9% | 88.0% |
| TA | 79.5% | 2* | 63.9% | 74.2% | 86.1% | 66.7% | 93.3% | 98.0% |
| PWJ | 76.1% | 3* | 66.7% | 74.4% | 77.6% | — | 86.1% | 78.3% |
| AC | 75.8% | 3* | 69.4% | 74.4% | — | 80.0% | 67.6% | 86.7% |
| AXP | 74.3% | 4 | 73.3% | 67.7% | 77.4% | 57.3% | 89.4% | 94.0% |
| SB | 72.8% | 5 | 87.0% | 80.7% | 63.1% | 46.7% | 83.3% | 79.6% |
| BNL | 72.1% | 6 | 70.4% | 75.0% | 62.7% | 60.0% | 78.6% | 88.3% |
| BSC | 71.2% | 7 | 72.2% | 76.3% | — | 50.0% | 68.3% | 83.3% |
| MER | 68.7% | 8 | 68.9% | 67.6% | 63.0% | 47.8% | 95.0% | 72.9% |
| MS | 66.0% | 9 | 75.0% | 66.7% | — | 46.7% | 83.3% | 69.4% |
| DRY | 65.3% | 10 | 44.4% | 55.7% | — | — | 66.1% | 61.5% |
| WEIGHTS: |  |  |  |  |  |  |  |  |
| 1991–92 | 100.0% |  | 8.9% | 35.6% | 15.8% | 14.9% | 14.9% | 9.9% |
| 1990–91 | 100.0% |  | 9.8% | 39.1% | 14.1% | 13.0% | 13.0% | 10.9% |

NOTE: Some companies in this survey do not have foreign operations and some do not have segments. Therefore, the weighting of the other sections is proportionately higher for such companies.

## QUARTILE RANKINGS

| Company | 1991 %Tile | Rank | 1990 %Tile | Rank | 1989 %Tile | Rank | 1988 %Tile | Rank | 1987 %Tile | Rank |
|---|---|---|---|---|---|---|---|---|---|---|
| **First Quartile:** | | | | | | | | | | |
| TROW | 80.4% | 1* | 88.0% | 1* | 81.6% | 3 | 62.0% | 10 | 49.5% | 13 |
| HI | 80.2% | 1* | 88.4% | 1* | 78.1% | 6 | 78.6% | 4 | 62.6% | 5 |
| PA | 79.5% | 2* | 87.0% | 2* | 81.4% | 4* | 71.2% | 7 | 54.6% | 10 |
| TA | 79.5% | 2* | 87.6% | 2* | 85.0% | 1 | 85.3% | 1 | 72.1% | 2 |
| **Second Quartile** | | | | | | | | | | |
| PWJ | 76.1% | 3* | 59.4% | 10 | 64.5% | 12* | 69.1% | 8* | 55.9% | 9 |
| AC | 75.8% | 3* | — | — | — | — | — | — | — | — |
| AXP | 74.3% | 4 | 82.6% | 3 | 81.5% | 4* | 72.3% | 6 | 61.4% | 6 |
| **Third Quartile:** | | | | | | | | | | |
| SB | 72.8% | 5 | 71.2% | 6 | 63.8% | 12* | 59.4% | 12 | 53.6% | 11 |
| BNL | 72.1% | 6 | 81.2% | 4 | 75.2% | 7 | 69.4% | 8* | 58.4% | 7 |
| BSC | 71.2% | 7 | 72.2% | 5 | 73.8% | 8 | 60.5% | 11 | 56.8% | 8* |
| **Fourth Quartile:** | | | | | | | | | | |
| MER | 68.7% | 8 | 66.8% | 7 | 66.5% | 10 | 64.1% | 9 | 67.2% | 4 |
| MS | 66.0% | 9 | 62.7% | 8 | 71.3% | 9 | 68.9% | 8* | 57.4% | 8* |
| DRY | 65.3% | 10 | 61.5% | 9 | 64.8% | 11 | 50.0% | 13 | 50.3% | 12* |
| Average: | 74.0% | | 77.2% | | 73.4% | | 69.9% | | 58.0% | |

**Deletions due to acquisitions, bankruptcies or other changes to public ownership:**

| | | | | | | | | | | |
|---|---|---|---|---|---|---|---|---|---|---|
| EFH | — | — | — | — | — | — | — | — | — | — |
| FBC | — | — | — | — | — | — | — | — | 56.8% | 8* |
| "OLD" PA | — | — | — | — | — | — | — | — | 50.0% | 12* |
| SLH | — | — | — | — | — | — | 69.5% | 8* | 71.3% | 3* |
| LFC | — | — | — | — | — | — | 83.8% | 2 | 71.2% | 3* |

**Transfers to other Subcommittees:**

| | | | | | | | | | | |
|---|---|---|---|---|---|---|---|---|---|---|
| FNM | — | — | 88.9% | 1* | 83.0% | 2 | 80.9% | 3 | 82.2% | 1 |
| SLM | — | — | 83.4% | 3 | 80.0% | 5 | 74.3% | 5 | 70.8% | 3* |

NOTES:
* = Indicates a tie in the ranking.
PA—"Old" Primerica was acquired by Commercial Credit in 1988, and Commercial Credit adopted the Primerica name and stock symbol.
FBC—First Boston was acquired by Credit Suisse in 1988.
SLH—Shearson Lehman Hutton was reacquired by American Express.
LFC—Lomas Financial declared bankruptcy in 1989.
FNM—Fannie Mae was transferred to the thrift and GSE group effective with 1991–92 survey.
SLM—Sallie Mae was transferred to the thrift and GSE group effective with 1991–92 survey.
NOTE: Some companies in this survey do not have foreign operations and some do not have segments. Therefore, the weighting of the other sections is proportionately higher for such companies.

## FINANCIAL SERVICES SUBCOMMITTEE

Nancy L. Young, CFA, Chair, New York
College Retirement Equities Fund

Michael W. Blumstein, CFA, New York
Morgan Stanley & Co.

Mary Jayne Byrne, CFA, Houston
Texas Commerce Investment Management Co.

William D. Cohen, New York
Lord, Abbett & Co.

Alison Deans, New York
Smith Barney, Harris Upham & Co., Inc.

Henry C. Dickson, CFA, Chicago
Kemper Securities Group, Inc.

Heather L. Dilbeck, CFA, New York
Bessemer Trust Company, N.A.

Mary F. Dunbrack, Boston
Baring America Asset Management Company, Inc.

L. W. Eckenfelder, CFA, San Francisco
Prudential Securities, Inc.

Richard S. Goleniewski, New York
Goldman Sachs & Co.

James Hanbury, CFA, New York
Wertheim Schroder & Co., Inc.

Samuel G. Liss, New York
Salomon Brothers, Inc.

Diane L. Merdian, Boston
Wellington Management Co.

Guy Moskowski, CFA, New York
Sanford C. Bernstein & Co.

Robert M. Rubino, Maryland
T. Rowe Price Associates

Caroline J. Smith, New York
Nomura Securities International Inc.

Nancy Spady, CFA, Chicago
Lincoln Capital Management Co.

Woodrow S. Tyler, CFA, Detroit
State of Michigan Retirement System

James P. Vandervort, Jr., CFA, Trenton
State of New Jersey Division of Investment

Andrew V. Vindigni, CFA, New York
General American Investors Company, Inc.

Thomas R. Wenzell, CFA, Chicago
Institutional Capital Corp.

# Food, Beverage & Tobacco

## Recommendation for Award

The Food, Beverage & Tobacco Subcommittee recommends that an Award for Excellence in Corporate Reporting be given to General Mills and PepsiCo, Inc. General Mills edged out PepsiCo by two tenths of one percent, but the score was based on one less evaluation (9 vs. 10 for PepsiCo), leading the subcommittee to proclaim the survey a tie for first place.

## Letter of Commendation

The subcommittee also recommends that UST, Inc. and Gerber Products both receive Letters of Commendation for a much improved effort during the past year. According to survey results, moving from the ninth spot in 1991 to the number three spot in 1992, UST, Inc. vaulted past giants such as Philip Morris, Sara Lee and Quaker Oats. Also sharing the spotlight for improvement is Gerber Products. Moving up six notches, (13th in 1991 to 7th in 1992), Gerber has demonstrated its commitment in establishing a strong program of quality reporting and overall communications to analysts.

## Evaluation Method

The Food, Beverage & Tobacco Subcommittee reevaluated the companies polled, with the addition of two tobacco companies and one additional beverage company. B.A.T Industries, which finished in the top ten, Universal Corporation (19th) and Grand Metropolitan (23rd), were added to the list for evaluation. The new questionnaire consisted of twenty-nine companies, fifteen of which are food companies, eight are beverage companies and six are tobacco companies.

To encourage greater participation, the subcommittee limited the survey to four categories: annual reports, interim reports, investor contact, and analyst group meetings and management accessibility. More than 75 questionnaires were sent to a cross section of buy-side and sell-side analysts monitoring these industries.

## Summary of Results

A summary of the scores for each of the four categories in the questionnaire appears at the conclusion of this report.

## Annual Report

For the second year in a row, PepsiCo's annual report was considered to be the most comprehensive, thus granting them not only the highest percentage of favorable votes (88.5%) in this category in 1992 but the highest score compiled in the last three surveys. General Mills and Sara Lee finished second and third, respectively, knocking off last year's runners-up, Quaker Oats (4th) and Philip Morris (5th).

Although Seagram finished dead last in this category, their one response skews the results. Therefore, for the third consecutive year, Archer-Daniels-Midland understandably was rated as having the worst annual report.

## Interim Reports

Detailed quarterly segment analysis of earnings and management's availability to discuss each business has enabled PepsiCo to dominate this category for the third straight year. Philip Morris, a distant second, improved from last year's third place, while Sara Lee dropped one place to finish third. Philip Morris continues to improve their quarterly reporting with a better and more informative segment breakdown.

Archer-Daniels-Midland's lack of complete quarterly income statement continues. As a result they also rank as the worst company in this important category. Not faring any better, Brown-Forman, Ralston Purina and Borden, which garnered responses indicating they all need improvement in this regard.

## Investor Relations

Gaining two places from last year, General Mills took top honors in the presenting of timely information, familiarity with current developments and objectives, and management accessibility. Rounding out the top three were PepsiCo, with yet another strong score, followed by the ever-improving UST, Inc. Two major changes were evident this year. First, 1991's winner Ralston Purina, who incidentally attained the highest percentage of favorable votes since the survey's inception (97%), plummeted to finish 22nd with a low of 45% of favorable votes. Likewise, falling from 6th place in 1991 to 18th this year, was Coca-Cola.

## Meetings and Management Availability

Availability of top management to the investment community improved in 1992, especially for General Mills, who finished first. Regular quarterly meetings were mentioned as the reason for PepsiCo's second place showing. Improving eight places from last year, Gerber Products placed third, with UST, Inc. and Hershey rounding out the top five.

### FOOD, BEVERAGE & TOBACCO
### EVALUATIONS AND SCORES—1991/92

| Company | # of Responses | Annual Report | | Interim Reports | | Investor Relations | | Meetings & Other | | Weighted Average |
|---|---|---|---|---|---|---|---|---|---|---|
| General Mills, Inc. | 9 | 85.0 | 2 | 81.7 | 4 | 91.7 | 1 | 87.0 | 1 | 86.4 |
| PepsiCo, Inc. | 10 | 88.5 | 1 | 85.0 | 1 | 90.0 | 2 | 81.3 | 2 | 86.2 |
| UST Inc. | 6 | 77.5 | 7 | 79.2 | 7 | 89.2 | 3 | 80.0 | 4 | 81.5 |
| Philip Morris | 10 | 80.0 | 5 | 84.0 | 2 | 87.5 | 4 | 70.0 | 10 | 80.4 |
| Sara Lee Corp. | 11 | 84.6 | 3 | 83.7 | 3 | 76.1 | 10 | 76.1 | 6 | 80.1 |
| Quaker Oats Co. | 10 | 82.0 | 4 | 79.5 | 6 | 76.0 | 11 | 72.7 | 8 | 77.6 |
| Gerber Products Co. | 11 | 76.9 | 7 | 74.6 | 8 | 74.1 | 13 | 81.2 | 3 | 76.7 |
| Hershey Foods Corp. | 6 | 76.7 | 8 | 69.2 | 11 | 76.7 | 8 | 77.8 | 5 | 75.1 |
| B.A.T. Industries p.l.c. | 3 | 75.0 | 10 | 65.0 | 16 | 87.5 | 4 | 70.0 | 10 | 74.4 |
| Campbell Soup Company | 7 | 74.3 | 11 | 72.2 | 9 | 81.5 | 6 | 65.7 | 11 | 73.4 |
| McDonald's Corp. | 4 | 75.0 | 10 | 81.3 | 5 | 76.3 | 9 | 60.8 | 13 | 73.4 |
| CPC International Inc. | 9 | 68.3 | 13 | 70.4 | 10 | 81.5 | 6 | 73.0 | 7 | 73.3 |
| ConAgra, Inc. | 9 | 67.8 | 15 | 66.7 | 15 | 80.5 | 7 | 71.5 | 9 | 71.6 |
| RJR Nabisco, Inc. | 7 | 67.9 | 14 | 62.5 | 18 | 82.9 | 5 | 70.0 | 10 | 70.8 |
| Anheuser-Busch Cos., Inc. | 9 | 75.6 | 9 | 68.9 | 12 | 75.6 | 12 | 55.2 | 16 | 68.8 |
| Coca-Cola Company | 7 | 79.3 | 6 | 62.2 | 20 | 60.7 | 18 | 62.4 | 12 | 66.2 |
| American Brands, Inc. | 5 | 73.8 | 12 | 68.8 | 13 | 73.8 | 14 | 47.5 | 21 | 66.0 |
| Kellogg Co. | 12 | 65.4 | 16 | 60.0 | 21 | 68.3 | 16 | 60.3 | 14 | 63.5 |
| Universal Corporation | 4 | 63.8 | 18 | 62.4 | 19 | 63.8 | 17 | 57.5 | 15 | 61.9 |
| Tyson Foods, Inc. | 5 | 64.0 | 17 | 63.0 | 17 | 73.0 | 15 | 37.3 | 23 | 59.3 |
| H.J. Heinz Company | 9 | 50.6 | 23 | 51.1 | 22 | 60.6 | 19 | 51.1 | 19 | 53.4 |
| Coca-Cola Enterprises | 6 | 60.0 | 19 | 67.5 | 14 | 40.0 | 24 | 43.3 | 19 | 52.7 |
| Grand Metropolitan PLC | 5 | 56.0 | 22 | 49.0 | 23 | 47.3 | 20 | 54.0 | 17 | 51.6 |
| Borden, Inc. | 8 | 56.3 | 21 | 48.2 | 24 | 45.5 | 21 | 52.0 | 18 | 50.5 |
| Brown-Forman Corp. | 2 | 60.0 | 19 | 42.5 | 26 | 35.0 | 25 | 50.0 | 20 | 46.9 |
| Ralston Purina | 9 | 48.4 | 25 | 47.2 | 25 | 45.0 | 22 | 23.0 | 24 | 40.9 |
| Archer-Daniels-Midland Co. | 7 | 45.0 | 26 | 30.0 | 28 | 44.9 | 23 | 40.6 | 22 | 40.1 |
| Adolph Coors | 1 | 50.0 | 24 | 40.0 | 27 | 35.0 | 25 | 10.0 | 25 | 33.8 |
| Seagram Company Ltd. | 1 | 40.0 | 27 | 20.0 | 29 | 30.0 | 26 | 10.0 | 25 | 25.0 |

## FOOD, BEVERAGE & TOBACCO SUBCOMMITTEE

Roy D. Burry, CFA, Co-Chair, New York
Kidder, Peabody & Co., Inc.

John M. McMillin III, CFA, Co-Chair, New York
Prudential Securities, Inc.

John Averill, Boston
Eaton Vance Management, Inc.

Peter J. Barry, New York
Rothschild, Inc.

William N. Booth, CFA, Boston
Wellington Management Co.

Lisa Falcone, Boston
Harvard Management

Nomi Ghez, New York
Goldman, Sachs & Co.

Stephen M. Long, New York
Kidder, Peabody & Co., Inc.

Joanna Schaif Rossien, New York
S.G. Warburg & Co., Inc.

Jane A. Shickich, New York
Prudential Securities, Inc.

# Foreign-Based Oil

This is the first year that the reporting/disclosure practices of the non-U.S. companies with ADR's have been rated. As companies were not aware of the rating criteria in advance of the publication of their 1991 annual reports, the committee did not feel it appropriate to give awards. Rather, we felt that we should make overall comments, familiarize companies with our evaluation methods and scoring, and announce intentions to formally rate reporting/disclosure practices next year. We view this as an outstanding opportunity to provide constructive input for the publication of 1992 annual reports and to help in the ongoing program of communications with investors. The committee intends to follow up shortly with companies to explain valuation benchmarks and to highlight investor perceptions.

This group of companies generally has reasonably to very good disclosure already. Companies rated are very prominent in their home countries and have been operating in the public eye for some time. Disclosure in the worldwide oil industry has advanced quite significantly over the last 20 years and the lessons learned by the U.S. based companies have clearly been shared with and used as helpful input by their foreign competitors. Accounting practices used worldwide in the petroleum industry are similar to U.S. GAAP and there is a pervasive worldwide culture unique to the oil industry, which results in surprisingly great similarity between U.S. and non-U.S. based companies. As a result, disclosure practices in a general sense are quite comparable to U.S. based companies. In preparation for U.S. share ownership, which is the common trait of the companies rated, accounting/reserves data have been more or less adapted to U.S. standards. Still, there is room for constructive criticism, as one would expect given the diverse set of nationalities and cultures involved with this group of companies.

## General Comments

The committee felt that the area where there is the most room for improvement was in the frequency and timing of interim reports and communications of business trends to investors on a timely basis. In general, quarterly/semi-annual/annual results are published later, in some cases significantly so, than U.S. companies. The French practice, for example, is to release partial data on a timely basis (i.e., less than one month after a period's close), but not to release sector and financial details for one or even two months later. Without the detail, the initial release is of limited analytical value. Norsk Hydro reports on a very timely basis. Repsol usually reports somewhat on the late side. Both of these latter companies do provide full detail when they release earnings. Most U.K. companies report semi-annually and do so quite awhile after the period has ended. Overall, these practices are in line with those of respective home markets but American investors, used to full detail within three to four weeks of the quarter's close, would prefer quicker and more detailed reports of operations. We realize there is a cost involved with doing this, but feel the market would be better informed and more efficient as a result.

Annual reports for the non-U.S. companies are generally published quite a bit later than American investors are accustomed to. There are local reasons why this is so but the committee felt that the later the annual report—which is the key source of published information—is published, the less value it has in explaining company results and in prediction of future results.

There should be a standardized system for translating results into U.S. dollars. American investors who own foreign securities should be aware of the risks and opportunities of investing outside the U.S. and, in theory, should not have to see earnings expressed in dollars. But it is to the advantage of the companies to interest as many investors as possible. In this regard, it is probably inevitable that dollar earnings should be expressed as well as earnings in home currency. As it is, some companies use end-rates, some use average rates that prevailed during the quarter, and some use a convenience rate. The SEC advocates convenience rates, but the committee finds the use of an average rate the most realistic and desirable, with the added advantage that it preserves the dollar earnings whereas other methods frequently result in restated dollar earnings. Given that oil is a dollar commodity, underlying earnings are actually in dollars so it seems reasonable to preserve original dollar earnings.

In general, the committee found the investor relations efforts of this group of companies competent and professional. American investors often express a preference for investor relations personnel to be stationed in the U.S. to ease communications. While it is a simple matter today to call anywhere in the world, time differences do limit opportunities to call Europe, for example. And travel budgets do not permit all investors to personally visit companies located outside the U.S. The reality is that the committee felt that company interests would be best served by having investor relations personnel also stationed in the U.S.

Notwithstanding the above comments, the committee felt that this group of companies pursued admirable efforts to communicate with American investors. Generally, the companies had made periodic visits to the U.S. to update investors and were judged as being quite accessible to analysts who visited abroad. The suggestions involve bringing this same level of information to investors who are not able to visit at home headquarters.

Overall, it was felt that price/volume data were not presented in sufficient detail (e.g., by country or reporting period) to make analysts confident in construction of their earnings models. Natural gas prices outside the U.S. are an area of non-disclosure, in particular. And it was felt that companies might consider additional business line disclosure, given that some business lines (e.g., Norsk Hydro's light metals and agricultural sectors, Total's Trading and Middle East) contain some very dissimilar activities.

Per share data were not always prominently featured nor was it always possible to easily ascertain the number of shares outstanding. This was not a problem for Norsk Hydro or Repsol, with constant numbers of shares outstanding, but was somewhat difficult for Elf and Total, which had been involved with share sales and other financial transactions. And BHP was judged to not present per share data consistently.

Interim reports did not consistently contain updated cash flow or balance sheet information. The committee felt that this was an area for major improvement.

The committee cited a desire that applicable exchange rates (i.e., average exchange rates for the reporting period and key end-rates) be prominently displayed in interim reports.

Lastly, the committee felt that it would be helpful to American investors if company disclosure routinely contained more references to home country developments, since American investors are frequently not aware of all of these. And it would be helpful if annual reports, etc., highlighted the companies' position in their home markets. This is more in the arena of education than corporate disclosure, per se, but would be welcomed nevertheless.

## Specific Company Comments

*The Broken Hill Proprietary Company, Ltd. (BHP)* has a unique, multi-industry business mix and as such is harder to analyze than single-sector companies. The committee felt that investors would be well-served by business line breakdowns beyond the current three. For example, the minerals sector actually involves several key commodities, often moving in different directions; additional disclosure between minerals (e.g., coal, copper, iron ore, etc.) would be helpful. Petroleum is an integrated business and a split between refining/marketing and exploration/production would facilitate understanding. BHP was mentioned as not clearly presenting per share data, particularly for ADR's.

BHP was judged as having an extensive and consistent investor relations effort, and this was very favorably commented on. Top management made great effort to be available to American investors and this was supplemented by a well-regarded U.S. based effort.

As to financial disclosure, BHP was mentioned for not providing interim cash flow or balance sheet measures. The Australian cash flow statement is presented quite differently from an American statement.

*Elf Aqitaine, Inc.*'s disclosure as to the results of oil and gas producing activities was cited as being particularly helpful. The committee also rated Elf's investor relations program and the frequency of visits of key executives to America as important positives. Elf's U.S. based investor relations program was praised.

If possible, investors would clearly appreciate more timely release of annual reports and quarterly reporting. A preference was expressed for interim balance sheet and cash flow data and more price/volume information.

Elf received high marks for frequency of press releases, highlighting ongoing developments.

*Lasmo plc* was applauded for its efforts to visit with U.S. investors. Top management showed good faith and consistency of approach. Lasmo's attempts to show its forward production profile were also highly rated.

The committee recommended that Lasmo also adapt its reserves definition to a U.S. basis and show earnings and cash flow on this basis.

*Norsk Hydro A.S.* was cited for its timely release of quarterly reports and its consistent and very helpful visits to American investors by key executives. The imminent move of investor relations personnel to the U.S. was applauded. Overall, Norsk Hydro's investor relations efforts were viewed very positively.

The committee felt that Norsk Hydro's business line disclosure should be broadened, given the large number of business lines that the company operates in. Fertilizers are in a much different cycle than other agricultural chemicals, for example, and no distinction is made between refining/marketing and exploration/production. Price/volume disclosure for oil/gas and other commodities could be improved.

*Repsol, S.A.* The committee viewed Repsol's investor relations efforts and disclosure practices as very strong. However, investors have opined that they thought it desirable that Repsol have an investor relations representative in the U.S. to facilitate communications. And it was felt that the refining/marketing segment used in business line reporting might be divided between refining and marketing/distribution, given the different factors and regulatory aspects affecting these business lines. The committee also found certain aspects of Repsol's quarterly reports were confusing when restatements were involved.

*Total Compagnie Francaise des Petroles.* The committee felt that Total's disclosure practices were somewhat inconsistent and that interim report disclosure was less complete than would be desired.

Total was applauded for its U.S. investor relations presence and for the frequency of visits by top management to the U.S.

As mentioned above, the grouping of Total's business lines results in some dissimilar businesses under the same caption and therefore some confusion as to how to evaluate trends (comment refers to the Middle East and Trading Group, which also includes metals).

### FOREIGN-BASED OIL SUBCOMMITTEE

Todd L. Bergman, CFA, Chair, New York
Goldman, Sachs & Company

Christopher Buckley, New York
Goldman, Sachs & Co.

Susan Graham, New York
Merrill Lynch

Michael Kerr, New York
Capital Guardian Trust Co.

Thomas P. Moore, Jr., CFA, Boston
State Street Research & Management Co.

# Health Care

## Recommendation for Award

For the second year in a row, the Health Care Subcommittee has recommended that Schering-Plough Corporation receive an Award for Excellence in Corporate Reporting in recognition of the overall high quality of its reporting and communications program.

Schering-Plough has long been an industry leader in providing quality information to the financial community. For the past several years, it has held annual meetings for investment professionals at which time senior management is available for open and frank discussions. The company has also been an innovator in disclosing detailed quarterly sales data by major product lines. Schering-Plough's "SGP Product Pipeline" and "Investor Bulletin" publications have been well received by analysts and portfolio managers; these reports have been emulated by other health care firms.

## Overall Comments

In addition to Schering-Plough, Pfizer, Warner-Lambert, Glaxo and Upjohn were also judged to have "A" rated programs. Pfizer has shown dramatic improvement in its communications program during the past two years, moving up from ninth to second place. Warner-Lambert and Upjohn have scored high in the subcommittee's evaluation for the past several years. Glaxo has recorded consistent improvement in its program since the committee first evaluated it in 1989. Johnson & Johnson also continued to rise in the ratings. The firms that ranked at the bottom end of the spectrum generally provided the investment community little, if any, access to senior management. In the opinion of the subcommittee, management accessibility has become increasingly important to in-depth financial analysis. Potential points in that sector comprised 35% of the total.

## Evaluation Procedures and Criteria

Seventeen major pharmaceutical and hospital supply companies were examined. The subcommittee was divided into three teams, each of which analyzed five or six companies. Another team reviewed the evaluations for consistency.

The subcommittee's evaluation form was adapted from guidelines suggested by the Corporate Information Committee and from those used by other subcommittees. The specific factors measured were updated this year to reflect several changes that have occurred in the industry. The weightings assigned were also revised slightly to reflect the growing importance of quarterly data. The overall evaluation was based on an analysis of three major parts of each company's communications program. The parts and the weightings assigned to each were:

| | Point Weighting |
|---|---|
| Annual reports and 10-Ks | 38 |
| Other published material (quarterly reports, 10-Qs, & other information) | 27 |
| Management contacts | 35 |
| Total | 100 |

The industry has made significant strides in improving the quality of quarterly statements. Whereas in 1984 less than one-half of the companies published segment data in their quarterly reports, all 17 provided such information in the current year. In addition, most firms now publish adequate balance sheets, income statements, and cash flow statements on a quarterly basis. The subcommittee believes, however, that discussion of quarterly sales and profit trends by business sectors should be expanded.

## Follow-Up Procedure

The subcommittee plans to make its evaluations available to the companies reviewed and offers to meet with managements that are interested in the results and the subcommittee's suggestions for strengthening their programs.

## HEALTH CARE ANALYSIS OF CORPORATE RATINGS, 1991

|  | Annual Report Narrative | Annual Report Quantitative | Other Published Material Quarterly | Other Published Material Other | Management Contact Individual | Management Contact Group | Letter Grade | Total Point Score 1991 | 1990 | 1989 | 1988 | 1987 |
|---|---|---|---|---|---|---|---|---|---|---|---|---|
| Points Available | 20 | 18 | 25 | 2 | 32 | 3 |  | 100 | 100 | 100 | 100 | 100 |
| Schering-Plough | 17 | 16 | 23 | 2 | 32 | 3 | A | 93 | 93 | 90 | 90 | 89 |
| Pfizer | 18 | 17 | 25 | 2 | 27 | 3 | A | 92 | 89 | 81 | 83 | 76 |
| Warner-Lambert | 15 | 14 | 22 | 2 | 32 | 3 | A | 88 | 90 | 93 | 92 | 92 |
| Glaxo Holdings | 17 | 16 | 22 | 1 | 28 | 3 | A | 87 | 86 | 85 | NR | NR |
| Upjohn | 19 | 15 | 19 | 2 | 32 | 0 | A | 87 | 92 | 91 | 90 | 91 |
| Eli Lilly | 16 | 15 | 21 | 1 | 32 | 0 | B | 85 | 87 | 86 | 84 | 85 |
| Marion Merrell Dow | 19 | 16 | 18 | 1 | 28 | 3 | B | 85 | 80 | 80 | 79 | 84 |
| Johnson & Johnson | 14 | 15 | 21 | 2 | 29 | 3 | B | 84 | 82 | 77 | 70 | 70 |
| Becton Dickinson | 15 | 15 | 20 | 1 | 29 | 3 | B | 83 | 81 | 80 | 80 | 86 |
| SmithKline Beecham | 19 | 11 | 20 | 1 | 28 | 3 | B | 82 | 85 | 78 | NR | NR |
| C.R. Bard | 16 | 13 | 17 | 2 | 30 | 3 | B | 81 | 83 | 84 | 84 | 85 |
| Merck & Co. | 18 | 14 | 19 | 2 | 25 | 2 | B | 80 | 78 | 75 | 75 | 78 |
| Abbott Laboratories | 12 | 15 | 15 | 1 | 32 | 1 | B | 76 | 81 | 84 | 81 | 79 |
| Baxter International | 15 | 12 | 17 | 1 | 29 | 0 | B | 74 | 86 | 83 | 83 | 81 |
| Bristol-Myers Squibb | 14 | 14 | 20 | 1 | 24 | 1 | B | 74 | 85 | 70 | 71 | 71 |
| Syntex | 17 | 13 | 24 | 1 | 13 | 3 | C | 71 | 81 | 81 | 88 | 89 |
| American Home Products | 13 | 13 | 19 | 2 | 22 | 0 | C | 69 | 69 | 69 | 74 | 75 |

NR Not Rated

## HEALTH CARE SUBCOMMITTEE

Kent Blair, Chair, New York
Donaldson, Lufkin & Jenrette

Barry Kurokawa, Denver
Invesco Trust Co.

Jason M. Pilalas, Los Angeles
Capital Guardian Research Company

Francis J. Morris, Wilmington
E.I. du Pont de Nemours & Co.

Barbara A. Ryan, New York
Alex. Brown & Sons, Inc.

Ronald M. Nordmann, New York
PaineWebber Inc.

Arthur J. Wichman, CFA, New York
J.P. Morgan Investment Management, Inc.

# Insurance

## Recommendation for Award

The Insurance Subcommittee recommended that Capital Holding Corporation receive an Award for Excellence in Corporate Reporting for the 1991 annual report period.

We believe that it is unprecedented, but for the fourth year in a row, Capital Holding has finished first and won this coveted award. In 1983, 1984 and 1987, the company also placed within the top five slots. Prior to Capital Holding's dominance of the top slot, the top rung finishers were dominated by the multiline and property-casualty companies.

In general, comments from subcommittee members showed a growing frustration with the lack of candor and insight into the numerous problems of both the life and property-casualty industries provided by many insurance management teams. There is a sense that too many companies are not being managed in an effective manner. One cannot help but ask what the boards of directors of many of these companies have been doing? To be sure, the continued slippage in the industry's reporting standards has done nothing to curb investor's disdain of managements.

Clearly, committee members noted numerous factors that helped to boost Capital Holding into the number one position again. One member summed it up very well by noting that "The company continues to provide excellent information on a timely basis." Top management is very accessible and is lauded for traveling around to meet with investors. For the most part, commentary is straightforward and they solicit queries from their owners. In general the sense is that Capital Holding does a good job of providing specific information about its basic businesses and investment portfolio. The operational commentary in the annual report and the layout of statistical information continue to be positively cited. Interim material has also been above average and timely. Furthermore, analyst sessions, particularly the annual strategic update, are crisp and focused with key management personnel always in attendance and available. Simply put, the company continuously attempts to address its problems and industry trends head on. While it is difficult to find any major faults with the company's progress in shareholder communication in recent years, there is nonetheless room for improvement.

Some frustration has been noted with respect to Capital's coyness on its allocation of capital and returns of its key business segments. Furthermore, management has not been as successful as some think they could be in allaying investor fears/unease over their banking operation and accumulation and investment group operation. A more succinct discussion of these dangling participles is overdue.

## Other Comments

In the runner-up position, one point away, was the SAFECO Corporation. SAFECO has been moving up in the rankings and finished third a year ago. Refreshing candor about what ails the property-casualty industry and in particular SAFECO's approach to the personal lines business (its dominant business operation) was often noted by committee members. Also providing the momentum was the timely availability of enhanced statistical data and ongoing analyst meetings. Access of top management was also cited. The shortfalls relate to the need/want of somewhat more specificity on its growing life insurance operation and how the various business units fit together under the corporate umbrella.

Like SAFECO, UNUM Corporation moved up a notch to the number three position, a laudable achievement for an entity that only became a public company a few years ago. Several committee members cited the comprehensive nature of the company's financial supplement and the fact that it is delivered on the day earnings are reported. Continuous interfacing with the investment community was also given high marks. Some subcommittee members indicated that the company's stature could be further enhanced by access to more operational personnel.

Rounding out the top five slots were the St. Paul Companies and NAC Re Corporation. The St. Paul Companies' statistical supplements and periodic "white papers" get recognition. Access to top management and more investor interface were noted as places for improvement. The ability of NAC Re Corporation to achieve a ranking within the top five ranks is very noteworthy. It shows that size and newness are not necessarily stumbling blocks. Indeed, members cite NAC Re's complete disclosure of their results, expectations for the future, strategy and industry issues. Some expansion of the quarterly statistical supplement and more analyst meetings were the shortcomings.

## Areas of Weakness

It is hard to believe, but the quality of the industry's reporting to shareholders continues to deteriorate. In too many instances, the state of the business and how individual carriers fit into the puzzle are not being discussed. Committee members continued to be unanimous in their contempt of the reporting jobs being done by managements with respect to acknowledging and discussing pertinent industry structural problems. Insights into goals, missed goals and achievements are rare animals. Likewise, tough questions about price cutting, capital needs and existence of necessary critical mass on various business segments go unanswered!

For the property-casualty business, laments were long and the solutions nil. Few annual reports chose to discuss the industry's suicidal pricing structure. Specifics about how individual carriers were faring with respect to pricing were never discussed. Insight into risk adjusted premium trends or at least the trends in deviations from ISO rates was appropriate. Succinct commentary about paid loss trends and the justification of compromised reserving standards remained convenient taboo items. Likewise, trends in retention levels and to what extent, if any, individual carriers used financial reinsurance fell through the cracks. Wouldn't it be interesting to see a table comparing calendar year and accident year underwriting results? Caution was sounded on the slowdown in net investment income growth, but we did not see intelligent discussions about its implications. Data on the susceptibility of fixed income portfolios to early calls would also have been useful. Growth in capital bases was a hot topic, but there were no discussions about the lack of statutory capital growth from operations as opposed to stock and bond market gains. Discussions about "niches" and "specialties" were still around, but insights into what critical mass was needed on various business segments and lines never got much ink. Companies still have not yet recognized that their annual reports are report cards. Successes and failures and appropriate supporting data should be included. At a bare minimum, some justification of the low ROE's being achieved is needed. Finally, a *simple* one page earnings per share summary untangling "non-recurring items" would be extremely helpful in getting some of the static out of some very garbled numbers.

Life insurance reports did not do much better. The continuing problems with commercial real estate highlighted inadequate prior disclosure and the life insurance industry's broad discretion for asset valuation. The ability to compare real estate and mortgage portfolios was an exercise in futility due to the intermingling of net and gross data and the lack of such disclosure. Many subcommittee members noted the absence of adequate comments concerning capital needs and allocation. This was particularly startling given the fact that risk based capital was being discussed by the regulatory authorities. Another omission that was astonishing was the industry's involvement in health care, both as a provider and a financier of coverage. As one committee member wrote, "The spotlight cannot get any brighter on an issue of major importance to consumers and politicians."

As we have noted in the past, the accounting and nomenclature in both the property-casualty and life insurance industries is at best obtuse to most investors. Annual reports must include glossaries and simple descriptions of what various ratios are meant to show. The SEC, FASB and AICPA all have an interest in the oversight of the insurance industry. Each of these organizations has its own agenda and their various pronouncements add to investor confusion. The lack of credible discussions on substantive industry accounting issues by company managements does little to enhance the industry's poor image among investors and regulators.

The insurance industry's corporate reporting continued to slip. The omissions were material and it was difficult not to assume that many managements were avoiding answering the difficult questions. One could only speculate about the reasons behind their motives. It could be a misreading of the severity of their company's financial health or it could be a delaying tactic hoping for an industry turnaround. In any event, the public's faith in financial institutions has been markedly diminished by the problems in the banking and savings and loan industries. At this juncture, there is no "federal net" to protect insurance policyholders and various members of Congress are taking a close look at the industry. All the more reason why the insurance industry must do a better job of disclosure.

Some committee members have expressed doubt about the usefulness of our work, citing the fact that for the most part the same companies were always congregated around the top of the list. Some adjustments were made to the rating categories and point scores beginning with the 1988 review. Specifically, an investor relations category was added to the rating process and some new companies were also added to the review. There has clearly been an increase in interest in this report by many investor relations personnel. The changing of the guard over the past three years seems to indicate that someone may indeed be watching our efforts. Unfortunately, the disinterest among those companies that have typically scored at the lower rungs of the ladder remains.

## Criteria

The Insurance Subcommittee continued to utilize a rating sheet that it has employed in previous years. Of the total possible 100 points, up to 50 points could have been awarded for annual reports and supplements. Another 16 were available for interim reports and other published material. A total of 34 points could be allocated for management availability including the new investor relations segment. The subcommittee emphasized that the evaluation sheet was purposely designed for *subjective* appraisal, since the very nature and diversity of the insurance group precludes highly objective scoring.

The evaluation began with two basic questions: (1) whether management had, to the reviewers' knowledge, in any of its official communications to shareholders misrepresented material facts adverse to the company, or (2) whether other management practices were materially misleading. One overall qualification question suggests that the reviewer not complete the rating schedule for any company obviously unacceptable but that there should be succinct comment about the most obvious report inadequacies and possible remedies.

"Our most important contribution should not be to award excellence but identify and communicate with those companies needing guidance in their reporting." This has been our objective, and this we will continue to do.

### INSURANCE SUBCOMMITTEE

Myron M. Picoult, Chair, New York
Oppenheimer & Co., Inc.

Alice L. Cornish, Hartford
Northington Partners, Inc.

Harry Fong, Hartford
Conning & Company

A. Michael Frinquelli, CFA, New York
Salomon Brothers, Inc.

Herbert E. Goodfriend, New York
KPMG Peat Marwick

Marian L. Kessler, Minneapolis
IDS Financial Services, Inc.

Donald G. Zerbarini, New York
Lord, Abbett & Co.

## 1991 SCORES
## 700 Point Maximum

| Points 1991 | Company | Rank 1990 | 1989 | 1988 | 1987 |
|---|---|---|---|---|---|
| 589 | Capital Holding Corporation | 1 | 1 | 1 | 5 |
| 588 | SAFECO Corporation | 3 | 6 | 8 | 8 |
| 566 | UNUM Corporation | 4 | 18 | NR | NR |
| 554 | St. Paul Companies | 6 | 8 | 10 | 12 |
| 542 | NAC Re Corporation | 9 | 15 | 18 | NR |
| 539 | Chubb Corporation | 5 | 7 | 7 | 2 |
| 528 | Lincoln National Corporation | 7 | 3 | 2 | 3 |
| 528 | USF&G Corporation | 15 | 21 | 14 | 17 |
| 525 | Aetna Life & Casualty | 10 | 2 | 4 | 1 |
| 522 | American International Group | 2 | 9 | 6 | 10 |
| 514 | Travelers Corporation | 8 | 10 | 11 | 9 |
| 513 | CIGNA Corporation | 11 | 4 | 9 | 7 |
| 512 | GEICO Corporation | 19 | 14 | 16 | 13 |
| 512 | Ohio Casualty Corporation | 14 | 11 | 13 | 11 |
| 506 | American General Corporation | 18 | 20 | 12 | 6 |
| 483 | Continental Corporation | 12 | 13 | 5 | 4 |
| 446 | Torchmark Corporation | 20 | 19 | 15 | 16 |
| 444 | Aon Corporation | 17 | 17 | 17 | 15 |
| 426 | Kemper Corporation | 13 | 16 | 3 | 14 |
| 425 | Conseco | 25 | NR | NR | NR |
| 425 | General Re Corporation | 21 | 12 | 20 | 19 |
| 417 | EXEL Limited | NR | NR | NR | NR |
| 408 | Marsh & McLennan Corporation | 16 | 22 | 21 | 18 |
| 370 | Alexander & Alexander | 22 | 25 | 25 | 20 |
| 364 | Jefferson-Pilot Corporation | 24 | 24 | 24 | 24 |
| 357 | Washington National Corporation | NR | NR | NR | NR |
| 345 | USLIFE Corporation | 23 | 23 | 23 | 25 |
| 315 | Liberty Corporation | 27 | NR | NR | NR |
| 264 | Protective Life Corp. | NR | NR | NR | NR |
| 263 | CNA Corporation | 28 | NR | NR | NR |

# International Pharmaceutical

This year initiates the formal evaluation of investor communications programs for several international pharmaceutical companies. Recognizing the relatively early stage of development for many of these programs, the committee is not issuing an award this year, seeking instead to establish a baseline for evaluation of progress while providing a framework for feedback on specific programs and suggestions for improvement.

## Evaluation Procedures

The subcommittee analyzed seven major pharmaceutical companies in this year's survey, with each annual report, related financial information and investor relations program evaluated by each member. The evaluation format allocated points as follows: annual report (45 points), other published materials (20 points) and management contacts (35 points), with some adjustments for discussion of currency and accounting disclosures. The evaluation system was generally consistent with procedures used by the current U.S. health care subcommittee.

## General Comments

Most of the reviewed international pharmaceutical companies are in still relatively early development of formal investor relations programs. As a result, the ratings of evaluated international drug companies compared unfavorably to ratings assigned to U.S. health care companies. For example, the 1990 health care subcommittee rating for 15 of 17 U.S. and U.K. companies received total point scores of 80 or above. Only Rhone-Poulenc Rorer generated a score in excess of 80 points in this year's international pharmaceutical survey. The overall quality of product line disclosures, balance sheet information, accounting interpretations and discussion of quarterly sales and profit trends are considered well below U.S. and selective U.K. benchmarks.

## Summary Reviews

*Rhone-Poulenc Rorer's* investor relations program received generally high marks, especially for management access and product line sales detail. Owing to the company's substantial European sales and expense exposure, greater discussion on currency exposures was suggested.

*Ciba-Geigy* has initiated a number of investor seminars in its effort to bridge the gap between its current disclosure practice and accepted North American standards. The company received favorable comments concerning increased management access and product line sales detail.

*Astra* received high marks for details of products, markets and research programs and share ownership disclosure in the annual report. Greater access to senior management and increased quarterly financial detail was encouraged.

*Wellcome plc.* Following this past year's equity offering, the company is suggested to schedule more group presentations while increasing product line detail in its annual report.

*Sandoz.* Although Sandoz has made substantial progress in its investor relations effort over the past year, lack of information remains the company's primary shortcoming. The company receives generally favorable comments concerning progress in arranging both group and individual meetings with analysts.

*Roche Holdings.* Based on its low relative rating, Roche needs to dramatically improve the quality of information to the investment community. Greater access to management outside of formal investor presentations was generally encouraged.

*Hoechst* also received very low ratings, reflecting limited information flow and lack of exposure within the North American investor community.

## Additional Information

The subcommittee will release information concerning the rating of companies reviewed and offer to meet with managements interested in suggestions for improving their communications programs.

## INTERNATIONAL PHARMACEUTICAL INDUSTRY

| Company | Annual Report Narrative 20 | Annual Report Quantitative 25 | Other Published Materials Quarterly 18 | Other Published Materials Other 2 | Management Contact Individual 30 | Management Contact Group 5 | Letter Grade | Total Point Score 100 |
|---|---|---|---|---|---|---|---|---|
| Rhone-Poulenc Rorer, Inc. | 17 | 17 | 16 | 2 | 26 | 5 | A | 83 |
| Astra Pharmaceutical | 15 | 19 | 13 | 2 | 21 | 3 | B | 73 |
| Ciba-Geigy Corp. | 13 | 15 | 12 | 2 | 26 | 5 | B | 73 |
| Wellcome PLC | 12 | 16 | 12 | 2 | 21 | 4 | C | 67 |
| Sandoz Ltd. | 12 | 11 | 9 | 1 | 23 | 5 | C | 61 |
| Roche Holdings AG | 13 | 14 | 10 | 1 | 14 | 2 | D | 54 |
| Hoechst AG | 12 | 13 | 9 | 1 | 15 | 2 | D | 52 |

## INTERNATIONAL PHARMACEUTICAL SUBCOMMITTEE

Kenneth R. Kulju, Chair, New York
UBS Securities, Inc.

Martin Hall, London
James Capel and Company

Steve R. Frank, CFA, St. Louis
Anderson, Hoagland and Company Investment Management

# Machinery

### Recommendation for Award

The Machinery Subcommittee recommended that Dover Corporation receive an Award for Excellence in Corporate Reporting for 1991. The company scored 87.0 points out of a possible total of 100. The company has historically scored high in the past few years and noteworthy progress was made in both the annual report and interim material components. It is worthy of note that the point separation among the high scoring companies continues to be relatively small. By contrast, a high percentage of the companies evaluated are found at the lower end of the rating scale and the point separation is large.

### Companies Evaluated

The Machinery Subcommittee evaluated 16 companies, the same as in the prior year. It is possible that the universe will expand in upcoming annual evaluations, as the dynamics of the marketplace is leading to an increase in the number of larger machinery companies returning to public ownership.

### Criteria and Scores

The categories and weightings used were unchanged from last year: annual report (40%); quarterly and other printed material (30%); and investor relations and other aspects (30%).

In the annual report section, companies that did not report ten years of historical data were penalized. Some discretion was exercised where, for example, the company had a major restructuring. Companies were penalized for inadequate segment reporting. A similar guideline was followed in the evaluation of the interim reporting. In the investor relations segment, it was clear again that those companies scored well where management was increasingly accessible. The role of the investor contact continues to increase in importance in the committee's evaluation.

In order to insure the fairness of the scores, each subcommittee member evaluated each company when sufficient knowledge was evident. The scores were then averaged.

### General Comments

Out of a possible 100 points, the average score for the 16 companies evaluated was 70.9, compared with 72.2 for the prior period. In the annual report segment, the average score was 26.1 out of a possible 40. In the quarterly and other printed material category, the average was 22.6 out of a possible 30. In the final category, which is a reflection of a more subjective evaluation, the average score was 22.2 out of a possible 30.

The field of companies evaluated was unchanged from last year. A view of the individual scores shows limited changes in most cases. It appears that year in and year out, there are the same companies falling into a group that make the top four. The remaining twelve trail off with a widening spread in the individual scores. As with the top four, there is a grouping that seems to be stuck in the rear.

The subcommittee acknowledges the increased means and methods of informing the investment community with prominent examples including: faxes, fact books, and the accelerating usage of conference calls. Coupled with the pending and actual accounting rule changes, it is apparent that the method of evaluation is subject to change as well. It will be a focus of discussion and proposals during the current year with any resultant changes in place in time for the next corporate reporting evaluation.

## ANALYSIS OF CORPORATE RATINGS, MACHINERY

| | Annual Report (40%) | Quarterly Material (30%) | IR & Other (30%) | Total (100%) | Rank 1991 | Rank 1990 | Rank 1989 | Rank 1988 | Rank 1987 |
|---|---|---|---|---|---|---|---|---|---|
| Dover Corporation | 36.7 | 27.0 | 23.3 | 87.0 | 1 | 3 | 1 | 4 | 3 |
| Ingersoll-Rand Company | 33.5 | 26.5 | 25.8 | 85.8 | 2 | 2 | 2 | 3 | 5 |
| Cummins Engine Company | 35.0 | 24.0 | 26.5 | 85.5 | 3 | 5 | 3 | 2 | 1 |
| TRINOVA Corporation | 35.0 | 26.3 | 23.0 | 84.3 | 4 | 1 | 4 | 5 | 4 |
| Parker Hannifin Corporation | 35.8 | 22.3 | 23.8 | 81.9 | 5 | 4 | 10 | 15 | 13 |
| Giddings & Lewis, Inc. | 30.0 | 23.0 | 28.0 | 81.0 | 6 | 11 | — | — | — |
| Harnischfeger Industries | 26.5 | 28.5 | 24.0 | 79.0 | 7 | 6 | 7 | 6 | 6 |
| Caterpillar, Inc. | 32.8 | 21.0 | 21.8 | 75.6 | 8 | 9 | 12 | 11 | 11 |
| Navistar International Corp. | 27.0 | 24.0 | 23.7 | 74.7 | 9 | 8 | 8 | 7 | 9 |
| Kennametal, Inc. | 26.0 | 21.0 | 25.0 | 72.0 | 10 | 13 | 15 | 12 | 10 |
| Cincinnati Milacron, Inc. | 24.8 | 18.2 | 28.5 | 71.5 | 11 | 7 | 9 | 14 | 15 |
| Deere & Company | 28.2 | 21.5 | 20.8 | 70.5 | 12 | 12 | 13 | 9 | 7 |
| Varity Corporation | 27.5 | 22.0 | 16.0 | 65.5 | 13 | 14 | 6 | 6 | 6 |
| Clark Equipment Company | 25.0 | 21.5 | 18.5 | 65.0 | 14 | 16 | 11 | 16 | 16 |
| PACCAR, Inc. | 24.0 | 19.7 | 13.0 | 56.7 | 15 | 15 | 16 | 17 | 17 |
| Briggs & Stratton Corp. | 24.0 | 15.0 | 13.0 | 52.0 | 16 | 10 | 14 | 13 | 14 |
| Average | 26.1 | 22.6 | 22.2 | 70.9 | | | | | |

## MACHINERY SUBCOMMITTEE

Paul Whelan, Chair, New York
Louis Nicoud & Associates

Larry D. Hollis, Milwaukee
Robert W. Baird & Co., Inc.

Eli S. Lustgarten, New York
PaineWebber Inc.

Michael J. Kelly, New York
J.P. Morgan Investment Management Inc.

# Media

## Summary and Recommendation for Award

The Media Subcommittee recommends that Knight-Ridder and Gannett receive Awards for Excellence in Corporate Reporting this year in recognition of the overall high quality of annual and quarterly written reports and their responsive communications programs with analysts on a regular basis. Knight-Ridder has either tied for first place or won outright in six of the last eight years, while Gannett joined the winner's circle last year for the first time. Both companies scored 82 out of 100 possible points, down slightly from the 85 that they both commanded in 1990.

Knight-Ridder was particularly strong in the Annual Report category, which counted for 40% of the total points available. The level of detail found in the segment data and financials and footnotes was cited as the best in the media industry. As was the case last year, the company was specifically praised for detailing its trailing 12 months numbers on quarterly statements and for breaking out the revenue of its major newspaper properties. Gannett's strongest showing was in the Investor Relations category, which counted for 30% of the total points available. IR was broken down into the personal contact who interacts with analysts and group presentations. Gannett came in first overall in each of those subcategories. Susan Watson was specifically praised for being very responsive and providing candid observations.

Besides Knight-Ridder and Gannett, five other companies stand out as examples for others to follow—Tribune, Capital Cities/ABC, Time/Warner, E.W. Scripps, and Times Mirror. All of these companies received scores of 75 or better and were clustered within a fairly tight range.

## Companies Reviewed and Evaluation Procedures

Like last year, 20 companies were evaluated, consisting of nine newspaper publishers, four information companies, and seven companies with primary interests in television, cable, and/or entertainment. Twenty-three members made up the Media Subcommittee this year, roughly the same number as last year. The same questionnaire was used as in the last couple of years, making the conclusions meaningful in relation to past years. Each analyst evaluated only the companies with which he or she was familiar, but at least six members scored each company.

The companies were evaluated on their performance in three areas: 40% of the score was determined by the annual report, 30% by interim and other publications, and 30% was due to the investor relations program. The annual report score was made of the content and candidness of the president's letter (5% weighting), the breakdown and descriptions of segment data (20%), and analysis and detail of financials and footnotes (15%). Interim and other publications were evaluated by judging the detail and timeliness of quarterly statements (20%) and other published material (10%). The final category, investor relations, was made up of the knowledge and responsiveness of the investor relations office (20%) and the frequency and content of group presentations (10%).

## General Comments

The corporate reporting and investor communications programs in the media industry were quite varied, but the newspaper companies consistently scored higher than the other two subcategories of the media group. Six out of the top ten ranked companies were newspaper publishers, and the lowest ranked newspaper company still came in 14th out of the 20 companies evaluated. Interestingly, however, relative to last year, the newspaper companies did not show quite as much dominance because of improving showings by some of the information and broadcasting/cable/entertainment companies.

The most common criticism cited by committee members regarding a company's financial reporting related to insufficient disclosure of operating profits and cash flow by segment on a quarterly basis. This has improved over the years, but a few companies could still improve in this regard. In addition, a few of the newspaper companies now provide monthly revenue breakdowns by segment. This was congratulated and encouraged on a broader basis. In the three broad areas evaluated, the average score in the Interim and Other Publications area represented

64% of the total points possible, while in the Annual Report and Investor Relations categories, close to 70% of total possible points were the average scores.

In general, those companies that received high accolades usually had extensive factbooks that provided additional detail on various media properties, very detailed annual reports, and/or monthly data that helped to reduce quarterly surprises. A good suggestion that has not yet been universally embraced is for the media companies to hold quarterly conference calls to discuss results. This saves time for companies and analysts and generally provides more information than is possible on shorter, individually placed calls.

## Specific Company Comments

Although Knight-Ridder and Gannett tied for first place again this year, there were some changes in rankings by a number of companies. Most improved in the survey this year were Time/Warner, Reuters Holdings, and CBS, all of which jumped five places higher than their rankings last year. The latter two are still ranked in the bottom half of the companies evaluated, but are clearly improving. Time/Warner, however, is now ranked fifth (essentially tying with E.W. Scripps) and was cited as having terrific quarterly meetings and a very strong investor relations program.

Also improving in overall rankings were McGraw-Hill and Dun & Bradstreet, which each jumped up by three places compared to last year. McGraw-Hill now ranks 9th compared to 17th two years ago, while Dun & Bradstreet improved a bit to 16th, but still trails levels achieved in 1988. Like last year, McGraw-Hill was praised for its quarterly meetings with analysts and for the ceasing of major restatements of earnings and restructurings.

The companies moving most notably south this year were The New York Times and Comcast. While management was cited as being very responsive to investors and the new quarterly conference calls were deemed very helpful, The New York Times fell to 12th place from 7th, primarily because of frustration with a lack of breaking-out amortization by segment and specific property detail in its annual report. Comcast also fell five places, from 14th to 19th, despite its helpful quarterly conference calls, because of a deficiency of information provided on its rapidly growing cellular business.

Finally, two other companies deserving mention are Tribune and Capital Cities/ABC. They ranked third and fourth, respectively, following the tying winners. Tribune came in third in both the Annual Report and Interim and Other Information categories due to the extensive amount of detail provided, especially in its monthly reports which are considered to be the best in the industry. Investor relations contact Joseph A. Hays came in second overall (tying with Joseph Fitzgerald at Capital Cities/ABC), just behind Gannett's contact, Susan Watson. In addition to doing very well in the Investor Relations category, Capital Cities/ABC came in second (behind Knight-Ridder) for the president's letter in its annual report.

## MEDIA INDUSTRY
### Ranking By Category

| | Company Type | Overall Ranking 100% | Annual Report 40% | Interim and Other Publications 30% | Investor Relations 30% | Rank By Company Type |
|---|---|---|---|---|---|---|
| Knight-Ridder | N | 1 (tie) | 1 | 1 (tie) | 5 | 1 (tie) |
| Gannett | N | 1 (tie) | 2 | 1 (tie) | 1 | 1 (tie) |
| Tribune | N | 3 | 3 | 3 | 4 | 3 |
| Capital Cities/ABC | B | 4 | 4 | 7 | 3 | 1 |
| Time/Warner Inc. | B | 5 | 7 | 6 | 2 | 2 |
| E. W. Scripps Co. | N | 6 | 5 | 4 | 8 | 4 |
| Times Mirror | N | 7 | 6 | 5 | 6 | 5 |
| Paramount Communications | B | 8 | 11 | 8 | 9 | 3 |
| McGraw-Hill | I | 9 | 9 | 9 | 14 | 1 |
| A. H. Belo | N | 10 | 10 | 10 | 13 | 7 |
| Affiliated Publications | N | 11 | 14 | 13 | 10 | 8 |
| New York Times | N | 12 | 15 | 12 | 12 | 9 |
| Reuters Holdings | I | 13 | 18 | 15 | 7 | 4 |
| Washington Post | N | 14 | 8 | 18 | 16 | 6 |
| CBS Inc. | B | 15 | 13 | 11 | 19 | 4 |
| Dun & Bradstreet | I | 16 | 16 | 14 | 17 | 3 |
| Dow Jones | I | 17 | 12 | 16 | 20 | 2 |
| The Walt Disney Co. | B | 18 | 17 | 17 | 18 | 5 |
| Comcast Corp. | B | 19 | 19 | 19 | 11 | 6 |
| Tele-Communications | B | 20 | 20 | 20 | 15 | 7 |

N—Newspaper Publisher
I—Information Publisher
B—Television, Cable, and/or Entertainment Company

## MEDIA INDUSTRY SCORING
### Weighted By Importance of Category

|  | Overall Ranking (100%) | Annual Report (40%) | Interim and Other Publications (30%) | Investor Relations (30%) | 1991 Rank | 1990 Rank | 1989 Rank | 1988 Rank | 1987 Rank |
|---|---|---|---|---|---|---|---|---|---|
| Knight-Ridder | 82 | 35 | 25 | 23 | 1 (tie) | 1 (tie) | 1 | 1 (tie) | 3 |
| Gannett | 82 | 33 | 25 | 25 | 1 (tie) | 1 (tie) | 3 | 3 | 4 |
| Tribune | 79 | 32 | 24 | 23 | 3 | 4 (tie) | 2 | 1 (tie) | 2 |
| Capital Cities/ABC | 77 | 31 | 22 | 24 | 4 | 4 (tie) | 4 | 5 | 5 |
| Time/Warner Inc. | 76 | 29 | 23 | 24 | 5 | 10 | 6 | 6 | 8 |
| E. W. Scripps Co. | 76 | 31 | 24 | 21 | 6 | 3 | 7 | — | — |
| Times Mirror | 75 | 29 | 23 | 22 | 7 | 6 | 5 | 4 | 1 |
| Paramount Communications | 68 | 26 | 21 | 21 | 8 | 9 | 8 | — | — |
| McGraw-Hill | 67 | 27 | 21 | 18 | 9 | 12 | 17 | 14 | 12 |
| A. H. Belo | 64 | 26 | 19 | 19 | 10 | 11 | 13 | 12 | 11 |
| Affiliated Publications | 62 | 24 | 17 | 21 | 11 | 8 | 9 | — | — |
| New York Times | 62 | 24 | 18 | 20 | 12 | 7 | 10 | 7 | 7 |
| Reuters Holdings | 61 | 23 | 17 | 22 | 13 | 18 | 12 | 9 | 13 |
| Washington Post | 60 | 28 | 15 | 18 | 14 | 13 | 15 | 11 | 10 |
| CBS Inc. | 60 | 25 | 18 | 17 | 15 | 20 | 20 | 15 | 16 |
| Dun & Bradstreet | 58 | 24 | 17 | 18 | 16 | 19 | 19 | 10 | 14 |
| Dow Jones | 58 | 26 | 16 | 16 | 17 | 16 | 14 | 8 | 9 |
| The Walt Disney Co. | 57 | 24 | 16 | 17 | 18 | 15 | 11 | — | — |
| Comcast Corp. | 54 | 22 | 12 | 21 | 19 | 14 | 16 | — | — |
| Tele-Communications | 49 | 20 | 11 | 18 | 20 | 17 | 18 | 13 | 15 |

## MEDIA SUBCOMMITTEE

Susan L. Decker, CFA, Chair, San Francisco
Donaldson, Lufkin & Jenrette, Inc.

Judith M. Anderson, CFA, Wilmington
E.I. duPont de Nemours & Co.

Lanny Baker, New York
Morgan Stanley

Christopher Dixon, New York
PaineWebber

Juliet S. Ellis, CFA, Houston
Texas Commerce Investment Management Company

Ted Finch, Boston
State Street Research & Management Co.

Karen Firestone, Boston
Fidelity Management & Research Co.

J. Michael Gaffney, CFA, Baltimore
USF&G Corporation

Mark D. Greenberg, CFA, New York
Scudder, Stevens & Clark, Inc.

Darice P. Grippo, CFA, Boston
MacDonald Grippo Riely

Bala S. Iyer, CFA, Detroit
National Bank of Detroit/ Trust Div.

James S. Kang, New York
Capital Guardian Research

Mark Kastan, CFA, New York
The Bank of New York

Robert B. Ladd, CFA, New York
Neuberger & Berman Management, Inc.

Jack Leibau, Pasadena
Primcap Management Co.

Dennis H. Liebowitz, New York
Donaldson, Lufkin & Jenrette, Inc.

Mark M. Manson, New York
Donaldson, Lufkin & Jenrette, Inc.

Laura Martin, Los Angeles
The Capital Group, Inc.

J. Kendrick Noble, Jr., CFA, New York
Noble Consultants, Inc.

John S. Reidy, CFA, New York
Smith Barney, Harris Upham & Co., Inc.

Jeffrey J. Russell, CFA, New York
Smith Barney, Harris Upham & Co., Inc.

Bruce E. Thorp, CFA, Philadelphia
Provident National Bank

Kim Williams, Boston
Wellington Management Co.

# Natural Gas

## DISTRIBUTION COMPANIES

### Recommendation

The Natural Gas Distribution Subcommittee recommends that the 1991 Award for Excellence be given to MCN Corporation. MCN, which tied for first place with National Fuel Gas in 1990, was the clear winner in 1991. It ranked number one in quarterly reports as well as in the annual report category where the subcommittee was particularly impressed with its performance in the area of financial statements and management discussion and analysis. The first time that the subcommittee included MCN in its evaluation process was in 1988, the year that the company was spun off from Primark. That year, as might be expected for a newly independent company, MCN ranked near the bottom of the pack, ninth among the eleven companies that the subcommittee considered. MCN is to be commended for the dramatic improvement that it has made in its corporate reporting activities since that time. Its diligent efforts to implement the suggestions of the subcommittee have been a contributing factor in its rapid rise in the rankings.

### General Comments

Brooklyn Union and Equitable Resources also continued to make steady progress in the rankings. These two companies came in sixth and seventh, respectively, in 1986. Last year, they tied for third place. This year, Equitable Resources remained in third place while Brooklyn Union moved up to the number two spot. Brooklyn Union puts out a first-rate statistical supplement which ranked number one in the Historical Data category for the second year in

### NATURAL GAS DISTRIBUTION COMPANIES
#### Statistical Evaluation Summary

|  | Maximum Score | ATG | BU | EQT | MCN | NFG | GAS | PET | PGL | UGI | WGL |
|---|---|---|---|---|---|---|---|---|---|---|---|
| Annual Report |  |  |  |  |  |  |  |  |  |  |  |
| General Impression | 50 | 33 | 40 | 40 | 44 | 35 | 47 | 35 | 31 | 42 | 36 |
| Shareholder Letter | 150 | 145 | 134 | 136 | 139 | 129 | 105 | 123 | 106 | 104 | 134 |
| Operational Discussion | 150 | 123 | 129 | 137 | 133 | 127 | 121 | 133 | 128 | 124 | 123 |
| Financial Statements/MD&A | 150 | 123 | 130 | 133 | 135 | 113 | 130 | 134 | 125 | 120 | 132 |
| Historical Data | 150 | 119 | 130 | 118 | 120 | 128 | 128 | 105 | 115 | 93 | 117 |
| Subtotal | 650 | 543 | 563 | 564 | 571 | 532 | 531 | 530 | 505 | 483 | 542 |
| Quarterly Statements | 150 | 98 | 132 | 125 | 134 | 119 | 121 | 125 | 105 | 114 | 128 |
| Subtotal | 800 | 641 | 695 | 689 | 705 | 651 | 652 | 655 | 610 | 597 | 670 |
| Investor Relations | 200 | 157 | 156 | 154 | 162 | 161 | 153 | 139 | 146 | 136 | 167 |
| Total | 1,000 | 798 | 851 | 843 | 867 | 812 | 805 | 794 | 756 | 733 | 837 |
| Ranking for Year 1991 |  | 7 | 2 | 3 | 1 | 5 | 6 | 8 | 9 | 10 | 4 |
| Ranking for Year 1990 |  | 4 | 3 | 3 | 1 | 1 | 2 | 7 | 8 | 6 | 5 |
| Ranking for Year 1989 |  | 5 | 6 | 9 | 7 | 3 | 2 | 1 | 10 | 11 | 4 |
| Ranking for Year 1988 |  | 4 | 6 | 8 | 9 | 3 | 1 | 2 | 10 | 11 | 4 |
| Ranking for Year 1987 |  | 4 | 7 | 6 | — | 5 | 2 | 1 | 10 | 9 | 3 |

Note: due to rounding columns may not add up

---

ATG-Atlanta Gas Light; BU-Brooklyn Union Gas; EQT-Equitable Resources; MCN-MCN Corporation; NFG-National Fuel Gas; GAS-NICOR Inc.; PET-Pacific Enterprises; PGL-Peoples Energy; UGI-UGI Corp; WGL-Washington Gas Light a row. Equitable Resources' fine performance is due in particular to its detailed and well-written review of operations. This effort has earned the company the number one ranking in the Operational Discussion category for the past two years.

In the Investor Relations category, there were several significant changes in rankings. Washington Gas Light, which was in the middle of the pack last year, moved up to the first place spot. We attribute this, at least in part, to its group meetings which were extremely timely. Key operating people were made available for candid discussions on important industry issues. MCN dropped to the second place spot in 1991, in part because it changed from a broad-based effort to one that targeted specific investors. National Fuel Gas and Nicor, which ranked second and third in 1990, slid to the number five and six spots, respectively, in 1991.

We anticipate that investor relations will continue to be a very competitive category in 1992, partly because of turnover in the industry. In recent months new investor contacts have been announced at several of the companies. A more important factor, however, is that the natural gas distribution companies are facing major changes in the way they conduct their business. The evolving structure of the natural gas industry presents new opportunities for them, but also additional risks. It will be a challenge for them to adequately educate investors, especially since the industry is so complex.

## Evaluation Procedures

The subcommittee included two new members, three holdover members and a new chair. This amount of turnover is not surprising given that the evaluation process requires a significant time commitment. Each subcommittee member evaluates all ten companies on investor relations and on two of the other categories. The result is that each category is evaluated by two analysts and their scores are averaged to determine the final score. For the investor relations category, the subcommittee also sent out simplified questionnaires to a large group of analysts who follow the industry. Their responses were averaged with those of the subcommittee members.

Following the compilation of the scores, the subcommittee spent two days meeting with the companies. During these meetings, each analyst had the opportunity to discuss the factors that influenced his scores and to make specific suggestions regarding how a given company could improve its reporting in the future. Eight of the ten companies that we evaluated took the time to meet with us.

## PIPELINES

## Recommendation for Award

The Natural Gas Pipeline Subcommittee recommends that Enron Corporation be given the 1991 Award for Excellence in Corporate Reporting. Enron received the highest overall score due, in part, to its first-place finish in the hotly competitive area of investor relations where Enron gets high marks for the accessibility and knowledgeability of its investor relations team. Enron ranked second in the area of financial reports where the subcommittee was particularly impressed with its shareholder letter and quarterly reports.

## General Comments

The subcommittee also wishes to commend Questar for its first-place ranking in financial reports. Questar received high scores in all of the categories related to the Annual Report, but its performance in the area of Quarterly Statements was clearly outstanding. Here the subcommittee appreciated the detailed discussion of the outlook as well as of the financial and operating results for the period. The subcommittee also applauds Questar's excellent fourth-quarter report. Detailed reports on fourth-quarter results are especially important in the gas industry where, because of the seasonal nature of the business, the results in the final quarter have a disproportionately large impact on earnings for the year.

In addition, several companies deserve recognition for strong performances in specific categories. Transco ranked first in Financial Statements while, for the second year in a row, Arkla received the highest score in Divisional Discussion. All but one of the companies that we evaluate now publish an annual factbook. That makes the Historical Data category very competitive and makes the first-place ranking of Consolidated Natural Gas within that category all the more impressive.

These are challenging times for the natural gas pipeline industry. Federal regulations require a massive restructuring of the services that pipelines may offer. High debt loads have forced some companies to cut the dividend on their common stock. The rating agencies, by downgrading, or threatening to downgrade, debt ratings have stimulated the financial restructuring of some major players in the industry. The bankruptcy filing of Columbia Gas has contributed to the air of uncertainty and has raised the level of scrutiny that the pipelines face from both investors and regulators. In its meetings with the companies, the subcommittee indicated that, in general, the level of disclosure regarding financial and gas supply contract obligations has been disappointing. Given the turbulent environment that confronts investors in the industry, the subcommittee is placing increased emphasis on full and timely disclosure in these areas. That increased emphasis will be evident in our review of corporate reporting for 1992 and will have an impact on scoring for the investor relations category as well as for the written materials.

## Evaluation Procedures

The subcommittee included two new members, three holdover members, and a new chair. The procedures followed were similar to those used by the natural gas distribution company subcommittee. Of the thirteen companies that were evaluated, twelve took the time to meet with the subcommittee to discuss the results and hear our suggestions.

### NATURAL GAS PIPELINE COMPANIES
### Statistical Evaluation Summary

| | Maximum Score | ALG | CG | CGP | CNG | E | ENE | ENS | PEL | SGO | SNT | STR | TGT | WMB |
|---|---|---|---|---|---|---|---|---|---|---|---|---|---|---|
| Annual Report | | | | | | | | | | | | | | |
| General Impression | 50 | 37 | 38 | 27 | 37 | 40 | 40 | 30 | 40 | 38 | 38 | 40 | 27 | 36 |
| Shareholder Letter | 100 | 85 | 85 | 82 | 87 | 90 | 92 | 81 | 87 | 82 | 85 | 90 | 89 | 84 |
| Divisional Discussion | 150 | 142 | 131 | 130 | 139 | 135 | 135 | 140 | 138 | 131 | 134 | 138 | 130 | 134 |
| Historical Data | 125 | 99 | 103 | 49 | 117 | 92 | 114 | 99 | 111 | 104 | 79 | 115 | 88 | 80 |
| Financial Statements | 125 | 101 | 98 | 51 | 94 | 118 | 103 | 107 | 107 | 103 | 86 | 116 | 61 | 80 |
| Subtotal | 550 | 463 | 453 | 337 | 473 | 474 | 483 | 456 | 482 | 458 | 421 | 498 | 394 | 413 |
| Quarterly Statements | 200 | 140 | 185 | 78 | 150 | 180 | 188 | 160 | 180 | 148 | 113 | 193 | 68 | 125 |
| Subtotal | 750 | 603 | 638 | 415 | 623 | 654 | 671 | 616 | 662 | 605 | 533 | 690 | 462 | 538 |
| Investor Relations | 250 | 141 | 150 | 155 | 221 | 192 | 227 | 154 | 196 | 159 | 188 | 189 | 168 | 159 |
| Total | 1,000 | 744 | 788 | 569 | 844 | 846 | 898 | 770 | 858 | 764 | 721 | 879 | 629 | 697 |
| Ranking for 1991 | | 9 | 6 | 13 | 5 | 4 | 1 | 7 | 3 | 8 | 10 | 2 | 12 | 11 |
| Ranking for 1990 | | 5 | 7 | 11 | 1 | 1 | 2 | 9 | 4 | 8 | 6 | 3 | 12 | 10 |
| Ranking for 1989 | | 10 | 5 | 13 | 3 | 1 | 2 | 8 | 4 | 12 | 7 | 6 | 11 | 9 |
| Ranking for 1988 | | 7 | 6 | 13 | 1 | 2 | 5 | 12 | 4 | 10 | 8 | 3 | 9 | 11 |
| Ranking for 1987 | | 14 | 6 | 13 | 2 | 1 | 8 | 11 | 4 | 9 | 12 | 3 | 10 | 7 |

Note: Due to rounding columns may not add up

ALG-Arkla, Inc; CG-Columbia Gas System; CGP-Coastal Corp; CNG-Consolidated Natural Gas; E-Transco Energy; ENE Enron Corp; ENS-ENSERCH Corp; PEL-Panhandle Eastern; SGO-Seagull Energy; SNT-Sonat; STR-Questar; TGT-Tenneco Inc; WMB-Williams Companies

# NATURAL GAS SUBCOMMITTEE

## Chair

Ronald F. Cassinari — M R Beal & Company

### Natural Gas Distribution Companies

| | |
|---|---|
| Susan Chapman, CFA, Chair | Forbes, Walsh, Kelly & Co., Inc., New York |
| Joanne M. Fairechio | Salomon Brothers, Inc., New York |
| Gary F. Hovis | Argus Research Corp., New York |
| D. Roger B. Liddell | Ingalls & Snyder, New York |
| Catharina T. Milostan | Prudential Securities, Inc., New York |
| Ralph G. Pellecchia | Fitch Investors Service, Inc., New York |

### Natural Gas Pipelines Companies

| | |
|---|---|
| Susan Chapman, CFA, Chair | Forbes, Walsh, Kelly & Co., Inc., New York |
| David Ahl | Daiwa Securities, New York |
| Michael G. Barbis, CFA | Wertheim Schroder & Co., New York |
| Carol M. Coale | Howard, Weil, Labouisse, Friedrichs, Inc., Houston |
| Gary F. Hovis | Argus Research Corp., New York |
| Ralph G. Pellecchia | Fitch Investors Service, Inc., New York |

# Nonferrous and Mining

## Recommendation for Award

After considerable evaluation and deliberation, the subcommittee recommends that an Award for Excellence in Corporate Reporting be awarded in each subsector: nonferrous metals, precious metals, and coal. While the subcommittee did not feel that any one company had reached the optimum level of disclosure in reporting, the overall level of information provided by each award winner was better than that in its peer group. In the nonferrous metals segment it was Freeport-McMoRan Copper & Gold Inc.; in the precious metals segment it was Amax Gold Inc.; and in the coal segment it was Ashland Coal Inc.

NONFERROUS METALS—Freeport-McMoRan Copper & Gold Inc. scored highly in all three reporting segments, but it was two important aspects of quarterly reporting that put them over the top. Management offers complete statements and full operating and production data in their first release of quarterly earnings, yet the release is timely.

PRECIOUS METALS—Amax Gold Inc. improved its score dramatically from last year's results and scored highly in all three reporting segments. It was clearly the leader in quarterly reports, an area of much emphasis by the committee. The significant improvement in the standings by Amax Gold was due to implementation of recommendations made by the subcommittee following a review of the 1990–91 survey with management.

COAL—Ashland Coal Inc. clearly deserves the award for the second consecutive year because it leads the industry in thorough and timely disclosure. Ashland Coal continues to improve its disclosure by providing more detailed information on its operating units. This continues to become more important as the company grows, especially since the growth is mainly through acquisitions. Also, its quarterly reports are very good, as is its investor relations program.

## Criteria For Review

The 32 companies included in the survey were evaluated on their reporting practices and investor communications. They were included in the survey because of general investment interest as well as size, capitalization, and float. Each company was reviewed by at least two, but in most cases, three or more analysts, with the results being weighted and averaged to compute a standard score. We believe that the results of the survey fairly rank the companies in order of investor perception as to the criteria reviewed.

The subcommittee used a comprehensive questionnaire for its study. The questionnaire was very detailed and specific, even more so than last year. In particular, a number of new questions were added to the quarterly section that compared the level of information given quarterly with that provided in the annual. The purpose was to re-emphasize the importance that analysts attach to prompt, complete quarterly information. The questionnaire also included a number of new questions about balance sheet and cash flow statement data in the 10-year historic summary in the annual report.

The subcommittee felt that balanced and informative reporting practice throughout the year was more desirable than one comprehensive annual document and weighted its views accordingly. The weightings by category were substantially changed from last year to reflect the increased importance placed upon timely dissemination of information. Quarterly and 10-Q reports and quarterly earnings press releases accounted for 45% of the overall score (up from 40% last year and 30% in 1989); annual and 10-K reports, 35% (no change); and investor relations and related aspects, including field trips and analysts meetings, 20% (down from 25%).

## General Comments

The subcommittee is pleased to see the number of company managements taking an interest in improving their ranking in this review. We appreciate the requests for information and hope that the discussions we have had have been helpful. The subcommittee would specifically like to applaud all of the aluminum producers' efforts to improve their quarterly reporting of shipment and averaged realized price data.

The scores in this year's survey varied widely by category. Some of the companies scored well on annual reports, only to stumble elsewhere. Others did better reporting quarterly than annually. There are four major areas in which the subcommittee feels there is significant room for improvement in industry reporting practices: 1) business segment reporting in quarterly reports; 2) discussion of corporate strategies and goals in the annual report; 3) disclosure of operational data on a quarterly basis, and 4) disclosure of full income, balance sheet, and cash flow data in the initial press release of quarterly earnings.

Given that segment reporting has been required for quite some time now and that investors would like to see more frequent reports of segment data, the subcommittee questions the failure of corporate managements to report this information on a quarterly basis. In some cases in our survey, it was the lack of good quarterly segment data that lowered the ranking of companies that otherwise have a strong performance. Some of the large companies have the most potential for improvement in this area.

## Subsector Reports

The individual subsector group reports follow. We have made an effort to divide the group into three sectors for better comparability among companies. The committee continues to believe that investor interests are better served by dividing the group into more homogeneous subsectors—nonferrous metals, precious metals, and coal.

## Companies Included in the Survey

A total of 32 companies from Australia, Canada, United Kingdom, and United States were included in this year's survey of the nonferrous and mining industry. These companies were chosen as representative of companies in the overall category, but are not a complete or exhaustive list. The subcommittee views the universe as fluid, and will review the list each year.

| Name of Company | Ticker Symbol |
|---|---|
| Nonferrous: | |
| Alcan Aluminium Ltd. | AL |
| Aluminum Company of America (Alcoa) | AA |
| Amax Inc. | AMX |
| Asarco Inc. | AR |
| CRA Limited | CRADY* |
| Cyprus Minerals Company | CYM |
| Freeport McMoRan Copper & Gold | FCX |
| Inco, Ltd. | N |
| Kaiser Aluminum Corporation | KLU |
| Magma Copper Company | MCU |
| MIM Holdings Limited | MIMOY* |
| Phelps Dodge Corp. | PD |
| Reynolds Metals Company | RLM |
| The RTZ Corp. PLC | RTZ* |
| Western Mining Corp. Holdings | WMC |
| Precious Metals: | |
| Amax Gold Inc. | AU |
| American Barrick Resources Corp. | ABX |
| Battle Mountain Gold Company | BMG |
| Coeur d'Alene Mines | CDE |
| Echo Bay Mines Ltd. | ECO |
| Hecla Mining Company | HL |
| Hemlo Gold Mines Inc. | HEM** |
| Homestake Mining Company | HM |
| LAC Minerals Limited | LAC |
| Newmont Mining Corp. | NEM |
| Pegasus Gold Inc. | PGU |
| Placer Dome Inc. | PDG |
| Coal: | |
| Addington Resources, Inc. | ADDR |
| Ashland Coal Inc. | ACI |
| NERCO, Inc. | NER |
| The Pittston Company | PCO |
| Westmoreland Coal Company | WCX |

\* Symbol for listed ADRs
\*\* Symbol for Toronto exchange

## NONFERROUS METALS COMPANIES
### Susan Bridges, CFA, Chair

This year, the subcommittee reviewed eleven North American companies and four overseas companies in the nonferrous segment. Ten committee members participated in the nonferrous subsegment review, and each company was reviewed by at least three analysts, except for the overseas companies, which were each reviewed by two analysts.

### General Comments

Overall scores ranged from 26.9 to 70.4, with an average score of 47.0 and a median score of 44.4. As has been true for several years now, the high-scoring companies were all copper producers, while aluminum and nickel producers tended to rank in the middle. The lowest ranking companies were all overseas.

## Annual Reporting

Scores on annual reporting ranged from 12.8 to 23.7, out of a possible 35. The average was 18.2 and the median 18.3.

The subcommittee feels that there is room for significant improvement in annual reporting in the following areas: (1) the companies' long-term and one-year strategies and goals and a discussion of last year's results in context of the stated objectives for that year; (2) identification of the major internal and external factors affecting the reporting period and the following year's outlook; (3) meaningful linkage between reported volume and price information and segment sales and profit; (4) more detail on operations (production, reserves, cut-off grade, average realized prices, and costs); and (5) more cash flow and balance sheet information in their ten-year histories.

The subcommittee was very disappointed to see how little improvement there had been in discussing strategies and reporting production data compared to last year, since these areas had been particularly identified in the last two reviews as needing improvement. It was also disappointed that very little attention was paid to its request for more historic cash flow and balance sheet data.

## Quarterly Reporting

Scores on quarterly reporting ranged from 6.3 to 33.1, out of a possible 45. The average was 19.0 and the median, 17.2.

The subcommittee feels that there is room for improvement in: (1) quarterly business segment reporting; (2) factual support for discussions of quarterly operating performance (particularly production, reserves, realized prices, costs, and the ability to relate management discussions about particular products or operations to reported numbers); and (3) the publication of full income statements, balance sheets, and cash flow statements in the initial earnings release. This year's questionnaire heavily penalized the failure to provide such information in the earnings release or the quarterly. The subcommittee believes that there is very little benefit to early reporting of an earnings number if analysts must wait for the 10-Q to get full financial statements and notes. (10-Q's are available 45 days after the close of the quarter.) Several companies are essentially able to provide 10-Q-level contents while reporting only a week to ten days later than those companies who provide only an earnings number.

## Investor Relations

Scores for investor relations ranged from 6.5 to 17.5, out of a possible 20. The average was 11.0 and the median, 10.4.

The wide disparity of results in this section is a function of the heavy weightings that the subcommittee placed on regular meetings between analysts and management and operating personnel. It was difficult to score well without such meetings. Furthermore, there was a strong correlation between companies that meet with analysts and the availability and

### NONFERROUS METALS COMPANY RANKINGS

| 1991–92 Rank | Company | Total Score | Annual Reports | Quarterly Reports | Investor Relations | 1989–90 Rank* | 1990–91 Rank |
|---|---|---|---|---|---|---|---|
| 1 | FCX | 70.4% | 21.5% | 33.1% | 15.8% | 1 | 2 |
| 2 | MCU | 68.8 | 20.2 | 31.1 | 17.5 | 12 | 4 |
| 3 | PD | 63.8 | 23.7 | 25.3 | 14.8 | 3 | 1 |
| 4 | AR | 57.9 | 18.3 | 29.2 | 10.5 | 5 | 3 |
| 5 | AL | 53.2 | 20.1 | 23.2 | 9.9 | 11 | 5 |
| 6 | AA | 49.6 | 20.4 | 17.2 | 11.9 | 7 | 7 |
| 7 | RLM | 45.8 | 20.5 | 16.8 | 8.5 | 8 | 9 |
| 8 | N | 44.4 | 16.3 | 21.5 | 6.5 | 6 | 8 |
| 9 | CYM | 43.6 | 17.8 | 15.4 | 10.4 | 10 | 10 |
| 10 | AMX | 42.4 | 15.3 | 12.7 | 14.4 | 1 | 6 |
| 11 | WMC | 40.9 | 16.9 | 11.9 | 12.1 | NA | 11 |
| 12 | KLU | 37.8 | 18.8 | 12.3 | 6.7 | NA | NA |
| 13 | CRA | 31.9 | 12.8 | 9.9 | 9.2 | NA | 12 |
| 14 | MIM | 26.9 | 13.0 | 6.3 | 7.6 | NA | 13 |
| 15 | RTZ | 26.9 | 17.4 | 19.4 | 9.9 | NA | 14 |

* The 1989–90 ranking was adjusted for the removal of the coal companies from this universe.

## PRECIOUS METALS COMPANY RANKINGS

| 1991–92 Rank | Company | Total Score | Annual Reports | Quarterly Reports | Investor Relations | 1990–91 Rank* |
|---|---|---|---|---|---|---|
| 1 | Amax Gold | 74.2% | 23.2% | 34.2% | 16.8% | 7 |
| 2 | Lac Minerals | 69.1 | 21.9 | 33.1 | 14.0 | 3 |
| 3 | Placer Dome | 68.6 | 23.1 | 30.3 | 15.2 | 8 |
| 4 | Echo Bay | 67.0 | 22.5 | 29.6 | 14.9 | 1 |
| 5 | American Barrick | 66.3 | 20.7 | 27.3 | 18.3 | 2 |
| 6 | Battle Mountain | 65.9 | 23.2 | 27.8 | 14.9 | 4 |
| 7 | Pegasus | 63.5 | 22.8 | 23.3 | 17.5 | 6 |
| 8 | Homestake | 60.5 | 20.9 | 24.8 | 14.8 | 9 |
| 9 | Newmont Mining | 59.2 | 19.5 | 23.9 | 15.8 | 5 |
| 10 | Hemlo Gold | 58.9 | 22.2 | 23.4 | 13.3 | 12 |
| 11 | Coeur d'Alene | 54.7 | 15.9 | 25.4 | 13.4 | 10 |
| 12 | Hecla | 51.9 | 17.8 | 20.9 | 13.1 | 11 |

*The 1990–91 ranking was adjusted to reflect fewer companies in the 1991–92 survey.

knowledgeability of the investor relations contact, which only served to widen the gap between the high and low scores.

## PRECIOUS METALS COMPANIES
### Lucille Palermo, CFA, Chair

The subcommittee reviewed 12 companies in the previous metals segment. Four committee members participated in the study, and each company was reviewed by three analysts.

Noteworthy in the results is the quantum leap taken by the winner, Amax Gold Inc., which moved to first place (with a score of 74.2%) from seventh place (54.8%) in 1990. The company reviewed its performance last year with the committee and clearly took decisive steps to improve results, such as putting out a full press release on quarterly results. In general, most companies improved their results this year, with the exception of American Barrick, which was penalized heavily for publishing only year-to-date results in its quarterlies.

The committee remains dismayed, however, at the wide variation in quality of reporting given the homogeneity of the business of this group. The members would like to see

- *Quarterly Reports* that contain financial statements as complete as those in the company's annual reports and that contain meaningful updates on capital expenditures, hedging positions, and individual operations, particularly vis-a-vis targets for the year.
- *Cost breakdowns* that include per-ton data, as well as the mining, milling, royalty, depreciation, on-site overhead, and reclamation components, both in the aggregate and for individual mines.
- *Specific corporate goals* and the strategies in place for achieving those goals together with the performance measurements to reflect management's success at achieving them.
- *Long term historical summaries* that include performance ratios such as return on assets, return on equity, book value etc., over a ten-year period.

### General Comments

Overall scores rose significantly for 1991, with a range of 51.9 to 74.2, compared with a range of 38.6 to 63.9 last year. The average score was 63.3 and the median was 63.0.

### Annual Reporting

Annual reporting scores ranged from 15.9 to 23.2, and averaged 21.1. The median was 20.5.

Companies could improve scores by elaborating on their corporate strategies and long-term goals and the performance ratios used to measure management's success at achieving those goals. Another way would be to include more items in the financial statements, particularly the balance sheet, statement of changes in cash flow, and historical summaries.

### Quarterly Reporting

Quarterly reporting scores ranged from 20.9 to 34.2, and averaged 27.0. The median was 27.6. Better discussion of individual operations and more complete financial statements would improve results for most companies.

## Investor Relations

Investor relation scores ranged from 13.1 to 18.3, and averaged 15.2. The median was 14.9.

More frequent company-sponsored presentations and organized field trips would improve many companies' results. For others a more proactive investor relations effort is required.

## COAL MINING COMPANIES
### Daniel A. Roling, CPA, CFA, Chair

The subcommittee once again included 5 companies in the coal mining segment of the Nonferrous and Mining Industry survey. Three committee members participated in the coal mining subsegment review.

Once again Ashland Coal Inc. is being recommended for an award. The subcommittee still believes, however, that there is room for additional improvement. The major criticism is limited to the press release for quarterly earnings, which does not contain a cash flow statement and lacks a clear presentation of shares outstanding and a reconciliation of fully diluted earnings per share. In addition, some subcommittee members would like to see more information on reserves, costs, and operating data on individual operations.

The ranking of the coal companies changed slightly with Westmoreland Coal Company moving from fourth place to third on the strength of its improvement in its annual report. It appears that management of Westmoreland Coal has taken an interest in improving its disclosure and shareholder relations program.

We continue to believe that it would be most useful for management to share with shareholders their strategic objectives for the company. Accordingly, the subcommittee was once again disappointed to see how little improvement was made in shareholder communications regarding corporate strategies. Also, very little improvement was made in improved reporting of production or operating data for diversified companies.

## General Comments

Overall scores ranged from 43.4 to 62.0, with an average score of 52.0 and a median score of 49.8.

## Annual Reporting

Scores on annual reporting ranged from 18.2 to 20.4, out of a possible 35. The average was 19.4 and the median, 19.6.

## Quarterly Reporting

Scores on quarterly reporting ranged from 17.0 to 27.9, out of a possible 45. The average was 21.9 and the median, 19.8.

## Investor Relations

Scores for Investor relations ranged from 7.2 to 14.6, out of a possible 20. The average was 10.6 and the median, 10.2.

### COAL MINING COMPANY RANKINGS

| 1991–92 Rank | Company Ticker Symbol | Total Score | Annual Reports | Quarterly Reports | Investor Relations | 1989–90 Rank | 1990–91 Rank |
|---|---|---|---|---|---|---|---|
| 1 | ACI | 62.0% | 19.6% | 27.9% | 14.6% | 1 | 1 |
| 2 | PCO | 55.9 | 18.2 | 27.5 | 10.2 | 2 | 2 |
| 3 | WCX | 49.8 | 20.3 | 19.8 | 9.7 | 4 | 4 |
| 4 | NER | 48.8 | 20.4 | 17.0 | 11.4 | 3 | 3 |
| 5 | ADDR | 43.4 | 18.5 | 17.8 | 7.2 | NA | 5 |

# NONFERROUS AND MINING INDUSTRY SUBCOMMITTEE

Daniel A. Roling, CPA, CFA, Chair
Merrill Lynch, New York

NONFERROUS METALS:
Susan Bridges, CFA, Chair, New York
Alliance Capital Management

J. Theodore Berkemeier, Los Angeles
Capital Guardian Research

Cole Lannum III, CFA, Saint Louis
Boatmen's Trust Company

Victor Lazarovici, New York
S.G. Warburg & Company

Elizabeth Mackay, CFA, New York
Bear, Stearns, & Co.

R. Douglas Moffat, CFA, Atlanta
The Robinson-Humphrey Co.

Anthony Rizzuto, Jr., New York
First Boston Corporation

Daniel A. Roling, CPA, CFA, New York
Merrill Lynch

G. David Underwood, CFA, Pittsburgh
C.S. McKee

Thomas M. Van Leeuwen, CFA, New York
Lehman Brothers

PRECIOUS METALS:
Lucille Palermo, CFA, Chair, New York
Van Eck Securities

Victor Flores, San Antonio
United Services Advisors, Inc.

Warren Myers, New York
Merrill Lynch

Alex Tershakovec, New York
Goldman Sachs & Co.

COAL:
Daniel A. Roling, CPA, CFA, Chair, New York
Merrill Lynch

Victor Flores, San Antonio
United Services Advisors, Inc.

Rafael A. Villagran, New York
Lehman Brothers

# Paper and Forest Products

## Recommendation for Award

The subcommittee recommends that Georgia-Pacific receive the Award for Excellence in Corporate Reporting in recognition of the overall high quality of the company's communication program.

Last year's runner-up, Georgia-Pacific narrowly edged out three time recipient Boise Cascade in this year's evaluation. Georgia-Pacific's financial communication program was judged to be fully comprehensive and sustained a high standard in all aspects. The company's written material provided a high degree of detail on the company's operations. The combination of the annual report and factbook was highlighted as particularly noteworthy by the subcommittee. The quarterly disclosures were complete and timely. The company conducted an active investor relations effort. The analyst contacts were knowledgeable, well informed, responsive to analysts' inquiries and facilitated meetings with senior management and operating personnel. Overall, the company's program demonstrated a commitment in all aspects to furnishing accurate, accessible and timely financial information.

## Evaluation Procedures

The subcommittee's evaluation form was developed from guidelines suggested by the Corporate Information Committee, incorporating issues pertinent to the industry. The form is reviewed annually to ensure that topical subjects, affecting the industry, are given due consideration. The evaluation procedure was based on a review of three elements of a company's financial communication program. Weightings were assigned to specific categories as follows:

|  | Weighting |
| --- | --- |
| Annual Reports, 10-K, and Factbook | 50% |
| Quarterly Reports | 25% |
| Investor Relations and Related Aspects | 25% |

Eight subcommittee members reviewed nineteen companies.

## Category I
## Annual Report, 10-K, and Factbook

Evaluation of the annual report focused on the chairman's letter, and discussion of corporate strategy. An objective review of the company's twelve-month performance was expected, as was a meaningful analysis of prospects for the coming year, together with the identification of critical contributing variables (both internal and external). A detailed outline of the company's strategy, its implementation and potential consequences were expected. Divisional sales and earnings information, capacity and production data, discussion of cost and historical pricing trends, detail on timber reserves and raw material self-sufficiency, and a review of capital expenditures and the resultant impact were also accorded a high degree of significance. A ten-year historical summary was considered essential, and bonus marks were awarded if data for eleven years were provided. Discussion of a company's environmental liability was expected. In addition, the subcommittee awarded bonus marks for innovative disclosures, while flagrant omissions were penalized. Discussion of changes in accounting policies and their impact were evaluated, with particular emphasis on disclosure with respect to SFAS 106. The content and relevancy of the factbook were evaluated.

## Category II
## Quarterly Reports

Analysis of the quarterly report emphasized quarterly sales and operating information on a segment basis. Production data and pricing information on a quarterly basis were expected. In addition, detailed quarterly income statements, balance sheets and cash flow statements for the quarter were considered necessary. The adequacy and quality of disclosure on the day of the earnings release were reviewed. Good commentary on operating results, including the identification of significant factors influencing results, and an update on capital expenditure plans where appropriate, were expected. In all instances, the level of detail was compared with that provided by the annual report. Publication of a fourth quarter report was considered necessary.

## Category III
## Investor Relations and Related Aspects

The category of investor relations and related aspects evaluated the timeliness and content of management presentations and company field trips. Analyst contacts were evaluated according to familiarity with current developments, objectivity and accessibility. The availability of a knowledgeable contact on the day of an earnings release or material development was judged to be essential. Access to senior management was also considered an important element. Related aspects in this category incorporated the evaluation of other information made available and included press releases on material developments, access to internal or industry studies, relevant articles on the company and copies of management presentations. Bonus marks were awarded for innovative delivery of information.

## General Comments

Overall, scores were somewhat higher this year in comparison with last year, reflecting a modest improvement in all categories, and continued an improving trend identified in last year's report. The industry's continued commitment to an active financial communication program is particularly encouraging, in light of the challenging operating environment which has negatively affected results in recent years. Companies which have reduced emphasis on investor relations during this period have been penalized as a result. Meaningful improvements in either scores or rankings were accomplished by Georgia-Pacific, Consolidated Papers, Federal Paper Board, James River, Kimberly Clark and Willamette Industries.

*Annual Reports and Factbooks*: The annual report and factbook presented by Georgia-Pacific was considered to be the most comprehensive combination. In particular, the subcommittee applauded complete information on unit production, capacity, segment sales data and historical pricing trends, as well as detailed footnotes and an extensive table of significant financial ratios. Additional exhibits considered worthy of mention include: capacity, production and market share information provided by Willamette Industries, financial footnotes presented by Temple-Inland, the flow chart incorporated by Mead, historical pricing trends and production data included by Louisiana Pacific, market information by product category and share from Kimberly Clark, Bowater's inclusion of detailed segment information, and segment profit and loss information from Boise Cascade.

The subcommittee highlighted the factbooks produced by Mead and Boise Cascade as merit worthy. The publication of a combined factbook and annual report by Weyerhaeuser received praise from the subcommittee. Temple-Inland and Bowater received commendation from the subcommittee for the level of detail provided in the annual report, 10-K or supplemental data which obviated the need for a factbook. The subcommittee continued to recommend that companies furnish a meaningful factbook to supplement or complement the information supplied in the annual report.

Criticisms of the subcommittee continued to focus on the chairman's letter and we would welcome a more in-depth analysis of the operating environment and business prospects. The subcommittee would encourage discussion of operations in an industry context.

*Quarterly Segment Information*: The absence of quarterly segment sales and earnings information continued to penalize company scores. The subcommittee continued to urge that companies make such information available and noted with appreciation that companies have responded favorably to the request. Scott Paper made quarterly segment information available for the first time. Although the subcommittee noted that Mead provided segment information on a half yearly basis, the lack of quarterly segment data continued to handicap an otherwise outstanding effort.

Boise Cascade received commendation from the subcommittee for the completeness and timeliness of its quarterly information. Quarter disclosures from Kimberly Clark, Consolidated Papers, Georgia-Pacific, Louisiana Pacific, Union Camp, Willamette Industries and Bowater were considered worthy of attention. Although quarterly information in the year under review presented by Bowater received commendation, the subcommittee noted with disappointment the recent hiatus in segment information. The subcommittee encouraged the quarterly conference call and fax delivery of press releases as efficient and timely methods of disseminating information.

*Investor Relations and Related Aspects*: Improved scores were particularly evident in this category. Over 50% of the companies under evaluation ranked in the first quartile for this category as compared with 37% a year ago and 39% two years ago. The investor relations effort within the industry was considered quite comprehensive. Investor relations contacts received generally high marks. Companies engaged in a comprehensive investor relations effort, including regularly scheduled meetings with the financial community and access to senior management, distinguished themselves in this category. Kimberly Clark was considered particularly outstanding in this regard. The analysts' field trip conducted during the year received high commendation. Boise Cascade, Mead, Temple-Inland, Federal Paper Board and Weyerhaeuser were cited by the subcommittee for their regular analysts meetings.

*Other Comments*: The subcommittee recognized the continued commitment to financial communications exhibited by Boise Cascade. In spite of a difficult operating environment, the company has made every effort to keep investors apprised of their situation.

The subcommittee called attention to the financial communication program conducted by Kimberly Clark. The company's high ranking demonstrated that it is possible to provide an appropriate level of detail without jeopardizing competitive position and should serve as an example to those companies reluctant to disclose specific information on those grounds.

The aim of the subcommittee is to provide the industry with an improved understanding of what is considered a satisfactory level of information by the financial community. The subcommittee has been most encouraged by the response of the industry to its suggestions. The challenging environment of the last several years has placed additional pressure on the financial communication programs of the industry and the subcommittee once again recognized the industry for maintaining a constructive approach to corporate communications during this period. The subcommittee again welcomed the opportunity to meet with companies to address specific issues.

## PAPER AND FOREST PRODUCTS INDUSTRY
### 1991-1992 Evaluations

| | I Annual Report, 10-Ks, and Fact Book Score | Rank | II Quarterly Reports Score | Rank | III Investor Relations and Related Aspects Score | Rank | Total Score | Rank | 1990 Rank | 1989 Rank | 1988 Rank | 1987 Rank |
|---|---|---|---|---|---|---|---|---|---|---|---|---|
| Boise Cascade | 35.0% | 3 | 22.0% | 1 | 22.0% | 2 | 79.0% | 2 | 1 | 1 | 1 | 3 |
| Bowater Incorporated | 29.1% | 13 | 18.7% | 10 | 18.0% | 11 | 65.8% | 13 | 6 | 8 | 7 | 5 |
| Champion International | 24.5% | 16 | 14.4% | 16 | 12.8% | 17 | 51.7% | 17 | 16 | 17 | 12 | 6 |
| Consolidated Papers | 33.0% | 5 | 21.0% | 3 | 19.0% | 8 | 73.0% | 4 | 11 | 13 | 9 | 7 |
| Federal Paper Board | 30.0% | 12 | 16.9% | 13 | 21.2% | 4 | 68.1% | 10 | 13 | 11 | 5 | NR |
| Georgia-Pacific | 39.5% | 1 | 20.7% | 4 | 21.8% | 3 | 82.0% | 1 | 2 | 6 | 1 | 8 |
| International Paper | 29.0% | 14 | 14.2% | 17 | 20.2% | 5 | 63.4% | 14 | 12 | 15 | 15 | 16 |
| James River Corporation | 25.2% | 15 | 19.7% | 6 | 15.6% | 16 | 60.5% | 15 | 18 | 18 | 16 | 14 |
| Kimberly-Clark | 31.5% | 7 | 21.9% | 2 | 22.7% | 1 | 76.1% | 3 | 4 | 5 | 3 | 4 |
| Louisiana Pacific Corp. | 30.5% | 11 | 20.2% | 5 | 18.0% | 11 | 68.7% | 9 | 9 | NR | NR | NR |
| Mead Corporation | 37.0% | 2 | 16.6% | 14 | 19.2% | 7 | 72.8% | 5 | 5 | 2 | 2 | 2 |
| Potlatch | 31.5% | 7 | 18.0% | 11 | 17.0% | 15 | 66.5% | 12 | 10 | 9 | 6 | NR |
| Scott Paper | 24.5% | 16 | 11.6% | 19 | 12.2% | 18 | 48.3% | 18 | 17 | 7 | 13 | 11 |
| Stone Container | 18.4% | 19 | 14.7% | 15 | 9.7% | 19 | 42.8% | 19 | 15 | 16 | 19 | NR |
| Temple-Inland | 31.4% | 10 | 18.8% | 9 | 17.8% | 13 | 68.0% | 11 | 8 | 3 | 8 | 9 |
| Union Camp | 32.5% | 6 | 19.4% | 7 | 19.0% | 8 | 70.9% | 7 | 7 | 4 | 11 | 12 |
| Westvaco Corporation | 23.0% | 18 | 12.5% | 18 | 17.5% | 14 | 53.0% | 16 | 19 | 12 | 17 | 13 |
| Weyerhaeuser Company | 35.0% | 3 | 17.1% | 12 | 20.1% | 6 | 72.2% | 6 | 3 | 14 | 14 | 15 |
| Willamette Industries | 31.5% | 7 | 18.9% | 8 | 18.9% | 10 | 69.3% | 8 | 14 | 10 | 10 | 10 |
| Maximum Score | 50.0% | | 25.0% | | 25.0% | | 100.0% | | | | | |

NR: Not Rated

## PAPER AND FOREST PRODUCTS SUBCOMMITTEE

Kim Williams, Chair, Boston
Wellington Management Company

Sherman Chao, New York
Merrill Lynch

Chris Corapi, New York
J.P. Morgan & Co., Inc.

C.A. Dillon, III, CFA, New York
First Manhattan Co.

Frank R. Dunau, CFA, Boston
Harvard Management Co., Inc.

Bruce Kirk, CFA, New York
S.G. Warburg & Co., Inc.

Lawrence A. Ross, CFA, New York
PaineWebber, Inc.

Richard S. Schneider, New York
Kidder Peabody & Co., Inc.

# Petroleum

This year, four subgroups—International Oils, Domestic Integrated Oils and Independent Refiners, Independent Oil and Gas Producers, and Oil Service and Contract Drillers—reviewed 42 companies.

The International Oil subcommittee made significant changes in both its questionnaire and weightings of results. This undertaking resulted in a survey that is better focused on issues which are most important to the industry as it exists today. Additionally, this subcommittee feels that its reconstructed scoring system enabled reviewers to more easily identify and value each company's unique strengths and weaknesses.

Surveys conducted by the other three subcommittees generally followed the questionnaires and scoring systems established in recent years, although some modifications were made to reflect changes in accounting standards and industry regulations.

## Recommendation for Awards for Excellence

The subcommittees recommended that the following Awards for Excellence be given for 1991–1992:

International Oil Cos.
   Award: Mobil Corporation
   Letter of Commendation: Exxon Corporation
Domestic Integrated Oil
   Cos. Award: Atlantic Richfield and Phillips Petroleum (tie)
   Letter of Commendation: Occidental Petroleum
Independent Refining Cos.
   Award: Ashland Oil
Independent Oil & Gas Producers Award: Enron Oil & Gas Company
Oil Service and Equipment
   Cos. Award: Baker Hughes
Oil & Gas Contract Drilling
   Cos. Award: Global Marine and Rowan Cos. (tie)

While there were repeat winners in the International Oils (Mobil), the Domestic Integrated Oils (Arco and Phillips) and the Contract Drillers (Rowan), it is interesting to note that in both the International Oils and the Domestic Oils the committees chose to recognize companies that have made major positive strides in their respective categories. Exxon (International Oils) was recommended to receive a Letter of Commendation for its very successful restructuring efforts in both the investor relations and corporate reporting areas. Exxon leapfrogged from seventh place (in both 1989 and 1990) to second place this year. A similar, if not quite as dramatic leap was taken by Occidental Petroleum (Domestic Oils) this year, as the company moved from eighth place (in 1989) to sixth place (in 1990) to third place this year. The Domestic Integrated Oils subcommittee, noting Occidental's highly successful efforts at improving both reporting practices and investor relations communications, has recommended that company for a Letter of Commendation.

## Review Sessions

To encourage an ongoing dialogue between the Corporate Information Committee and company managements, all subcommittees meet with investor relations managers and other senior corporate officers to review the results of their surveys in detail. The meetings provide a forum for companies to respond to the evaluations and to offer suggestions for amending the process, as well as to gain a deeper understanding of how companies are perceived by the investment community. Although in the main these sessions are viewed by both our committees and the companies as being very positive and valuable, it should be noted that some companies' compensation and bonus for investor relations executives are based on placement in the CIC surveys. Our committees have tried repeatedly to make clear that turning this ongoing process into a contest is not the goal or intention of either the committees or AIMR. Rather, participation in the evaluation process should emphasize the continuing process of refining written and oral communications between companies and the investment community.

## The Role of NAPIA

The National Association of Petroleum Investment Analysts continues to maintain a high profile in the evaluation process. The NAPIA Board of Directors takes an active role in trying to persuade the organization's members to take part in the exercise and the chairman of the Corporate Information Committee is a member of the Board.

## Subsector Reports

The individual subsector group reports follow. All of the subcommittee members clearly agree with the Chairman of the international oils subsector's statement that "the quality and volumes of corporate reporting have made enormous evolutionary strides." Indeed, the independent oil and gas producers Chairman believes that "most of the companies [surveyed] deserve honorable mentions for the quality of their reporting and their investor relations efforts . . . " and the integrated oils subcommittee "applauds all of the companies for their efforts" and "believes that the overall efforts of all the companies ...is certainly worthy of praise."

Therefore, the suggestions for improvement that were made were all in terms of refining a process that basically works quite well. Our committees felt that the specificity and volume of quarterly information could be improved upon, and that more detailed information regarding both oil and natural gas price realizations and production costs, as well as more specific pricing information and contract price levels on the oil service side would be extremely helpful.

In closing, we would like to point out that the overall quality of investor relations efforts was given very high priority by all of our committees. We wish to commend all of the companies in the Petroleum industry for their close attention to these efforts and to thank both company personnel and the members of our committees for their continuing work toward the common goal of clear and consistent communication and information flow.

## TABLE 1
## COMPANIES REVIEWED

**International Oil Companies (7)**

Amoco Corporation
British Petroleum Company
Chevron Corporation
Exxon Corporation
Mobil Corporation
Royal Dutch/Shell Group
Texaco Inc.

**Independent Refiners (4)**

Ashland Oil
Diamond ShammRock Refining & Marketing
Sun Companies
Valero Energy

**Oil and Gas Drilling Companies (5)**

Energy Service Co. (ENSCO)
Global Marine
Nabors Industries
Parking Drilling Co.
Rowan Companies

**Domestic Integrated Oil Companies (8)**

Amerada Hess Corporation
Atlantic Richfield Company
Kerr-McGee Corporation
Murphy Oil Corporation
Occidental Petroleum Corporation
Pennzoil Company
Phillips Petroleum Company
Unocal

**Oil Service & Equipment (9)**

Baker-Hughes Inc.
Baroid Corporation
Dresser Industries
Enterra Corporation
Halliburton Companies
McDermott International
Schlumberger Ltd.
Smith International
Tidewater

**Independent Oil & Gas Producers (9)**

Anadarko Petroleum
Apache Corporation
Burlington Resources
Enron Oil & Gas Company
Louisiana Land & Exploration
Maxus Energy
Oryx Energy Company
Santa Fe Energy Resources
Union Texas Petroleum

## TABLE II
## PETROLEUM SUBCOMMITTEE MEMBERS

### Chair

| | |
|---|---|
| Janet Rasmussen | Wertheim Schroder & Co., New York |

### International Oil Companies

| | |
|---|---|
| John D. Hervey, Chair | Donaldson, Lufkin & Jenrette, New York |
| Terry Fires Bovarnick, CFA | E.I. DuPont de Nemours & Co., Wilmington |
| Ellen K. Hannan | Bessemer Trust Co., N.A., New York |
| Robert M. Shearer, CFA | Fiduciary Trust Co. Int'l, New York |
| Mary Anne Sudol, CFA | Fitch Investors Service, Inc., New York |
| Simon Trimble | Lehman Brothers, New York |

### Domestic Integrated and Independent Refining Companies

| | |
|---|---|
| Richard W. Cohen, Chair | RAS Securities Corp., New York |
| Michael Schilling | M. Schilling & Co., New York |
| Douglas T. Terreson, CFA | Putnam Management Co., Boston |
| Elizabeth Vale, CFA | CoreStates Investment Advisers, Philadelphia |

### Oil Service and Contract Drilling Companies

| | |
|---|---|
| Jeffrey R. Freedman, Chair | Smith Barney, Harris Upham & Co., Inc., New York |
| Anthony Giammalva | Weiss, Peck & Greer, New York |
| R. Michael Henzi | State Street Management & Research Co., Boston |
| Kenneth S. Miller | Shearson Lehman Hutton, Inc., New York |
| Kevin D. Simpson, CFA | Wertheim Schroder & Co., New York |

### Independent Oil and Gas Producers

| | |
|---|---|
| Michael G. Barbis, CFA, Chair | Wertheim Schroder & Co., New York |
| Karl Bandtel | Wellington Management Co., Boston |
| J. Dale Harvey | Capital Research & Management Co., Los Angeles |
| Martin Jacobs, CFA | Brinson Partners, Inc., Chicago |
| Bryan R. Martin | Fidelity Management & Research, Boston |
| John J. Myers, CFA | Southcoast Capital Corp., Austin |
| Michael Schilling | M. Schilling & Co., New York |

## INTERNATIONAL OIL COMPANIES

### John D. Hervey, Chair

### Recommendation for Awards

For the 1991 reporting year, the subcommittee for the international oil companies recommends that Mobil receive an Award for Excellence in corporate reporting. Further, we recommend that Exxon be awarded a commendation for its marked improvements as the company restructured its investor relations focus and redoubled its efforts in corporate reporting, finishing in second place. Given the very close scores of the top three companies, Chevron is accorded special recognition for its third place finish, solidly maintaining a position in the top tier of scores over the past 5 years.

### General Comments

In 1991, as in recent years, the international oil companies should again be recognized for their superior efforts in written and oral disclosure. Recognizing that the quality and volumes of corporate reporting have made enormous evolutionary strides, our first task as a committee was to revamp our survey questionnaire to better address the industry's development. This process left us with a poll that better isolates areas that can be constructively improved rather than focusing on items that have already been encompassed by the companies as reporting standards.

Further, we have attempted to redirect the scoring process so as to better recognize that just as operations differ from one company to the next, so too do the reporting responsibilities vary within the industry. Therefore, we changed the scoring process this year from a straight point system to a percentage base. The companies' final ranking was based on each score as a percentage of applicable points scored.

Based on the results from the three sections of our survey we make the following observations:

- Mobil scored first in Part I, the annual disclosure section, which is based on scrutiny of the companies' annual reports, financial supplements and 10-K documents. Exxon and Texaco also did quite well, scoring second and third, respectively. This section is by far the most heavily weighted in the survey, representing approximately half of the total points awarded.

- While Mobil placed among the top several scores in most of the subsections to Part I, it was the company's superior reporting in the chemicals arena that assured the top credit. Not only was better chemical's sector reporting a primary suggestion from last year's committee, but there is still considerable room for improvement among all of the companies rated. An improvement here would be especially beneficial to the relative scores of Amoco and Exxon.

- Chevron was the top scoring company in Part II of our survey, quarterly and interim publications. Chevron had the top rating in three of the four subsections, management commentary, financial information and operating information. Although the same names populate the top three slots here as in Part I, the order has changed as Mobil and Exxon scored second and third, respectively. This section included an optional score for publications of a general industry nature which only counted if applicable (but in no case did the optional credit count to lower a company's percentage score). Royal Dutch and British Petroleum were given the highest recognition for their general industry publications.

- Although the scores for most of Part II were both very close and exceptionally strong, it was the *operating information* subsection that most differentiated the group rather than *management commentary* or *financial information*. The key operating measures causing much of the disparity were price realization disclosure for crude, natural gas and NGLs (by geography) and chemical margin and volume data. Clearly this section represents an area for future emphasis for several of the companies. Improving their quarterly operating information represents an opportunity for British Petroleum, Royal Dutch/Shell and Amoco to make meaningful strides toward raising their relative performance.

- Although the top four scores in Part III, which measures the investor relations effort, were squeezed within 5%, top honors went to Chevron. Texaco, Royal Dutch/Shell and Exxon all deserve recognition for the second, third and fourth respective positions. This part of the survey is broken into two subsections: *investor relations contact evaluations* and *company meetings*. Based on the scores for each subsection, there appears to be little correlation between the two. Chevron and Texaco were within 2% of each other at the top of the investor relations score, both well ahead of the next closest company. Mobil, Royal Dutch/Shell and Exxon were given the highest credits for their company meetings.

- As we mentioned above, committee members were particularly impressed by Exxon's improvement from last year. Having occupied the last place ranking since 1987, Exxon's second place finish in this 1991 survey—a year that saw many of the other participants make noticeable qualitative gains—is especially noteworthy.

Sincere thanks are extended to the committee members for their hours of work and to the participating companies for their cooperation, extensive efforts and responsive attitudes. Based on the results of this year's survey, it is particularly gratifying to note that this process continues to have a favorable impact on corporate reporting and disclosure.

## INTERNATIONAL OIL COMPANIES
### 1991 Scoresheet Results

|  | AN | BP | CHV | XON | MOB | RD/SC | TX |
|---|---|---|---|---|---|---|---|
| **PART I: Annual Report, Statistical Supplement, and 10-K** | | | | | | | |
| A. Management Commentary | 63% | 74% | 73% | 77% | 74% | 73% | 73% |
| B. Financial Information | 68% | 59% | 58% | 67% | 71% | 37% | 57% |
| C. Operating Income | | | | | | | |
|   1. Exploration & Production | 68% | 72% | 64% | 85% | 75% | 72% | 82% |
|   2. Refining, Marketing & Transportation | 56% | 50% | 62% | 71% | 67% | 62% | 65% |
|   3. Chemicals | 34% | 42% | 49% | 31% | 68% | 48% | 23% |
|   4. Other (LNG, Coal, Metals, etc.) | N/A | 60% | 68% | 75% | 62% | 79% | N/A |
| Total Part I    Weight: 51% | 59.6% | 60.1% | 61.6% | 68.7% | 71.2% | 59.1% | 62.0% |
| **PART II: Quarterly Reports and Interim Publications** | | | | | | | |
| A. Management Commentary | 70% | 70% | 75% | 75% | 75% | 70% | 75% |
| B. Financial Information | 70% | 61% | 72% | 70% | 71% | 58% | 71% |
| C. Operating Information | 52% | 34% | 75% | 62% | 68% | 49% | 56% |
| D. Interim & General Publications | 59% | 81% | 71% | 66% | 75% | 85% | 60% |
| Total Part II    Weight: 27% | 62.6% | 56.1% | 73.6% | 67.4% | 71.3% | 61.2% | 65.9% |
| **PART III: Investor Relations Effort** | | | | | | | |
| A. Investor Relations Contacts | 62% | 66% | 86% | 75% | 57% | 79% | 84% |
| B. Company Meetings for Analysts | 33% | 58% | 69% | 73% | 75% | 73% | 70% |
| Total Part III    Weight: 22% | 46.6% | 61.3% | 77.0% | 73.7% | 66.4% | 75.7% | 76.3% |
| Grand Total    Weight: 100% | 57.3% | 59.2% | 68.5% | 69.4% | 70.1% | 63.3% | 66.3% |
| Rank for 1991 | 7 | 6 | 3 | 2 | 1 | 5 | 4 |
| Rank for 1990 | 5 | 3 | 1* | 7 | 1* | 6 | 4 |
| Rank for 1989 | 3 | 4 | 1 | 7 | 6 | 5 | 2 |
| Rank for 1988 | 3 | 2 | 1 | 7 | 6 | 4 | 5 |
| Rank for 1987 | 4 | 2 | 3 | 7 | 5 | 1 | 6 |

\*-Tie

AN-Amoco; BP-British Petroleum; CHV-Chevron; XON-Exxon; MOB-Mobil; RD/SC-Royal Dutch/Shell; TX-Texaco

# DOMESTIC INTEGRATED OIL AND INDEPENDENT REFINING COMPANIES

## Richard W. Cohen, Chair

### Recommendation for Awards

The review of the 1991 Corporate Information Subcommittee for the Domestic Integrated Oil Companies was divided into two groups of companies—the Domestic Integrated Group (8 companies) and the Independent Refining Group (4 companies). Based upon the results the subcommittee applauds all of the companies for their efforts with respect to their annual and quarterly reporting. While individual company investor relations efforts varied widely and not all of the companies held an annual analyst meeting, the subcommittee found that the companies were more than cooperative and quite timely in their disclosure practices. Several of the companies are now also providing either or both a quarterly or semi-annual update meeting or a conference call to keep analysts better informed.

In the Domestic Integrated Group, the subcommittee is recommending that Atlantic Richfield and Phillips Petroleum receive Awards of Excellence. These two companies have continued to set the standard for this group. In addition, because of the substantial improvement in its effort during the year 1991, Occidental Petroleum is recommended for a Letter of Commendation. This recommendation is reflective of the company's effort to improve its reporting and its relationship with the financial community.

In the Independent Refining Group, the subcommittee recommends an Award of Excellence be given to Ashland Oil for its overall effort in financial reporting and investor relations. In addition, Valero and Sun Company are deserving of commendation for their outstanding efforts during 1991.

### General Comments

Because of the restructuring which has taken place in the domestic oil industry over the past several years, we believe that the companies should try to provide more information relative to their intermediate and long term strategy. Because of the concern over oil producing prospects in the United States and overseas, the committee would like to see more discussion of future production profiles and what measures are being implemented to manage this problem. In addition, a more detailed breakdown of pricing and production costs on a per barrel basis might be helpful. While capital spending has been broken down by segment, key projects with their associated capital costs would provide an added focus for readers. One participant noted that a company had made available an excellent five year statistical supplement that also incorporated a very helpful assessment of the completion dates and benefits from a number of major capital projects. These are very important tools for analysts.

The industry generally has become more attentive to initiating meetings with the investment community at frequent intervals during the course of the year. Atlantic Richfield, Occidental Petroleum, Phillips, Unocal, Ashland and Sun deserve praise for their regular annual meetings with the investment community. Focus meetings on specific topics that touch on company activities such as those held by Kerr-McGee as well as quarterly meetings by Valero, Phillips and Atlantic Richfield are certainly worthwhile and are to be commended. All the participating companies are encouraged to provide a forum at which the investment community is exposed to management thinking and strategy. Obviously, this will allow them to assess individual company prospects for the future.

For these two sectors of the petroleum industry, the subcommittee believes that the overall effort of all the companies and those individuals charged with the investor relations effort and the corporate reporting function are certainly worthy of praise.

## DOMESTIC INTEGRATED OIL COMPANIES
### Evaluation of Corporate Reporting for 1991

|  | AHC | ARC | KMG | MUR | OXY | PZL | P | UCL |
|---|---|---|---|---|---|---|---|---|
| PART I: Annual Report, Statistical Supplement & 10-K (54%) | 41.0% | 48.8% | 47.5% | 46.9% | 46.2% | 43.9% | 49.9% | 44.0% |
| PART II: Quarterly Reports, and Interim Publications (19%) | 14.7% | 17.3% | 17.0% | 16.9% | 14.5% | 15.0% | 17.8% | 15.7% |
| PART III: Investor Relations Effort (27%) | 16.6% | 25.5% | 17.3% | 15.5% | 24.9% | 17.0% | 23.6% | 22.7% |
| Grand Total (100%) | 72.3% | 91.6% | 81.8% | 79.3% | 85.6% | 75.9% | 91.3% | 82.4% |
| Rank for 1991 | 8 | 1 | 5 | 6 | 3 | 7 | 2 | 4 |
| Rank for 1990 | 8 | 1 | 4 | 7 | 6 | 5 | 2 | 3 |
| Rank for 1989 | 10 | 3 | 6 | 4 | 8 | 9 | 1 | 7 |
| Rank for 1988 | 10 | 1 | 4 | 7 | 9 | 6 | 3 | 5 |
| Rank for 1987 | 11 | 3 | 7 | 2 | 9 | 4 | 6 | 10 |

AHC-Amerada Hess; ARC-Atlantic Richfield; KMG-KerrMcGee; MUR-Murphy Oil; OXY-Occidental Petroleum; PZL-Pennzoil; P-Phillips; UCL-Unocal

## INDEPENDENT REFINING COMPANIES
### Evaluation of Corporate Reporting for 1991

|  | ASH | DRM | SUN | VLO |
|---|---|---|---|---|
| PART I: Annual Report, Statistical Supplement & 10-K (45%) | 40.4% | 34.4% | 37.4% | 39.2% |
| PART II: Quarterly Reports, and Interim Publications (20%) | 18.9% | 14.8% | 16.1% | 15.3% |
| PART III: Investor Relations Effort (35%) | 31.8% | 22.5% | 33.6% | 33.8% |
| Grand Total (100%) | 91.1% | 71.7% | 87.1% | 88.3% |
| Rank for 1991 | 1 | 4 | 3 | 2 |
| Rank for 1990 | 2 | 4 | 1 | 3 |

Companies not reviewed as a separate group until 1990

ASH-Ashland Oil; DRM-Diamond Shamrock; SUN-Sun Co.; VLO-Valero

# INDEPENDENT OIL AND GAS COMPANIES

## Michael G. Barbis, CFA, Chair

## Recommendation for Awards

After a one year interruption, the Exploration and Production Subcommittee went back to work and reviewed nine companies. The Subcommittee recommends that Enron Oil and Gas receive an Award for Excellence in Corporate Reporting for 1991. In the opinion of the reviewers, most of the companies deserve honorable mentions for the quality of their reporting and their investor relations efforts.

The subcommittee reviewed nine companies this year. Anadarko Petroleum, Apache Corp., Burlington Resources, Louisiana Land and Exploration, Maxus Energy and Oryx Energy were all reviewed in 1989. Enron Oil and Gas and Santa Fe Energy Resources were newcomers to the survey this year, and Union Texas Petroleum returned to the survey after last being reviewed in 1988. Mitchell Energy and Development and Triton Oil were asked to participate in the survey but did not disseminate information to enough of the committee members for the group to properly complete their evaluations, hence they were deleted from the final review process.

## General Comments

The committee felt that all of the exploration and production companies should be commended for the increased frequency of investor relations contacts— via conference calls, analyst meetings and company visits. Reviewers appreciated, in particular, companies efforts to discuss broad issues within the natural gas industry. The group also noted that financial reporting had improved for virtually all of the companies surveyed.

Several companies in the survey were penalized for financial reporting problems caused by the way in which information on specific corporate events was disseminated. In particular Burlington Resources's spin-off of El Paso Natural Gas and Santa Fe's acquisition of Adobe Resources were cited.

Enron Oil and Gas, the recipient of this year's award, scored well across the board— placing first in investor relations and second in both annual and quarterly reporting. Reviewers liked their numerous meetings at a variety of locations as well as good access to both operating and financial personnel.

Anadarko Petroleum, which was a very close runner up, was cited for its solid investor relations contact as well as its particularly good management commentary in its Annual Report and its Supplemental Fact Book.

The committee suggested five specific areas in which it would like to see improvement in exploration and production companies' financial reporting. They were: (1) discussion of natural gas liquids revenues and reserves; (2) financial and operating statistics of gas gathering and gas processing operations; (3) more detailed descriptions and statistics of natural gas sales and marketing; (4) better and clearer descriptions of non-recurring items (particularly asset sales) and; (5) the addition of quarterly reports for fourth quarters.

### INDEPENDENT OIL AND GAS PRODUCERS
### Evaluation of Corporate Reporting for 1991

|  | Weight | APC | APA | BR | EOG | LLX | MXS | ORX | SFR | UTH |
|---|---|---|---|---|---|---|---|---|---|---|
| PART I: Annual Report, Statistical Supplement and 10-K |  |  |  |  |  |  |  |  |  |  |
| A. Management Commentary | 100.0 | 86.7 | 77.7 | 68.3 | 86.7 | 64.0 | 60.0 | 67.3 | 48.3 | 65.0 |
| B. Financial Information | 200.0 | 185.0 | 184.7 | 155.3 | 188.3 | 166.0 | 151.3 | 165.7 | 155.0 | 160.0 |
| C. Statistical & Operating Information | 200.0 | 141.0 | 133.0 | 55.0 | 136.0 | 128.0 | 142.0 | 140.0 | 94.0 | 115.0 |
| Total Part I | 500.0 | 412.7 | 395.3 | 278.7 | 411.0 | 358.0 | 353.3 | 373.0 | 297.3 | 340.0 |
| PART II: Quarterly Reports and Interim Publications |  |  |  |  |  |  |  |  |  |  |
| Total Part II | 300.0 | 237.0 | 237.0 | 220.0 | 237.0 | 226.0 | 217.0 | 213.0 | 205.0 | 240.0 |
| PART III: Investor Relations Effort |  |  |  |  |  |  |  |  |  |  |
| A. Investor Relations Effort | 115.0 | 95.4 | 95.0 | 79.0 | 105.0 | 104.3 | 88.0 | 90.0 | 91.0 | 103.0 |
| B. Management's Responsiveness | 85.0 | 59.0 | 62.5 | 58.4 | 75.0 | 66.8 | 60.1 | 61.4 | 60.6 | 56.3 |
| Total Part III | 200.0 | 154.4 | 157.5 | 137.4 | 180.0 | 171.0 | 148.1 | 151.4 | 151.6 | 159.3 |
| Grand Total | 1,000.0 | 804.1 | 789.8 | 636.1 | 828.0 | 755.0 | 718.4 | 737.4 | 653.9 | 739.3 |
| Rank for 1991 |  | 2 | 3 | 9 | 1 | 4 | 7 | 6 | 8 | 5 |
| Rank for 1990 |  | N/A | N/A | N/A | N/A | N/A | N/A | N/A | N/A | N/A |
| Rank for 1989 |  | 1 | 7 | 8 | N/A | 3 | 2 | 5 | N/A | N/A |
| Rank for 1988 |  | 1 | 7 | N/A | N/A | 2 | 3 | N/A | N/A | N/A |
| Rank for 1987 |  | 2 | 6 | N/A | N/A | 1 | 3 | N/A | N/A | N/A |

APC-Anadarko; APA-Apache; BR-Burlington Resources; EOG-Enron Oil & Gas; LLX-Louisiana Land & Exploration; MXS-Maxus; ORX-Oryx; SFR-Santa Fe Resources; UTH-Union Texas Petroleum

# OIL SERVICE & EQUIPMENT COMPANIES AND CONTRACT DRILLING COMPANIES

## Jeffrey R. Freedman, Chair

### Recommendation for Awards

Once again, the oil service/contract drilling subcommittee separated the companies surveyed into two subgroups—Oil Service & Equipment and Contract Drilling companies. The rationale, which was also used last year, was that forming separate groups would allow for more equitable comparisons, as the methodology and reporting practices of the two types of companies are significantly different. Two companies (Smith International and Tidewater) were added to the list in the Oil Service category this year, one company (Energy Service Co.) was added to the Contract Drilling category.

For the 1991 reporting year, the subcommittee recommends that Baker Hughes receive the Award for Excellence in the Oil Service & Equipment category. This company clearly set the standard for this group. Baker Hughes was given the highest praise in each of the three categories encompassed in our survey—and was particularly cited for maintaining high visibility in its investor relations effort. Global-Marine and Rowan Companies (a virtual tie) are both recommended to receive Awards for Excellence in the Contract Drilling category. Only 14 points separated these two companies, and on a percentage basis they were virtually indistinguishable. It should be noted, however, that when broken out by category, Global Marine's score in the Investor Relations section of the survey was several percentage points higher than Rowan's was, while in the Annual Report section the opposite was true.

### General Comments

We would like to mention that the difference in total points received among the companies that placed second (Baroid), third (Dresser) and fourth (Enterra) in the Oil Service category was very narrow (22 points in total). We believe that these high scores reflect the outstanding efforts of all of these companies in both financial reporting and investor relations.

Our reviewers felt that, on the whole, all of the companies surveyed deserve to be cited for progress that they are indeed making toward improving communication with the investment community. Areas that need improvement on the financial reporting side all have to do with dissemination of specific information, that is, the breaking out of information in more detail on both geographic and operating segment bases. Information regarding pricing would also be quite helpful in both the oil service and contract drilling groups.

It should also be noted that, within the Investor Relations section of the oil service group's survey, more than half of the companies surveyed (Baker Hughes, Baroid, Dresser, Enterra and Schlumberger) received very high scores in investor relations contacts. The scores were extremely uneven in terms of companies' visibility in the investment community, i.e., company sponsored meetings and seminars.

## OIL SERVICE & EQUIPMENT COMPANIES
### Evaluation of Corporate Reporting for 1991
### Average Weighted Scores

| | % Weight | BHI | BRC | DI | EN | HAL | MDR | SLB | SII | TDW |
|---|---|---|---|---|---|---|---|---|---|---|
| PART I: Annual Report & 10-K | | | | | | | | | | |
| Management Commentary | 10.0 | 309 | 272 | 274 | 264 | 214 | 228 | 222 | 266 | 228 |
| Financial Information | 17.5 | 493 | 457 | 464 | 494 | 424 | 411 | 348 | 327 | 350 |
| Operating Information | 15.0 | 306 | 272 | 255 | 257 | 193 | 220 | 217 | 236 | 168 |
| Total Part I | 42.5 | 1,108 | 1,001 | 993 | 1,015 | 831 | 859 | 787 | 829 | 746 |
| | | | | | | | | | | |
| PART II: Quarterly Reports & Interim Publications | | | | | | | | | | |
| Management Commentary & Financial Information | 17.5 | 486 | 438 | 368 | 454 | 400 | 372 | 298 | 295 | 301 |
| Operating Information | 10.0 | 197 | 179 | 171 | 183 | 155 | 149 | 55 | 87 | 138 |
| Interim Publications | 5.0 | 122 | 80 | 116 | 80 | 88 | 100 | 78 | 68 | 45 |
| Total Part II | 32.5 | 805 | 697 | 655 | 717 | 643 | 621 | 431 | 450 | 484 |
| | | | | | | | | | | |
| PART III: Investor Relations Effort | | | | | | | | | | |
| Investor Relations Contacts | 15.0 | 461 | 430 | 386 | 414 | 226 | 260 | 335 | 292 | 184 |
| Company Meetings/Analyst Presentations | 10.0 | 305 | 210 | 300 | 170 | 205 | 140 | 140 | 146 | 163 |
| Total Part III | 25.0 | 766 | 640 | 686 | 584 | 431 | 400 | 475 | 438 | 347 |
| | | | | | | | | | | |
| Grand Total | 100.0 | 2,679 | 2,338 | 2,334 | 2,316 | 1,905 | 1,880 | 1,693 | 1,717 | 1,577 |
| | | | | | | | | | | |
| Rank for 1991 | | 1 | 2 | 3 | 4 | 5 | 6 | 8 | 7 | 9 |
| Rank for 1990 | | 2 | 3 | 1 | 5 | 4 | 7 | 6 | N/M | N/M |
| Rank for 1989 | | 3 | N/M | 2 | N/M | 6 | 7 | 8 | N/M | N/M |
| Rank for 1988 | | 4 | N/M | 2 | N/M | 7 | 6 | 8 | N/M | N/M |
| Rank for 1987 | | 5 | N/M | 3 | N/M | 7 | 4 | 8 | N/M | N/M |

N/M-Not Meaningful
BHI-Baker Hughes; BRC-Bariod; DI-Dresser; EN-Enterra; HAL-Halliburton; MDR-McDermott; SLB-Schlumberger; SII-Smith International; TDW-Tidewater

## OIL AND GAS DRILLING COMPANIES
### Evaluation of Corporate Reporting for 1991
### Average Weighted Scores

|  | % Weight | ESV | GLM | NBR | PKD | RDC |
|---|---|---|---|---|---|---|
| PART I: Annual Report & 10-K |  |  |  |  |  |  |
| Management Commentary | 10.0 | 241 | 269 | 246 | 259 | 351 |
| Financial Information | 17.5 | 446 | 378 | 282 | 368 | 417 |
| Operating Information | 15.0 | 307 | 358 | 261 | 282 | 356 |
| Total Part I | 42.5 | 994 | 1,005 | 789 | 909 | 1,124 |
| PART II: Quarterly Reports & Interim Publications |  |  |  |  |  |  |
| Management Commentary & Financial Information | 17.5 | 384 | 431 | 292 | 344 | 423 |
| Operating Information | 10.0 | 171 | 196 | 120 | 154 | 217 |
| Interim Publications | 5.0 | 104 | 122 | 50 | 100 | 94 |
| Total Part II | 32.5 | 659 | 749 | 462 | 598 | 734 |
| PART III: Investor Relations Effort |  |  |  |  |  |  |
| Investor Relations Contacts | 15.0 | 398 | 504 | 381 | 342 | 392 |
| Company Meetings/Analyst Presentations | 10.0 | 155 | 226 | 138 | 175 | 221 |
| Total Part III | 25.0 | 553 | 730 | 519 | 517 | 613 |
| Grand Total | 100.0 | 2,206 | 2,484 | 1,770 | 2,024 | 2,471 |
| Rank for 1991 |  | 2 | 1* | 4 | 3 | 1* |
| Rank for 1990 |  | N/M | 2 | 4 | 3 | 1 |

1*-Tie
N/M-Not Meaningful: Companies were not evaluated as a separate group until 1990.
ESV-Energy Service; GLM-Global Marine; NBR-Nabors Industries; PKD-Parker Drilling; RDC-Rowan Cos.

# Railroad

## Recommendation for Award

The Railroad Subcommittee recommended that one company, Consolidated Rail Corporation, receive an Award for Excellence in Corporate Reporting for 1991–92.

The subcommittee reviewed eight companies:

Burlington Northern Inc.
CSX Corporation
Consolidated Rail Corp.
Illinois Central Corp.
Kansas City Southern Industries, Inc.
Norfolk Southern Corp.
Santa Fe Pacific Corp.
Union Pacific Corp.

## Evaluation Procedures

The following point system was used:

| | |
|---|---:|
| Group I —Required Published Material | 40 |
| Group II —Published Material Not Required | 30 |
| Group III—Other Corporate Information | 20 |
| Group IV—Extra Credit | 10 |
| Total | 100 |

Material included in each of the groups was defined as follows:

I. Annual reports, factbooks, proxy statements, 10-K forms to the SEC, and R-1 forms to the ICC. Important considerations included the president's letter, financial summary, detail on railroad results, as well as on any diversified interests.

II. Interim reports, annual meeting reports, including questions and answers, quarterly newsletters to financial analysts, speeches before analysts societies and other groups, etc.

III. Other material of two types, corporate information contacts initiated by management and corporate communications initiated by the financial analyst. The former included the frequency and quality of periodic meetings with railroad analysts, or with securities analyst groups. Another consideration was the last field trip held. From the individual analyst's standpoint, emphasis was placed on the quality of interviews, response to phone calls, and the availability of a contact.

The quantitative results of the Railroad Industry Subcommittee evaluation appear at the end of the report.

## General Comments

Some modifications were made to the scoring system, including the evaluation of background data on officers/directors—a small area that cost almost every company a point. Apart from setting aside 10 points for extra credit, the president's letter in the annual report is now getting closer scrutiny.

Once again there was inadequate discussion of rate increases and yields in most railroad annual reports. Nonetheless, most of the companies' overall efforts have continued to improve significantly in recent years, especially with the use of factbooks.

*Conrail* maintained its first place rating as a result of leading scores in all categories. One of the weak areas in its published materials was insufficient comparisons on competitive market penetration. There was also a minor shortfall in timely details regarding an end-of-year write-off, and the earnings per share calculation without the write-off was not clearly quantified in the annual report or the annual factbook. However, the factbook provided excellent descriptions of revenue and cost trends including comments on future trends (which garnered extra credit points). Maximum scores typified its other corporate information, which was noteworthy for informative quarterly meetings, with frank answers to questions, and a productive but compact rail trip each year.

*Union Pacific* was a close second for the third consecutive year. The annual report and president's letter improved noticeably and were more expansive. The company's factbooks received high marks and other published materials were virtually faultless. The Group III ratings were again hurt by the CEO's occasional absence from its excellent quarterly meetings. It was also noted that the verbal discussions of nonrecurring quarterly items might be aided by the use of footnotes in handouts. The previous use of exclusive field trips has been improved recently to allow broader analyst participation.

*CSX Corp.* was rated number three for the third consecutive year but the spread from first to fourth place remains quite narrow. The company's Group III rating continues to suffer from absence of regular quarterly meetings which most other railroads now have. Some subcommittee members also thought the semi-annual analyst meetings in New York need to be better focused. On the positive side, the company's quarterly flash reports were complimented for their timely dispatch and thoroughness. One suggested area of improvement on financial data was a separate profit center breakout for CSX Intermodal, which now accounts for 14% of rail revenues.

*Norfolk Southern* continued to receive high marks for its published materials but the absence of a recent field trip on the railroad lowered its Group III rating. Furthermore, as noted last year, its quarterly factbook could be improved by showing separate quarterly data instead of cumulative year-to-date figures after the first three months of the year.

*Santa Fe Pacific* improved its rankings one notch to fifth place, aided by the establishment of informative quarterly meetings with analysts. From an annual report viewpoint, the president's letter could have been more expansive and there was only a five year historic table of financial results. It would also be useful to have more than three years of data shown in the annual statistical supplement, where comparable figures are available.

*Burlington Northern* fell to sixth place from fifth place as the annual report could have benefitted from more discussion of legislative/regulatory developments and the company's prospects. In addition, only five years of data were shown in the financial summary. While recent field trips were a positive under Group III, there was a general perception that the company's volatile financial performance necessitated extra effort to avoid surprising the financial community.

*Illinois Central.* This is the first time we have evaluated this company and it is already showing signs of improving. From a Group I approach, the president's letter was somewhat brief as was the financial highlights discussion. In addition, traffic volumes were shown in percentage terms whereas actual ton miles can also be useful. The absence of a factbook puts Illinois Central at a disadvantage compared to most other railroads as did the absence, until recently, of a dedicated investor relations person. The recent limited field trip (mostly sell side) is another step in the right direction but a broader analyst participation will hopefully be achieved in the future.

*Kansas City Southern* continued to achieve reasonably good ratings on its primary published material, but more details would help on rail tonnage/revenues by commodity. Group II and III valuations were hurt by the limited number of releases on operations and infrequent appearances before analysts. However, such shortcomings are typical for smaller companies and an analyst meeting was scheduled for October 1992.

*It should be noted that there is one new subcommittee member, and we have now allocated 10 points for extra credit, which may distort numerical comparisons with prior years.*

## AVERAGE EVALUATION BY RAILROAD SUBCOMMITTEE MEMBERS

|  | Group I | Group II | Group III | Group IV | Total* | 1991 Rank | 1990 Rank | 1989 Rank | 1988 Rank | 1987 Rank |
|---|---|---|---|---|---|---|---|---|---|---|
| Conrail | 37.6 | 27.1 | 18.4 | 7.7 | 90.9 | 1 | 1 | 3 | 2 | 2 |
| Union Pacific | 37.0 | 26.9 | 17.4 | 7.1 | 88.4 | 2 | 2 | 2 | 4 | 6 |
| CSX Corp. | 37.3 | 26.1 | 18.1 | 6.1 | 87.7 | 3 | 3 | 3 | 2 | 2 |
| Norfolk Southern | 36.9 | 26.6 | 16.9 | 4.7 | 85.0 | 4 | 4 | 1 | 1 | 1 |
| Santa Fe Pacific | 32.3 | 25.0 | 16.6 | 3.6 | 77.4 | 5 | 6 | 5 | 5 | 4 |
| Burlington Northern | 32.6 | 23.3 | 14.9 | 1.4 | 72.1 | 6 | 5 | 6 | 6 | 7 |
| Illinois Central | 33.0 | 21.3 | 14.0 | 1.3 | 69.5 | 7 | NA | NA | NA | NA |
| Kansas City Southern | 34.3 | 18.3 | 12.5 | 1.3 | 66.3 | 8 | 7 | 7 | 7 | 8 |
| Maximum Possible | 40.0 | 30.0 | 20.0 | 10.0 | 100.0 | | | | | |

*May not add because of rounding

## RAILROAD SUBCOMMITTEE

Michael H. Lloyd, CFA, Chair, New York
County NatWest Securities USA

Thomas J. Donnelly, CFA, New York
J.P. Morgan Investment Management, Inc.

Remy M. Fisher, Chicago
Kemper Financial Services, Inc.

Anthony Hatch, New York
PaineWebber, Mitchell, Hutchins, Inc.

James S. Kang, New York
Capital Guardian Research Co.

Addo H. Kuhlmann, New York
Fiduciary Trust Co. Int'l

Graeme Lidgerwood, New York
The First Boston Corp.

# Retail Trade

## Recommendations for Awards

The Retail Trade Subcommittee recommends that Awards for Excellence in Corporate Reporting for 1991 be presented to:

Toys "R" Us
Home Depot

Toys "R" Us and Home Depot replaced Wal-Mart and Dayton Hudson, last year's first and second place finishers, for excellence in corporate relations and reporting. Toys "R" Us rose from the number three position in 1990 on the strength of its investor relations program. The company was particularly active in participating in investor relations-oriented forums. In addition, our survey suggests that top management maintained a high level of accessibility throughout the year enabling the investment community to stay current on the company's developments. Toys also garnered an especially high grade for the quality of its current and interim reports. The Home Depot recorded the biggest improvement in ranking of the top-rated companies in the survey, rising from sixth place in 1990 to second place last year. Like Toys "R" Us, Home Depot's management was very active in participating in seminars, retail field trips and other investor-oriented forums. The company also scored high for the quality of its annual report and interim financial publications. The Association for Investment Management and Research (AIMR) has placed increased focus on quarterly reports, business segment information as well as other published material not required by the regulatory bodies. In these areas, both Toys "R" Us and Home Depot have shown steady improvement.

## Evaluation Procedures

To assure fair and complete evaluations, every company was graded on a 100 point basis for each of the three reporting criteria—"annual reports," "interim reports" and "other aspects." These raw scores were then multiplied by the preference weightings selected by each subcommittee member, according to the importance that he or she attributed to each factor. The weightings were within recommended ranges of 40–50% for the annual report, 30–40% for interim reports and 20–30% for other aspects. The average of the individual scores yielded the final rating. The following table details the scores by total and by each major criterion. In keeping with the suggestions of the AIMR Corporate Information Committee, membership of the subcommittee continues to reflect broad geographical representation. Moreover, the number of companies evaluated has been expanded to include the rapidly growing membership warehouse club sector, to include more specialty retailers and additional department store chains. To be specific, in recent years Charming Shoppes, Costco Wholesale, The Gap, The Home Depot, Kroger, Merry-Go-Round, Mercantile Stores, Waban, Speigel, Standard Brands Paint, TJX, Tiffany, Toys "R" Us, and Walgreen were added to the universe of companies reviewed. We believe that the credibility of the evaluation procedure has been strengthened by the increased representation of the warehouse club chains, the most rapidly growing subsector of retailing. Our evaluation process paid particular attention to the quantity and quality of segment data disclosure and analysis in quarterly and annual reports and in other publications. The overall appraisal scores this year were generally higher, and we would note the year-to-year improvement made by several companies—notably Melville, Tiffany and Nordstrom.

The criteria that the Subcommittee used to evaluate the reporting systems included the following factors, a number of which are either relatively new or revised:

## Annual Report, Form 10-K and Other SEC Filings

Management comments—scope, relevance, philosophy.
Industry environment—positives, negatives, outlook.
Description of operations—emphasis, changes, policies, future plans.
Quantitative—reporting by segments, divisional breakdowns.
—comparable-store sales data.
—store square footage detail; openings/closings; expansion plans.
—thoroughness of income statement, balance sheet and cash flow statements.
—lease information (both capital and operating leases).
—pension fund liabilities (including a critical look at all areas of pension reporting).
—clear description of pertinent retail industry statistics.

—accounting policies.
—income tax reconciliation.
—retiree healthcare liabilities.

**Interim Reports**

Quarterly reports—timeliness, detail, quality, quantitative aspects. (Any inadequacies in these reports were noted, given their growing importance in an increasingly volatile economic environment.)

Summaries, factbooks, speeches, etc.—quality and availability.

Press releases—regularity, new developments, availability.

Other reports, prospectus, stockholder communications.

**Other Aspects**

Attitude, cooperation with analysts.

Analyst investor presentations—timeliness, consistency, effectiveness, frequency.

Availability of corporate and divisional top management.

## Previous Subcommittee Recommendations Have Been Adopted By Several Companies

We are pleased to announce that several recommendations made by the Subcommittee in recent years have been adopted by certain retail companies, including:

1. Greater disclosure of divisional results. Since 1982, Sears has provided operating results for each of its business segments, and TJX began to follow this disclosure policy in 1983. In 1984, K mart moved toward the adoption of this policy and in 1985, other retailers such as Melville followed in this direction. During the 1986–1988 period, we cited Dayton Hudson and May Department Stores for excellent disclosure of business segment results. In 1989, Toys "R" Us and Wal-Mart provided improved business segment information. Most recently, K mart released sales and operating earnings for each of its specialty store divisions.

2. Reporting of monthly sales. Over the last several years, a number of retailers, including The Limited, The Gap, and The Neiman Marcus Group have initiated releases of monthly sales results. Most major retailers now report sales—both total and same-store results—on a monthly basis.

## Results of Evaluation

Generally speaking, the Subcommittee believes that financial reporting within the retail industry continues to show improvement. Quarterly reports have become more detailed, while the increased number of firms reporting monthly sales has helped analysts to estimate quarterly trends in profitability. However, the Committee believes that further improvements can be made in the following areas:

1. The release of monthly sales data including divisional data is encouraged for those companies that presently do not provide this information.

2. The breakout of results for the seasonally important fourth quarter in separate reports is very helpful, but only a handful of retailers provide such data at the present time.

3. The quarterly and annual release of complete divisional operating results is helpful with the availability of such information recommended.

4. Greater disclosure of lease information, both capital and operating leases, including data regarding the present value of operating leases.

## Subcommittee Communication Program

As in the past, the Subcommittee plans to contact the companies that received low scores to suggest changes in their reporting and communication systems. We also intend to discuss the following items with many of the other companies in our universe: improved financial reporting; more effective investor relations; and accounting issues, particularly how retailers can adopt one generally accepted concept for lease accounting. Additionally, in line with AIMR's general approach, we will review with company managements the methods for improving the quality of annual and quarterly segment data disclosure and analysis.

## RETAIL TRADE SCORES-1991

| | Total | Annual Report | Interim Reports | Other Aspects | 1991 Rank | 1990 Rank | 1989 Rank | 1988 Rank | 1987 Rank |
|---|---|---|---|---|---|---|---|---|---|
| Toys "R" Us | 96.5 | 39.1 | 24.6 | 32.8 | 1 | 3 | 2 | 3 | 1 |
| Home Depot | 96.3 | 39.0 | 24.5 | 32.8 | 2 | 6 | 6 | 2 | 11 |
| Wal-Mart Stores, Inc. | 96.0 | 38.9 | 24.5 | 32.6 | 3 | 1 | 1 | 4 | 2 |
| Dayton Hudson | 95.8 | 38.7 | 24.3 | 32.8 | 4 | 2 | 3 | 5 | 4 |
| May Department Stores Co. | 95.4 | 38.3 | 24.5 | 32.6 | 5 | 4 | 5 | 6 | 3 |
| J. C. Penney | 95.1 | 38.0 | 24.5 | 32.6 | 6 | 9 | 7 | 8 | 6 |
| The Limited | 94.9 | 38.0 | 24.4 | 32.5 | 7 | 5 | 4 | 1 | 12 |
| K mart Corp. | 94.7 | 37.3 | 24.5 | 32.9 | 8 | 7 | 11 | 9 | 10 |
| Woolworth Corporation | 94.5 | 37.5 | 24.3 | 32.7 | 9 | 8 | 8 | 10 | 5 |
| Melville Corp. | 94.1 | 37.6 | 24.0 | 32.5 | 10 | 14 | 13 | 11 | 8 |
| Tiffany & Co. | 93.2 | 37.0 | 23.9 | 32.3 | 11 | 16 | 17 | — | — |
| Sears, Roebuck & Co. | 93.1 | 36.8 | 23.8 | 32.5 | 12 | 11 | 9 | 7 | 7 |
| Rite Aid | 92.6 | 36.5 | 23.7 | 32.4 | 13 | 13 | 14 | 14 | 15 |
| The TJX Companies, Inc. | 92.1 | 36.4 | 23.5 | 32.2 | 14 | 17 | 16 | — | — |
| Albertson's | 91.7 | 36.0 | 23.3 | 32.4 | 15 | 10 | 10 | 13 | 16 |
| Dillard Department Stores, Inc. | 91.1 | 35.7 | 23.1 | 32.3 | 16 | 12 | 15 | 16 | 14 |
| The Great A&P Tea Co., Inc. | 90.9 | 35.5 | 23.0 | 32.4 | 17 | 20 | 26 | 22 | — |
| Spiegel, Inc. | 90.6 | 35.0 | 23.2 | 32.4 | 18 | 22 | — | — | — |
| Nordstrom | 90.3 | 35.2 | 23.3 | 31.8 | 19 | 23 | 19 | 17 | 20 |
| The Neiman Marcus Group | 89.9 | 34.5 | 23.2 | 32.2 | 20 | 21 | 21 | 20 | 23 |
| Longs Drug Stores | 89.5 | 34.2 | 23.2 | 32.1 | 21 | 19 | 23 | 23 | 22 |
| Merry-Go-Round Enterprises | 89.1 | 33.8 | 23.0 | 32.3 | 22 | 18 | — | — | — |
| The Kroger Co. | 88.0 | 33.5 | 22.9 | 31.6 | 23 | 27 | — | — | — |
| The Gap, Inc. | 87.2 | 33.0 | 22.8 | 31.4 | 24 | 34 | — | — | — |
| Mercantile Stores Co., Inc. | 87.1 | 33.3 | 22.6 | 31.2 | 25 | 24 | 27 | 25 | — |
| Costco Wholesale | 86.0 | 32.5 | 22.5 | 31.0 | 26 | — | — | — | — |
| Waban Inc. | 82.4 | 30.0 | 22.0 | 30.4 | 27 | — | — | — | — |
| Super Valu Stores, Inc. | 81.2 | 29.5 | 21.7 | 30.0 | 28 | 26 | 20 | 18 | 17 |
| Walgreen Co. | 80.3 | 29.8 | 21.3 | 29.2 | 29 | 29 | — | — | — |
| Winn-Dixie Stores, Inc. | 78.7 | 29.2 | 21.2 | 28.3 | 30 | 25 | 28 | 28 | 26 |
| Charming Shoppes, Inc. | 77.1 | 28.5 | 21.0 | 27.6 | 31 | 32 | — | — | — |
| Price Company | 76.9 | 28.6 | 20.8 | 27.5 | 32 | 31 | 29 | 27 | 21 |
| Edison Brothers | 76.5 | 28.3 | 20.5 | 27.7 | 33 | 28 | 25 | 24 | 27 |
| Petrie Stores | 76.3 | 28.1 | 20.3 | 27.9 | 34 | 30 | 31 | 31 | 29 |

## RETAIL TRADE SUBCOMMITTEE

Jeffrey M. Feiner, CFA, Chair, New York
Salomon Bros., Inc.

Francis T. Bailey, New York
Mutual Life Insurance Co. of New York

Harry Clayton Barr, CFA, Boston
Keystone Custodian Funds, Inc.

Gary W. Bender, CFA, Denver
Colorado Public Employees Retirement Association

Richard M. Bernstein, CFA, Baltimore
Mercantile-Safe Deposit & Trust Co.

Dave Burshtan, Houston
Texas Commerce Bank

Brent Clum, Baltimore
T. Rowe Price Associates, Inc.

Thomas M. Cole, Chicago
Brinson Partners, Inc.

John D. Connolly, CFA, W. Conshohocken
Miller, Anderson & Sherrerd

Joseph M. Corrado, CFA, Boston
Standish, Ayer & Wood, Inc.

Nancy M. Crouse, CFA, Philadelphia
CoreStates Investment Advisers

Philip Seymour Dano, CFA, Detroit
Woodbridge Capital Management

Kay S. Doremus, Atlanta
Trusco Capital Management

Steven P. Eastwood, CFA, Columbus
Public Employees Retirement System of Ohio

Mary English, Boston
Fidelity Management & Research Co.

David J. Gilson, CFA, Minneapolis
IDS Financial Services, Inc.

Evan G. Harrel, CFA, Houston
Fayez Sarofim & Co.

Lawrence J. Haverty, Jr., CFA, Boston
State Street Research & Management Co.

Brian Helmer, Hartford
Connecticut National Bank

Leonard S. Hirsch, New York
Neuberger & Berman

Brian S. James, CFA, Boston
Loomis Sayles & Co., Inc.

John B. Kosecoff, New York
Lord, Abbett & Co.

Gretchen S. Lash, CFA, Houston
American Capital Asset Management, Inc.

Peter D. Miselis, CFA, Springfield, MA
Massachusetts Mutual Life Insurance Co.

Jeanne Mockard, Boston
Putnam Management Co.

Elaine Rees, CFA, New York
The Dreyfus Corporation

Rita I. Reid, New York
Metropolitan Life Insurance Co.

Jean Richards, Hartford
Aetna Life & Casualty Co.

Colin L. Robinson, Providence
Rhode Island Hospital Trust National Bank

Brian Rohman, New York
Citibank N.A.

Valerie Ross, New York
Bessemer Trust Company, N.A.

Donald J. Solow, CFA, New York
J.P. Morgan Investment Management, Inc.

Joanne Stager, Los Angeles
Trust Company of The West

B. Holland Timmins, III, CFA, Austin
University of Texas System

William C. Tlucek, CFA, New York
Lehman Ark Management Co., Inc.

# Software/Data Services

## Summary

First Financial Management Corporation emerged as the first two-time award winner for corporate reporting in the software and data services group. Competition was tough though since many companies continue to improve their investor relations efforts and the quality of information disclosed to investors.

- This year, the committee emphasized quarterly disclosure of full financial statements and revenue breakdowns on a quarterly basis as well. A number of companies are still providing only summary income statements on report day with no expense detail, and in some cases, no balance sheet (Automatic Data Processing, Policy Management Systems Corp., and Systems Software Associates, Inc.). The committee believes that taking the few extra days to compile a more complete report would be more beneficial to the investment community than rushing to report minimal summary information. This avoids the risk of reaching one conclusion based on summary data and another once the details are available.
- Relatedly, the committee gave special recognition to companies such as Symix Systems that included a full quarterly income statement in the annual report. This practice is a great convenience for investors who can view the quarterly pattern of the business (revenues and expenses) quickly. This practice can also obviate the need for investors to procure a set of quarterly reports to achieve the same purpose.
- Conference call input has also proved valuable. The committee wishes to encourage the use of conference calls following quarterly reports and material events as is currently prevalent in the industry. Conference call access remains an issue as some companies limit access to the call which would seem to frustrate the fairness objective.
- A critical area of disclosure for investors, segment breakdowns, is improving but still far from ideal. The customary services and product breakdown required by the SEC is now standard, but some companies provide much more useful categorization. The committee wishes to encourage revenue segmentation by product line, operating system, hardware platform, geography, customer size, deal size, and other such criteria.
- Oracle Corporation and Consilium still lead the way in revenue segmentation. Oracle provides breakdowns by operating systems, geography, and product type as well as other useful operating data. Consilium breaks out its sales by functional module, major product lines, and customer industry. Computer Sciences Corp. and First Financial Management in the Services area provide useful breakdowns by lines of business on a quarterly basis. First Financial even provides operating income by segment on a quarterly basis and forecasts the same going forward.
- Investor relations programs continue to improve. Several investor relations officers have become pro-active in providing information to analysts in the form of fact sheets, news articles, and other data of interest (Consilium, LEGENT Corporation, American Management Systems, Inc.). Unfortunately, a few seem strangely hard to reach by phone. The committee wishes to re-emphasize the key expected benefit of having a separate IR position: improved responsiveness to investor inquiries.
- The committee is concerned about the quantity and quality of information provided to investor relations officials by management. Investors will be reluctant to rely on investor relations input if they feel management has not shared adequate information and perspective about the business with the IR official. A few companies have started to rotate operations executives through the IR function to provide more substantive information and background to interested investors. The committee wished to encourage this practice.
- Full day analyst meetings on an annual or quarterly basis are becoming more popular and more useful. Electronic Data Systems and Computer Sciences conduct particularly well organized analyst meetings. Electronic Data Systems was noted for its comprehensive overview of the business and breakout sessions for the various business units. Automatic Data was noted for effective quarterly analyst meetings and conference calls, and Policy Management's

annual analyst meeting was noted as particularly fact-filled and useful.
- Other areas needing improvement include the quality and timeliness of restatements following acquisitions. Given the consolidation taking place in the industry and the increasing frequency of acquisition, the committee wished to encourage companies to provide detailed, restated numbers and details about special charges as soon as practicable.

## Recommendation for Award

This year's Award for Excellence in Corporate Reporting in the software and services industry goes to *First Financial Management* of Atlanta, Georgia. The company's segmentation of revenues and operating income as well as forecasts on the same bases earned it the distinction of our first repeat winner.

The company faced up squarely to its restatement of its financials after an accounting error in a subsidiary. It discussed the issue openly and provided details in the opening pages of its annual report. The committee feels this candor should be encouraged.

The company makes frequent acquisitions and has provided insight into the strategy behind the acquisitions and detailed financial data in a timely fashion.

The company's analyst meetings are useful but not frequent enough. The committee would like to see such meetings on at least an annual basis. Management accessibility could be better at the operating level.

Overall, the committee felt First Financial Management's consistency, openness, and responsiveness to investors was notable and should be encouraged.

## The Runners Up

*Novell, Inc.* was the runner up this year and has steadily improved its investor relations efforts. The company provides useful segment breakdowns on conference calls but the data should be consistent. Rather than a verbal quantification of some aspects of the business, the committee prefers to see a consistent, written breakdown of revenues on a quarterly basis. The company's ability to discuss its strategy was noted as impressive and management accessibility is considered good. Guidance on earnings estimates has been reasonably good.

*BMC Software* also is a perennial contender for the award. As the second runner up, BMC was noted for its good segment information and its proactive step of disclosing upgrade fees. No other vendor has disclosed such information in the annual report or 10-K. The company has been accurate with earnings guidance and access to management was noted as particularly good. The committee thought the company could discuss the competitive environment more candidly. Compared to its competitor Platinum Technology, according to some committee members, BMC seems to downplay the competitive environment.

*Cognos, Inc.*, the third runner up, provides useful revenue breakdowns via conference call, but the committee felt this data should be faxed or mailed to investors. The company also faced its difficult business conditions candidly and provided explanations to investors as needed. Guidance on earnings could have been more detailed and accurate, but this may be a function of the company's difficult business climate.

## Other Company Observations

- LEGENT Corporation was noted for its particularly insightful explanation of its strategy in its annual report. The committee felt it was well written and provided an understandable overview of a complex business. Earnings guidance was accurate and useful.
- The committee was divided over Oracle Systems Corporation's handling of its financial restatement. Some felt the company dragged its feet on the issue and could have provided more information sooner about the size of the charge. Others felt little else could have been done given the state of the company's financial records at the time. In other matters, the committee felt Oracle had improved its information flow with periodic product briefings and analyst meetings. Guidance on earnings however was nonexistent.
- Systems Software Associates, Inc. was noted for its lack of accessibility in general. The lack of a CFO and investor relations function has made obtaining information difficult. However, the company held its first analyst meeting in years and we were encouraged by this event. However, committee members felt the company was unnecessarily restrictive in deciding who could attend the meeting.
- Ask Computer Systems, Inc. was commended on its detailed revenue breakdowns by product

and geography. Earnings guidance and explanations of acquisition effect have been above average. On the negative side, the company is perennially slow to get its annual report out (the company failed to publish one at all in fiscal 1991).
- The committee felt Platinum Technology was unusually direct and open about discussing its business climate. A few members thought the company could spend less time bashing competitors and focus on its own business while others found the candor about the competitive environment useful.
- Electronic Data Systems was recognized for its analyst meetings and management accessibility. Given the size of the company, the committee felt that management was fairly accessible and the investor relations function extremely responsive.
- Computer Associates was recognized for its improved quarterly information provided to investors. The segment breakdowns and material distributed at analyst meetings have been useful. However, earnings and expense guidance has been lacking and the company was slow to quantify the effect of its accounting change.

## Evaluation Process

The committee surveyed 53 companies this year compared with last year's 57. The decline was partially a result of several mergers in the industry. Some recent public offerings were not eligible for consideration because they have not published annuals or 10-Ks yet.

Each company was asked to mail materials to two designated members of the committee. At least two members of the panel examined the quantity and type of information provided by each company. The first round evaluations addressed objective measures such as the information content and presentation of the annual report, 10-K, 10-Q, and quarterly faxes. Scores were adjusted by a multiplier based on the average of all graders to remove the possible skewing effect of any one grader.

The 15 companies that had the highest score in the first round were reviewed again in the second round. The second round evaluation focused on more qualitative factors such as the following:
1. How much incremental insight into the company's business did management provide?
2. How useful was the segment information?
3. How well did the company face bad news?
4. How accessible was management to investors?
5. How timely and accurate was the company's guidance?
6. Did the management sponsor an "analyst/investors' day," attend conferences, or otherwise make itself available to investors?

### SOFTWARE/DATA SERVICES SUBCOMMITTEE RANKINGS

| 1991 Rank | Company Name | 1991 Score | 1990 Rank | 1989 Rank |
|---|---|---|---|---|
| 1 | First Financial Management | 116.0 | 11 | 2 |
| 2 | Novell Corporation | 115.0 | 16 | 9 |
| 3 | BMC Software | 109.0 | 7 | 28 |
| 4 | Cognos Incorporated | 107.0 | 3 | 42 |
| 5 | Electronic Data Systems | 106.7 | 28 | 33 |
| 6 | Borland International | 105.8 | 20 | 21 |
| 7 | Consilium | 105.6 | 1 | 25 |
| 8 | Adobe Systems, Inc. | 105.0 | 21 | 54 |
| 9 | Oracle Corporation | 105.0 | 43 | 10 |
| 10 | Sungard Data Systems, Inc. | 103.1 | 2 | 24 |
| 11 | Aldus Corporation | 99.0 | ** | ** |
| 12 | Cadence Design Systems, Inc. | 98.6 | 14 | 1 |
| 13 | Autodesk, Inc. | 98.5 | 37 | 3 |
| 14 | Electronic Arts | 98.5 | 5 | 48 |
| 15 | Computer Sciences Corp. | 97.8 | 8 | 5 |
| 16 | HBO & Company | 97.8 | 31 | 14 |
| 17 | Platinum Technology, Inc. | 97.8 | ** | ** |
| 18 | Equifax, Inc. | 97.6 | 15 | 4 |

| 1991 Rank | Company Name | 1991 Score | 1990 Rank | 1989 Rank |
|---|---|---|---|---|
| 19 | CAERE | 97.6 | 17 | 30 |
| 20 | Hogan Systems, Inc. | 97.6 | 33 | 48 |
| 21 | Analysts International | 96.4 | 45 | 47 |
| 22 | Easel Corporation | 96.4 | ** | ** |
| 23 | Sterling Software, Inc. | 95.3 | 10 | 8 |
| 24 | Keane, Inc. | 95.3 | 22 | 37 |
| 25 | Lotus Development Corp. | 95.3 | 40 | 11 |
| 26 | Symix Systems | 95.0 | ** | ** |
| 27 | SEI Corporation | 94.3 | 36 | 54 |
| 28 | KnowledgeWare, Inc. | 94.0 | 42 | 39 |
| 29 | Landmark Graphics | 93.2 | 19 | 48 |
| 30 | American Management Systems, Inc. | 93.0 | 23 | 6 |
| 31 | Boole & Babbage, Inc. | 93.0 | 44 | 33 |
| 32 | Microsoft Corporation | 93.0 | 9 | 18 |
| 33 | Shared Medical Systems | 91.8 | 39 | 32 |
| 34 | Informix Software, Inc. | 91.5 | 30 | 16 |
| 35 | Structural Dynamics | 90.7 | 24 | 54 |
| 36 | LEGENT Corporation | 90.4 | 13 | 17 |
| 37 | Software Toolworks, Inc. | 90.1 | ** | ** |
| 38 | Triad Systems Corporation | 90.1 | 32 | 44 |
| 39 | Logicon Incorporated | 87.2 | 34 | 31 |
| 40 | Software Publishing Corp. | 86.1 | 18 | 12 |
| 41 | Symantec Corporation | 86.1 | 35 | 26 |
| 42 | Computer Task Group, Inc. | 84.9 | ** | ** |
| 43 | Systems Center, Inc. | 83.8 | 41 | 27 |
| 44 | Interleaf, Inc. | 81.6 | 26 | 48 |
| 45 | Automatic Data Processing | 78.6 | 27 | 23 |
| 46 | Policy Management Systems Corp. | 78.5 | 29 | 13 |
| 47 | Computer Associates | 78.4 | 46 | 41 |
| 48 | Paychex, Inc. | 78.0 | 47 | 36 |
| 49 | American Software, Inc. | 76.9 | 25 | 22 |
| 50 | Systems Software Associates, Inc. | 71.2 | 38 | 19 |
| 51 | Intersolv | 67.4 | ** | ** |
| 52 | FiServe Incorporated | 61.1 | 48 | 46 |
| 53 | ASK Computer Systems, Inc. | 60.8 | 49 | 48 |

** Didn't evaluate: IPO or lack of submission

## SOFTWARE/DATA SERVICES SUBCOMMITTEE

Charles E. Phillips, Jr., CFA, Chair, Stamford
SoundView Financial Group, Inc.

Andrew C. Brosseau, CFA, Boston
Cowen & Company

Thomas J. Erickson, CFA, Minneapolis
Wessels, Arnolds, & Henderson

Thomas A. Galvin, New York
Forstmann-Leff Assoc., Inc.

Louis Giglio, New York
Bear, Stearns & Co., Inc.

Jill Hauser, Baltimore
T. Rowe Price

William J. Maselunas, CFA, Boston
Loomis Sayles & Co., Inc.

Mary McCaffrey, New York
C.J. Lawrence

Timothy R. McCollum, CFA, New York
Dean Witter Reynolds, Inc.

# Specialty Chemical

## Recommendation for Award

The Specialty Chemical Subcommittee recommends that the Award for Excellence in Corporate Reporting for 1991-92 be awarded to Dexter Corporation for the second consecutive year. In 1990-91, Dexter shared honors with Morton International. This year, the company outscored all companies in the survey.

*Dexter Corporation* wins this year's award mostly on the basis of its highly regarded annual and quarterly reports, as it received more moderate scores for personal contact and other published material. Its unique segment reporting by end market, geography, and product line helped analysts understand what was occurring at the company. Quarterly reports were viewed as "mini-annuals." Also appreciated was the company's candor with dealing with negative developments in a year where the company faced several challenges. As in past years, accessibility was an issue, although helpfulness was not.

## Evaluation Method and General Observations

This report covers corporate information activities from mid-1991 through mid-1992. Sixteen companies were evaluated this year compared with eighteen last year. Dropped from last year's survey were Millipore Corporation and Pall Corporation. The separation companies are covered by fewer specialty chemical analysts, making a fair survey more onerous. Pall had been a previous multi-year winner of the Award for Excellence and finished seventh last year. Millipore finished eighth. Also discontinued was M.A. Hanna, which has yet to become a standard company for coverage. Added this year was International Specialty Products, or ISP. Several analysts initiated coverage after the initial public offering last year.

The new and simpler format, first adopted last year, was used again. Companies were evaluated on the basis of the following criteria:

*Annual Report* (40%)—Key issues are management's review of the year and outlook for the following year. Points are awarded for lucid discussion of factors driving the company's business and a candid discussion of challenges. Operating data by segment, including income, explanations of acquisition activities, and a full summary table were important. Extra points could be awarded for innovative disclosure.

*Quarterly Reports* (25%)—Most important is a matching of annual report segmentation and a discussion of trends in the quarter and outlook. A fourth quarter report was considered a plus.

*Alternative Communications* (15%)—The company's initiative in sending out marketing information, earnings and news releases, and a factbook were evaluated. The category contained analysis of a company's use of facsimile and First Call. Mailing of SEC documents was expected.

*Personal Contact* (20%)—The investor contact was the primary person evaluated, although access to management and quality of analyst meetings were considered. Frank discussion of negative events and a post-quarter conference call were critical to a high score.

Some trends were the increasing segmentation of business results on a quarterly basis, such as at Ferro Corporation, and growing use of conference calls and First Call. Annual reports were considered equal to last year, as the recession may have contributed to a reluctance to become more ambitious as to content. Grace's decision to curtail quarterly reports and the confusion concerning acquisitions and divestitures at Grace, and to a lesser extent, Great Lakes Chemical, were noted disappointments. ISP was criticized for not disclosing business trends until nearly closing the quarter.

As for movement between Divisions, Ferro qualified for First Division honors for the first time, while Grace and Loctite fell to the Third Division. Nalco Chemical falls out of the First Division into the Second, again with controversy as to the quality of personal contact. Overall scores were more disparate than last year, with a higher percentage of scores above 70 and a higher number below 60. Annual report scores were a bit lower, but those for additional information rose.

First Division companies all have excellent investor relations programs. Most in this division repeat from last year, with the exception of Ferro Corporation which makes it for the first time. Scores were all over 70 points. Last year, companies with over 68 points qualified. In alphabetical order, the companies are:

*Air Products and Chemical* raised its overall score this year, but once again finishes just below the corporate award winner. The annual report was considered highly, although lack of quarterly segment reporting and timing of the quarterly analyst meeting were negatives.

*Ecolab* finishes in the First Division as last year. The divestiture of ChemLawn challenged the company as far as restatements and contacting analysts, and the company was judged to have been exemplary. Quarterly reports were highly valued and the new investor contact, who had been the contact several years before, was commended.

*H.B. Fuller* once again improves its ranking to fourth from fifth. Scores were consistent this year, compared to last year's disparity. The annual was deemed to be improved, as were quarterly reports. Once again, mailings of the conference call transcript were appreciated, as was the work of the investor contact.

*Ferro Corporation*, which had declined a ranking in each of the past two years, came away in the fifth spot this year. Improvements were noted in releasing segment data each quarter and the addition of a conference call with senior management. The annual received high marks.

*Morton International*, last year's winner, remains in the First Division. Its scores across the categories were consistently high, but especially noteworthy were the personal contact marks. The investor relations director and the CFO are responsive to analysts and the company was among the first in this group to have a post-quarter conference call. A request was made for a more detailed President's Letter that sets some goals for the year or the next few years.

Second Division companies had scores between 60 and 69. These were all deemed to be "good" marks. In alphabetical order, they are:

*Avery Dennison* improves to the Second Division, in its second year as a combined entity. Respondents noted that the company reached out to confused investors. The conference calls, and especially the analyst meeting, were highly valuable. However, in the words of one evaluator, the company "desperately needs to report sales and operating earnings by business each quarter." The investor contact improved his score, presumably as an effort to correct last year's substandard marks. Being a subscriber to First Call also helped.

*Betz Laboratories* finishes in the Second Division again, but improves its score for the second year in a row. The most desired change was the addition of quarterly results by segment. The annual report score improved, although it was not immediately obvious why. The company was judged to be accessible, although there was a desire to have an informed back-up to the busy CFO.

*Great Lakes Chemical* returns to the Second Division, after falling into the Third last year. Again, the most common complaint was a lack of quarterly, or in that event annual, segment reporting. This situation did improve, however, in the last annual report. Respondents would like to see a factbook from Great Lakes, outlining the diverse businesses and their overall contribution. The company contacts were viewed positively, if not a bit promotional, but praised for maintaining contacts regardless of the analyst's rating.

*Lubrizol* posted one of the best turnarounds of the survey, rising to the Second Division with a dramatic increase in score. The annual report, particularly the discussion of trends in the business, was highly valued. Breakdown of sales in each geographic area by product line was a first. The President's Letter hit all the bases and the summary was complete. Quarterlies were viewed as somewhat less helpful, as investors would like a price/volume/mix analysis. The company still suffers from not having a factbook, but scored highly for investor access to marketing documents, earnings releases, and personal contact. The new investor contact receives high marks, although presentations were deemed only moderately helpful.

*Nalco Chemical* slips to the Second Division, although its score is similar to last year. Again, the quarterly report was viewed favorably. As to segments, analysts appreciated the sales breakdown but would like more guidance on margins. The President's Letter could use more elucidation of company goals. The capital expenditure table was highlighted. The investor contacts are still controversial, as some analysts find it difficult to get in touch with them or receive the information they need. The company added a contact in addition to the CFO recently, which may help the situation.

Third Division programs were found to be needing improvement. Scores were below 60. Companies included are:

*ChemDesign* stays in the Third Division with a small investor relations program. The annual report was viewed to be skimpy and vague concerning company problems. Quarterly reports were OK, but direct contact was found lacking. A quarterly conference call was appreciated, but the information that is passed was viewed as not always helpful. All in all, respondents noted improvements for this still young and struggling public company.

*W.R. Grace* drops to the Third Division this year, after finishing in the middle of the pack in the last three. Several specific problems came up, including late restating of results for acquisitions and divestitures, loss of the quarterly meeting, lack of segment reporting in the specialty chemicals business, and, most importantly, discontinuance of the quarterly report. The new investor contact was viewed reasonably favorably, although group meetings were not. Lack of a factbook hurt the total score.

*International Specialty Products* was evaluated for the first time. The annual report lacked substance and lacked a summary table. Lack of segment reporting was noted. Most upsetting to respondents was the refusal to discuss quarterly business trends until the last week of the quarter. The corporate information program is young and expected to improve.

*Loctite Corporation* drops to the Third Division this year. The annual report received a much lower score, owing to an inadequate discussion of segment results and capital expenditures. There was no segmentation of income except by geography. The investor contact, who is also the CFO, was believed to have the facts, but sometimes difficult to track down and extract those facts from. Without a factbook or conference call, getting a high score will be difficult.

*Sigma Aldrich* was again in the Third Division, as its investor relations program is practically nonexistent. Quarterly reports were viewed as totally inadequate and the company does not seek contact with analysts. Any contact is restricted to the CEO and CFO and must be on the company's terms, as they do not attend meetings.

## SPECIALTY CHEMICAL COMPANIES
### Rating Analysis of 1991 Corporate Information Program

| 1991 Rank | Company | Total Score | Annual Report | Quarterly Reports | Other Published Material | Personal Contact | 1990 Score | 1990 Rank | 1989 Rank | 1988 Rank |
|---|---|---|---|---|---|---|---|---|---|---|
| | Maximum Possible Score | 100.0 | 40.0 | 25.0 | 15.0 | 20.0 | | | | |
| 1 | Dexter | 78.8 | 30.0 | 22.7 | 12.8 | 13.3 | 75.7 | 1* | 3 | 6 |
| 2 | Air Products & Chemical | 78.3 | 30.2 | 20.4 | 10.3 | 17.3 | 71.4 | 3 | 10 | 1* |
| 3 | Morton International | 74.5 | 23.2 | 20.0 | 12.3 | 19.0 | 75.7 | 1* | 4 | 3 |
| 4 | H. B. Fuller | 74.0 | 25.0 | 19.7 | 12.3 | 17.0 | 69.1 | 5 | 7 | 10 |
| 5 | Ferro | 70.7 | 26.4 | 15.3 | 12.7 | 16.3 | 64.8 | 9 | 8 | 7* |
| 6 | Ecolab | 70.1 | 22.4 | 20.0 | 11.7 | 16.0 | 69.6 | 4 | 5 | 11* |
| 7 | Great Lakes Chemical | 67.6 | 28.6 | 15.9 | 8.3 | 14.8 | 58.5 | 14 | 9 | 14 |
| 8 | Nalco Chemical | 65.9 | 23.6 | 22.5 | 10.7 | 9.1 | 68.3 | 6 | 2 | 4* |
| 9 | Betz Laboratories | 65.4 | 26.7 | 15.6 | 8.7 | 14.4 | 63.7 | 12 | 14 | 15* |
| 10 | Lubrizol | 65.4 | 27.8 | 15.0 | 9.8 | 12.8 | 57.7 | 16 | 16 | 17 |
| 11 | Avery Dennison | 64.8 | 27.1 | 13.7 | 10.3 | 13.7 | 58.0 | 15 | 18 | 4* |
| 12 | Loctite | 46.6 | 16.5 | 11.2 | 7.8 | 11.1 | 62.7 | 13 | 11 | 7* |
| 13 | International Specialty Products | 46.5 | 17.8 | 9.5 | 6.5 | 12.7 | NR | NR | NR | NR |
| 14 | ChemDesign | 44.7 | 17.5 | 11.0 | 6.7 | 9.5 | 53.6 | 17 | 13 | NR |
| 15 | W.R. Grace & Co. | 38.6 | 18.8 | 0.0 | 6.4 | 13.4 | 63.8 | 11 | 12 | 11* |
| 16 | Sigma Aldrich Corp. | 35.6 | 14.8 | 5.5 | 4.5 | 10.8 | 27.8 | 18 | NR | NR |
| Average 1991 | | 61.7 | 23.5 | 14.9 | 9.5 | 13.8 | | | | |
| 1990 | | 63.2 | 24.6 | 15.0 | 8.9 | 14.7 | | | | |
| 1989 | | 65.3 | 23.4 | 16.7 | 5.4 | 19.7 | | | | |

NR-Not Rated
*-Tie

### SPECIALTY CHEMICAL SUBCOMMITTEE

Stuart M. Pulvirent, Chair, New York
Lehman Brothers

Jeff Cianci, New York
Bear, Stearns & Co., Inc.

Rosemarie J. Morbelli, CFA, New York
Ingalls & Snyder

Karen Lane Gilsenan, New York
Morgan Stanley & Co., Inc.

Kimberly Ritrievi, Ph.D, New York
Donaldson Lufkin & Jenrette Securities Corp.

Robert D. Hardiman, CFA, New York
Merrill Lynch

James F. Spencer, CFA, Boston
Wertheim Schroder & Co., Inc.

## Appendix A
## CHECKLIST OF CRITERIA FOR EVALUATING FINANCIAL COMMUNICATIONS EFFORT

**Qualification Questions (mandatory for each subcommittee's evaluation form)**

1. To your knowledge, during the past year has the management of this company suppressed or misrepresented material facts adverse to the company and/or its operations or outlook?

2. In your opinion, are any accounting or other managerial practices of this company materially misleading?

3. In your opinion, is this company unduly dilatory with respect to its press releases and/or earnings statements?

(If you have answered any of these questions in the affirmative, do not proceed with the rating of this company but contact the subcommittee chairman. An affirmative answer to one of the questions by two or more subcommittee members will disqualify the company from being considered in this year's rating.)

Note: The percentage weights appearing after each major category title (below) can be distributed to subcategories in whatever manner seems appropriate to each subcommittee.

**I. Annual Published Information** (40% to 50% of total weight)

*A. Annual Report*

1. **Financial Highlights**—(is it clear and unambiguous?)

2. **President's Letter Review**—(Does it hit the highlights of the year in an objective manner? Is it relevant to the company's results and candid in appraising problems?)

It should include:

a. Review of the year.
b. Insights into operating rates, unit production levels and selling prices.
c. Acquisitions and divestments, if any.
d. Government business, if material.
e. Capital expenditures program; start-up expenses.
f. Research and development efforts.
g. Employment costs, labor relations, union contracts.
h. Energy cost and availability.
i. Environmental and OSHA costs.
j. Backlogs.
k. New products.
l. Legislative and regulatory developments.
m. Outlook.
n. Unusual income or expense.

3. **Officers and Directors**

a. Age, background, responsibilities of officers.
b. Description of company organization.
c. Outside affiliations of directors.
d. Principal personnel changes.

4. **Statement of Corporate Goals**

What are the short- and long-term corporate goals and how and when does management expect to achieve them? (This section could be included in several areas of the report but separate treatment is preferred.)

5. **Discussions of Divisional and/or Segment Operations**

a. How complete is the breakdown of sales, materials, costs, overhead, and earnings?
b. Are the segments logical for analytical purposes? Do they parallel lines of business?
c. Are unusual developments explained with management's response included?
d. Note comparisons with relevant industry developments to include:
   1. Market size and growth.
   2. Market penetration.
   3. Geographical divergencies.
e. Foreign operations:
   1. Revenues, including export sales.
   2. Consolidated foreign earnings vs. equity interest.
   3. Market and/or regional trends.
   4. Tax status.

**6. Financial Summary and Footnotes**

a. Statement of accounting principles, including explanation of changes and their effects.
b. Adjustments to EPS for dilution.
c. Affiliates-operating information.
d. Consolidated finance subsidiaries-disclosure of separate balance sheet information and operating results.
e. Cash flows statement (FAS 95).
f. Tax accounting-investment tax credits identified; breakdown of current and deferred for US and non US tax jurisdictions; reconciliation of effective and statutory tax rates; impact of changes in tax law; early application of FAS 96.
g. Clarity of explanation of currency exchange rate accounting.
   1. Impact on earnings from Balance Sheet translation if any.
   2. Indication of "Operating" or Income Statement Effect of exchange rate fluctuations.
h. Property accounts and depreciation policies:
   1. Methods and asset lives used for tax and for financial reporting.
   2. Quantification of effect on reported earnings of use of different method and/or asset lives for tax purposes.
i. Investments: composition and market values disclosed.
j. Inventories: method of valuation and identifying different methods for various product or geographic segments.
k. Leases, rentals: terms and liability.
l. Debt repayment schedules.
m. Pension funds: costs charged to income, interest rate and wage inflation assumptions; amount of any unfunded past service liability; amortization period for unfunded liability (FAS 87).
n. Other postemployment benefits: pay-as-you-go amount, discussion of potential liability and impact of FASB Standard 106, including plans to fund, or amend plans, and Standard 112.
o. Capital expenditure programs and forecasts, including costs for environmental purposes.
p. Acquisitions and divestitures (if material):
   1. Description of activity and operating results.
   2. Type of financial transaction.
   3. Effect on reported sales and earnings.
   4. Quantification of purchase acquisitions or small poolings that do not require restatement of prior years' results. (When restating for pooling, both old and new data are useful for comparison.)
q. Year-end adjustments.
r. Restatement of quarterly reports to year-end accounting basis.
s. Research and development and new products; amount and types of outlays and forecasts.
t. Contingent liabilities, particularly environmental.
u. Derivation of number of shares used for calculating primary and fully-diluted earnings per share.
v. Disclosures of the fair values of financial instruments (FAS 107).
w. Goodwill-amount being amortized and number of years.
x. Ten-year statistical summary:
   1. Adequacy of income statement and balance sheet detail.
   2. Helpfulness of "nonstatement" data (e.g. number of employees, adjusted number of shares, price of stock, capital expenditures, etc.)

B. *10-Ks, 10-Qs and Other Required Published Information*

**II. Quarterly and Other Published Information Not Required** (30% to 40% of total weight)

A. *Quarterly Reports*
   1. Depth of commentary on operating results and developments.
   2. Discussion of new products, management changes, problem areas.
   3. Degree of detail of profit and loss statement including divisional or segmental breakdown.
   4. Inclusion of a balance sheet and cash flow statement.

5. Restatement of all prior and current year quarters for major pooling acquisitions and quantification of effect of purchase acquisitions and/or disposals.

6. Breakout of nonrecurring or exceptional income or expense items including effects from inventory valuation and foreign currency translation factors.

7. Explicit statement of accounting principles underlying the quarterly statements.

8. Timeliness of receiving reports.

9. Separate fourth quarter report.

B. *Other Published Material*

1. Availability of proxy statements (even though this is required public information).

2. Annual meeting report: available with questions and answers and identity of those posing questions.

3. Addresses to analysts' groups: available with questions and answers.

4. Statistical supplements and fact books.

5. Company magazines, newsletters, explanatory pamphlets.

6. Press releases: Are they sent to shareholders and analysts? Are they timely? Do they include earnings numbers?

7. How are documents filed with public agencies made available (SEC, Federal Trade Commission, Dept. of Labor, court cases, etc.)? Does the company disseminate all material information in 10-K, 10-Q, and similar reports?

III. **Other Aspects** (20% to 30% of total weight)

A. Is there a designated and advertised individual(s) for shareholder and analyst contacts?

B. Interviews:
   1. Knowledgeability and responsiveness of company contact.
   2. Access to policymakers and operational people.
   3. Candor in discussing negative developments.

C. Presentations to analyst groups: frequency and content.

D. Company-sponsored field trips and meetings.

E. Annual meetings:
   1. Accessibility.
   2. Worthwhile to shareholders and analysts?

**1991 Annual Report Georgia-Pacific Corp.**

## Appendix B

SALES AND OPERATING PROFITS BY INDUSTRY SEGMENT

| (Millions) | 1991 | | 1990 | | 1989 | | 1988 | |
|---|---|---|---|---|---|---|---|---|
| **NET SALES** | | | | | | | | |
| **PULP AND PAPER** | | | | | | | | |
| Containerboard and packaging | $ 2,008 | 17% | $ 2,440 | 19% | $ 1,578 | 15% | $1,433 | 15% |
| Communication papers | 1,134 | 10 | 1,360 | 11 | 983 | 10 | 796 | 8 |
| Tissue | 664 | 6 | 719 | 6 | 679 | 7 | 590 | 6 |
| Market pulp | 645 | 6 | 779 | 6 | 728 | 7 | 533 | 6 |
| Paper distribution and envelopes | 1,218 | 10 | 1,027 | 8 | — | — | — | — |
| Other | 420 | 4 | 377 | 3 | 74 | 1 | 84 | 1 |
| | 6,089 | 53 | 6,702 | 53 | 4,042 | 40 | 3,436 | 36 |
| **BUILDING PRODUCTS** | | | | | | | | |
| Wood panels | 2,097 | 18 | 2,296 | 18 | 2,488 | 24 | 2,442 | 26 |
| Lumber | 1,819 | 16 | 1,966 | 16 | 2,109 | 21 | 2,134 | 22 |
| Chemicals | 223 | 2 | 247 | 2 | 253 | 3 | 241 | 2 |
| Gypsum products | 222 | 2 | 270 | 2 | 299 | 3 | 305 | 3 |
| Roofing | 183 | 2 | 192 | 2 | 194 | 2 | 189 | 2 |
| Other | 861 | 7 | 952 | 7 | 745 | 7 | 718 | 8 |
| | 5,405 | 47 | 5,923 | 47 | 6,088 | 60 | 6,029 | 63 |
| OTHER OPERATIONS | 30 | — | 40 | — | 41 | — | 44 | 1 |
| CONTINUING OPERATIONS | $11,524 | 100% | $12,665 | 100% | $10,171 | 100% | $9,509 | 100% |
| | | | | | | | | |
| **OPERATING PROFITS*** | | | | | | | | |
| Pulp and paper | $ 362 | 34% | $ 979 | 67% | $ 917 | 63% | $ 616 | 58% |
| Building products | 344 | 32 | 423 | 29 | 533 | 36 | 428 | 41 |
| Other operations | 17 | 2 | 17 | 1 | 15 | 1 | 10 | 1 |
| Other income (expense)** | 344 | 32 | 48 | 3 | — | — | — | — |
| CONTINUING OPERATIONS | $ 1,067 | 100% | $ 1,467 | 100% | $ 1,465 | 100% | $1,054 | 100% |

*OPERATING PROFITS ARE BEFORE INCOME TAXES, INTEREST, COST OF ACCOUNTS RECEIVABLE SALE PROGRAM, GENERAL CORPORATE EXPENSES, UNUSUAL ITEMS, EXTRAORDINARY ITEMS AND ACCOUNTING CHANGES.

**OTHER INCOME (EXPENSE) INCLUDES $344 MILLION OF PRETAX GAINS IN 1991 AND A NET $48 MILLON PRETAX GAIN IN 1990 RESULTING FROM ASSET DIVESTITURES, AND PRETAX RESTRUCTURING CHARGES OF $135 MILLION AND $18 MILLION, RESPECTIVELY, IN 1983 AND 1982. IF THESE AMOUNTS HAD BEEN INCLUDED IN SEGMENT OPERATING PROFITS, PULP AND PAPER OPERATING PROFITS WOULD HAVE BEEN $546 MILLION IN 1991, $939 MILLION IN 1990, $13 MILLION IN 1983 AND $41 MILLION IN 1982; BUILDING PRODUCTS OPERATING PROFITS WOULD HAVE BEEN $504 MILLION IN 1991, $511 MILLION IN 1990, $277 MILLION IN 1983 AND $128 MILLION IN 1982; AND OTHER OPERATIONS OPERATING PROFITS WOULD HAVE BEEN $13 MILLION IN 1983 AND $25 MILLION IN 1982.

©1992 Georgia-Pacific Corporation. Used by permission.

1991 Annual Report Georgia-Pacific Corp.

GEORGIA-PACIFIC CORPORATION AND SUBSIDIARIES

YEAR ENDED DECEMBER 31

| 1987 | | 1986 | | 1985 | | 1984 | | 1983 | | 1982 | | 1981 | |
|---|---|---|---|---|---|---|---|---|---|---|---|---|---|
| $1,246 | 15% | $1,029 | 15% | $1,037 | 15% | $ 909 | 13% | $ 647 | 11% | $ 605 | 12% | $ 569 | 12% |
| 621 | 7 | 461 | 6 | 356 | 5 | 445 | 7 | 450 | 7 | 437 | 9 | 375 | 7 |
| 539 | 6 | 502 | 7 | 514 | 8 | 507 | 8 | 449 | 7 | 429 | 8 | 388 | 8 |
| 314 | 4 | 221 | 3 | 157 | 2 | 225 | 3 | 191 | 3 | 187 | 4 | 248 | 5 |
| — | — | — | — | — | — | — | — | — | — | — | — | — | — |
| 90 | 1 | 68 | 1 | 70 | 1 | 25 | — | 31 | 1 | 29 | 1 | 37 | 1 |
| 2,810 | 33 | 2,281 | 32 | 2,134 | 31 | 2,111 | 31 | 1,768 | 29 | 1,687 | 34 | 1,617 | 33 |
| 2,355 | 28 | 1,864 | 26 | 1,666 | 25 | 1,637 | 25 | 1,560 | 26 | 1,217 | 24 | 1,230 | 25 |
| 2,002 | 23 | 1,676 | 23 | 1,434 | 21 | 1,461 | 22 | 1,424 | 24 | 1,003 | 20 | 1,017 | 20 |
| 189 | 2 | 155 | 2 | 173 | 3 | 186 | 3 | 162 | 3 | 136 | 3 | 139 | 3 |
| 361 | 4 | 375 | 5 | 377 | 6 | 360 | 5 | 269 | 4 | 183 | 4 | 193 | 4 |
| 194 | 2 | 230 | 3 | 260 | 4 | 268 | 4 | 222 | 4 | 197 | 4 | 144 | 3 |
| 654 | 8 | 553 | 8 | 560 | 8 | 540 | 8 | 506 | 8 | 450 | 9 | 438 | 9 |
| 5,755 | 67 | 4,853 | 67 | 4,470 | 67 | 4,452 | 67 | 4,143 | 69 | 3,186 | 64 | 3,161 | 64 |
| 38 | — | 89 | 1 | 112 | 2 | 119 | 2 | 129 | 2 | 130 | 2 | 136 | 3 |
| $8,603 | 100% | $7,223 | 100% | $6,716 | 100% | $6,682 | 100% | $6,040 | 100% | $5,003 | 100% | $4,914 | 100% |
| $ 383 | 41% | $ 146 | 22% | $ 29 | 6% | $ 202 | 34% | $ 71 | 23% | $ 44 | 23% | $ 118 | 41% |
| 533 | 58 | 500 | 73 | 391 | 86 | 379 | 63 | 354 | 117 | 136 | 70 | 141 | 48 |
| 10 | 1 | 35 | 5 | 35 | 8 | 20 | 3 | 13 | 4 | 32 | 16 | 33 | 11 |
| — | — | — | — | — | — | — | — | (135) | (44) | (18) | (9) | — | — |
| $ 926 | 100% | $ 681 | 100% | $ 455 | 100% | $ 601 | 100% | $ 303 | 100% | $ 194 | 100% | $ 292 | 100% |

## 1991 COMPARED WITH 1990

Sales of the Specialty Materials & Services Group increased $20 million, or 6%. The net effect of acquired or divested businesses increased sales by $10.6 million. Net of acquired or divested businesses, sales increased 3% comprising a 2% increase in unit volume and price increases averaging 1%. Sales of nonwoven products were strong in 1991 compared with 1990 while sales of magnetic materials were weak. Operating income decreased $26.9 million, or 58%. The decrease was primarily due to the provision for environmental settlement costs and related legal fees of $25.1 million in 1991 compared with $3.8 million in 1990. This provision is associated with a future settlement of a lawsuit and other matters arising out of alleged violations of environmental laws at the company's nonwovens facility in Windsor Locks. Divestiture and restructuring activities also unfavorably impacted operating income by $6.3 million over 1990. The cost of these activities decreased operating income by $3.3 million in 1991 due to a restructuring and realignment of operations, and increased operating income by $3 million in 1990 due to a gain on the sale of our European water management systems business offset by restructuring charges.

Sales of the Specialty Coatings & Encapsulants Group decreased $0.6 million from 1990. The effect of acquired businesses increased sales by $12.4 million. Net of acquired businesses, sales decreased 4% comprising a 7% decrease in unit volume offset by price increases averaging 3%. Operating income decreased $13.1 million, or 39%. Gross margins decreased primarily due to the decreased sales volume offset in part by average selling price increases which exceeded raw material cost increases. Increased marketing and administrative and R&D expenses impacted operating income unfavorably in 1991.

Sales of the Specialty Plastics & Composites Group decreased $9.2 million from 1990, or 9%. Net of acquired or divested businesses and the effect of the joint venture with Solvay, sales increased 3% primarily attributable to price increases. Operating income decreased $21.9 million. Divestiture and restructuring activities decreased operating income by $17.2 million over 1990. A $12.6 million provision related to the anticipated loss on the sale of the company's pultrusions and composites businesses, as well as restructuring costs of $2.6 million primarily associated with the realignment and integration costs of operations, decreased operating income in 1991. In 1990, divestiture and restructuring activity increased operating income $2 million. Lower gross margins due to the net impact of acquired or divested businesses and higher marketing and administrative expenses associated with recently acquired businesses also contributed to decreased operating income in 1991.

LTI sales increased in 1991 by $19.6 million, or 13%. Volume accounted for an 11% increase in sales and price increases averaged 2%. Products for molecular biology and cell culture were strong in 1991. Operating income decreased 2%. Increased gross margin dollars primarily due to higher sales volume were more than offset by increased marketing and administrative and R&D expenses and a charge of $1.2 million for restructuring. Gross margin as a percentage of sales was lower in 1991 due to unit costs for fetal bovine serum (FBS) increasing at a greater rate than unit selling prices.

## 1990 COMPARED WITH 1989

Sales of the Specialty Materials & Services Group increased $42.3 million from 1989, or 15%. Net of acquired businesses, sales increased $23.1 million, or 8%. Volume increases averaged 3%, price increases averaged 3% and currency translation effects increased sales 2%. Operating income increased $1 million, or 2%. Divestiture and restructuring activities increased operating income $2.8 million over 1989. These activities included a gain on the sale of our European water management systems business offset by restructuring charges related to the write-off of fixed assets made redundant as a result of our cogeneration facility and the costs of an early retirement program. Almost completely offsetting this increase in operating income were higher environmental settlement costs and related legal fees in 1990 compared with 1989 of $2.7 million associated with our domestic nonwovens facility. Gross margin as a percent of sales decreased in 1990 as a result of lower margins at our acquired nonwovens Swedish operation and the cogeneration facility in Windsor Locks.

Sales of the Specialty Coatings & Encapsulants Group increased $49.1 million from 1989, or 17%. Net of acquired or divested businesses, sales increased 11% comprising currency translation increases of 5%, volume increases averaging 3% and price increases averaging 3%. Operating income increased $6.9 million, or 26%. This increase was primarily due to average selling price increases greater than raw material cost increases, increased volume and the favorable impact of higher translation rates on international results.

Sales of the Specialty Plastics & Composites Group decreased $49.3 million from 1989, or 32%. Net of acquired or divested businesses and the effect of the joint venture with Solvay, sales decreased 2%. Volume decreases of 5% were offset by average price increases of 3%. Operating income increased slightly from 1989. Divestiture and restructuring activities increased operating income by $2 million in 1990 which included a gain from the sale of the company's PVC business offset by restructuring charges primarily associated with the write-down of intangibles, costs of exiting unprofitable ventures and a provision for integrating recently acquired businesses.

LTI sales increased in 1990 by $17.1 million, or 13%. Volume accounted for a 12% increase in sales and currency translation effects accounted for a 5% increase. Price decreases averaged 4%. Operating income increased $0.7 million, or 4%.

## 1989 COMPARED WITH 1988

Sales of the Specialty Materials & Services Group increased $2.3 million from 1988, or 1%. Net of divested businesses, sales increased 3%. Price increases averaged 4% and volume increases averaged 1%. Currency translation effects offset these favorable variances by decreasing sales 2%. Operating income decreased $3.3 million, or 7%, compared with 1988. This decrease was primarily due to the sale of the nonwoven's microfiber glass business. Lower gross margins in the nonwovens business in 1989 resulted from increased raw material and manufacturing operating costs.

Sales of the Specialty Coatings & Encapsulants Group increased $22 million from 1988, or 8%. Volume increases averaged 10% and price increases averaged 1%. Currency translation effects decreased sales 3%. Operating income increased $3.7 million, or 16%. This increase was primarily due to improved gross margins attributable to increased sales volume. Offsetting these increases were the unfavorable impact of lower translation rates on international results, and the provisions taken for product performance claims and the write-down of inventory totaling approximately $.05 per share.

Sales of the Specialty Plastics & Composites Group decreased $7.6 million from 1988, or 5%. Net of acquired businesses, sales decreased 6%. Volume decreases averaged 8% while price increases averaged 2%. Operating income increased $1.6 million, or 49%. This increase was attributable to the favorable impact of the reversal in 1989 of unneeded reserves for the replacement of defective product. Also, included was a capital gain. Restructuring reserves established in 1988 impacted the comparison of operating income favorably in 1989. These favorable effects were offset in part by a deterioration in gross margins attributable to lower sales volume due to the slowdown in the automotive market, competitive market pressures and increased raw material costs.

LTI sales increased in 1989 by $4.8 million, or 4%. Volume accounted for a 9% increase in sales. Currency translation effects accounted for a decrease of 3%, and price decreases averaged 2%. Operating income increased $0.7 million, or 4%. Gross margins increased due to the reduced cost of FBS and the related favorable LIFO impact. Offsetting this favorable result in 1989 were increased marketing, administrative and R&D costs.

# 1991 Annual Report The Dexter Corp.

| In thousands of dollars | 1991 | 1990 | 1989 | 1988 | 1987 |
|---|---:|---:|---:|---:|---:|
| **NET SALES** | | | | | |
| Specialty Materials & Services | $338,236 | $318,282 | $276,023 | $273,709 | $250,665 |
| Specialty Coatings & Encapsulants | 334,363 | 335,008 | 285,905 | 263,888 | 242,055 |
| Specialty Plastics & Composites | 94,196 | 103,353 | 152,638 | 160,283 | 144,778 |
| Life Technologies | 170,939 | 151,303 | 134,158 | 129,386 | 120,212 |
| Consolidated | $937,734 | $907,946 | $848,724 | $827,266 | $757,710 |
| Unit Volume and Product Mix Change | 0% | 3% | 3% | 4% | 17% |
| Field Sales Force | 434 | 458 | 501 | 508 | 523 |
| **DEPRECIATION AND AMORTIZATION** | | | | | |
| Specialty Materials & Services | $ 14,912 | $ 12,538 | $ 8,931 | $ 8,422 | $ 7,958 |
| Specialty Coatings & Encapsulants | 10,330 | 8,402 | 6,415 | 6,115 | 5,727 |
| Specialty Plastics & Composites | 4,673 | 5,899 | 7,815 | 7,123 | 6,472 |
| Life Technologies | 3,931 | 3,275 | 2,896 | 2,193 | 2,431 |
| General Corporate | 249 | 158 | 186 | 496 | 187 |
| Consolidated | $ 34,095 | $ 30,272 | $ 26,243 | $ 24,349 | $ 22,775 |
| **RESEARCH AND DEVELOPMENT** | | | | | |
| Specialty Materials & Services | $ 6,097 | $ 5,793 | $ 5,160 | $ 5,053 | $ 5,064 |
| Specialty Coatings & Encapsulants | 17,225 | 15,464 | 13,140 | 12,712 | 11,658 |
| Specialty Plastics & Composites | 5,760 | 6,109 | 7,743 | 6,208 | 4,744 |
| Life Technologies | 12,974 | 12,514 | 11,316 | 8,712 | 7,224 |
| Consolidated | $ 42,056 | $ 39,880 | $ 37,359 | $ 32,685 | $ 28,690 |
| Laboratory Staff | 470 | 504 | 525 | 506 | 504 |
| **DIVESTITURE AND RESTRUCTURING ACTIVITIES**—(loss) gain | | | | | |
| Specialty Materials & Services | $ (3,287) | $ 2,980 | $ 211 | $ 1,272 | $ 788 |
| Specialty Coatings & Encapsulants | (1,636) | (460) | (87) | (1,151) | (1,035) |
| Specialty Plastics & Composites | (15,249) | 2,008 | 566 | (2,362) | (2,173) |
| Life Technologies | (1,200) | (156) | | 607 | |
| General Corporate | (1,084) | (828) | 903 | (1,560) | 597 |
| Consolidated | $ (22,456) | $ 3,544 | $ 1,593 | $ (3,194) | $ (1,823) |
| **CONSOLIDATED OPERATING INCOME (LOSS)** | | | | | |
| Specialty Materials & Services* | $ 19,345 | $ 46,239 | $ 45,228 | $ 48,632 | $ 44,353 |
| Specialty Coatings & Encapsulants | 20,244 | 33,298 | 26,395 | 22,696 | 25,188 |
| Specialty Plastics & Composites | (16,965) | 4,935 | 4,892 | 3,275 | 10,929 |
| Life Technologies | 18,273 | 18,575 | 17,843 | 17,190 | 16,612 |
| Consolidated Operating Income | 40,897 | 103,047 | 94,358 | 91,793 | 97,082 |
| Other Income, net | 3,453 | 7,769 | 7,290 | 5,199 | 6,642 |
| Interest Expense | (16,800) | (17,484) | (10,926) | (12,178) | (14,127) |
| General Corporate Expense | (16,358) | (15,925) | (13,079) | (12,891) | (12,739) |
| Consolidated Income before Taxes | $ 11,192 | $ 77,407 | $ 77,643 | $ 71,923 | $ 76,858 |

* Reduced by provision for environmental settlement costs and related legal fees of $25,068 in 1991, $3,773 in 1990 and $1,093 in 1989.

| | 1991 | 1990 | 1989 | 1988 | 1987 |
|---|---:|---:|---:|---:|---:|
| **CAPITAL EXPENDITURES** | | | | | |
| Specialty Materials & Services | $ 21,945 | $ 18,298 | $ 7,848 | $ 4,214 | $ 8,199 |
| Specialty Coatings & Encapsulants | 15,216 | 11,463 | 6,349 | 7,674 | 4,732 |
| Specialty Plastics & Composites | 11,887 | 7,455 | 13,576 | 7,030 | 5,965 |
| Life Technologies | 9,188 | 6,604 | 4,990 | 6,957 | 4,637 |
| General Corporate and Other* | 3,513 | 90 | 356 | 270 | 86 |
| Consolidated | $ 61,749 | $ 43,910 | $ 33,119 | $ 26,145 | $ 23,619 |

* Includes capital expenditures of discontinued operations in 1988 and 1987.

| | 1991 | 1990 | 1989 | 1988 | 1987 |
|---|---:|---:|---:|---:|---:|
| **ASSETS AT YEAR-END** | | | | | |
| Specialty Materials & Services* | $266,722 | $259,456 | $214,748 | $153,852 | $156,124 |
| Specialty Coatings & Encapsulants | 218,478 | 201,071 | 151,187 | 139,887 | 139,165 |
| Specialty Plastics & Composites | 80,138 | 78,610 | 158,433 | 158,265 | 145,098 |
| Life Technologies | 110,633 | 95,632 | 81,231 | 79,965 | 66,583 |
| Consolidated Operating Assets | 675,971 | 634,769 | 605,599 | 531,969 | 506,970 |
| General Corporate and Other** | 108,500 | 127,614 | 88,891 | 94,422 | 105,547 |
| Consolidated Assets | 784,471 | 762,383 | 694,490 | 626,391 | 612,517 |
| Consolidated Liabilities | (470,689) | (418,685) | (369,209) | (319,165) | (318,729) |
| Net Assets | $313,782 | $343,698 | $325,281 | $307,226 | $293,788 |

* Includes assets relating to the Windsor Locks Cogeneration facility beginning in 1989.
** Corporate assets consist primarily of cash, securities and investments, including corporate assets of Life Technologies. Other assets include the investment in the joint venture with Solvay & Cie S.A. of $35,795 in 1991 and $34,347 in 1990, and the assets of discontinued operations of $20,681 in 1988 and $23,234 in 1987.

Operations outside the United States are becoming increasingly important to Dexter giving geographic diversification to sales and earnings. Profits attributable to operations in countries outside the United States account for all of 1991 operating profits as profits from U.S. operations were completely offset by the environmental, divestiture and restructuring provisions. In recent years, profits attributable to operations in countries outside the United States represent a disproportionately higher percent of the total than sales or assets.

### 1991 COMPARED WITH 1990

Net sales increased in Western Europe and the Pacific Area but decreased in North America. In North America, net sales increased in the Specialty Materials & Services Group and at LTI but decreased in the Specialty Coatings & Encapsulants Group and the Specialty Plastics & Composites Group. The decrease in the Specialty Plastics & Composites Group was primarily due to the net effect of acquired or divested businesses and the formation of the joint venture with Solvay & Cie S.A. in 1990. All product groups contributed to the $34.4 million increase in sales outside of North America. Net sales increased in Western Europe in 1991 largely due to the net impact of 1990 acquisitions. Net sales outside of North America were 36% of consolidated net sales in 1991 and 33% in 1990. Export sales increased by $8 million to $52 million and represented 6% of consolidated net sales in 1991.

Operating income increased in the Pacific Area and decreased in Western Europe. The loss of $0.1 million in North America resulted from profits from operations being completely offset by the $25.1 million charge for environmental settlement costs and related legal fees, a $12.6 million provision related to the anticipated loss on the sale of the company's pultrusions and composites businesses and restructuring charges. Operating income decreased in Western Europe in 1991 in the Specialty Materials & Services Group and in the Specialty Plastics & Composites Group and increased at LTI and in the Specialty Coatings & Encapsulants Group. Operating income of the Specialty Materials & Services Group in Western Europe included a one-time gain on the sale of our European water management systems business in 1990. Operating income in 1991 was favorably impacted by a full year's results from its 1990 nonwovens acquisition in Sweden. Operating income increased 7% in the Pacific Area.

Total net assets decreased 9%, or $29.9 million, over 1990. Net assets increased in Western Europe and the Pacific Area by 1% and 3%, respectively. Net assets in North America decreased due to the $25.1 million charge for environmental settlement costs and the related legal fees and the $12.6 million provision related to the anticipated loss on the sale of the company's pultrusions and composites businesses. Corporate assets decreased in all geographic areas. The principle reason for the decrease in corporate assets in North America was the special cash dividend paid by Life Technologies to minority interest shareholders which decreased cash by $23.3 million. Net assets outside of North America were 43% of total net assets in 1991 compared with 39% in 1990.

### 1990 COMPARED WITH 1989

Net sales increased in Western Europe and the Pacific Area but decreased in North America. In North America, net sales increased in all product groups except in the Specialty Plastics & Composites Group. Sales decreased primarily due to the formation of the joint venture with Solvay & Cie S.A. which resulted in the elimination of the thermoplastic polyolefin business' sales from consolidation and the sale of the polyvinyl chloride compounding business. Sales outside of North America increased $62.1 million principally due to higher currency translation rates, which contributed $26 million to this increase, and the nonwovens acquisition in Sweden. Net sales outside of North America were 33% of total net sales in 1990 and 28% in 1989. Export sales decreased by $13 million to $44 million and represented 5% of consolidated net sales in 1990. This decrease was due mainly to the elimination of the thermoplastic polyolefin business' sales from consolidation.

Operating income increased in North America and Western Europe but decreased in the Pacific Area. The operating income of the Specialty Materials & Services Group in Western Europe included a gain on the sale of our European water management systems business and was also impacted favorably by an acquisition in Sweden. Higher currency translation rates also increased operating income in Western Europe. Operating income decreased 32% in the Pacific Area. Lower margins resulting from the introduction of new food packaging products in the Pacific Area, as well as increased manufacturing and selling costs associated with these products in Singapore, decreased operating income. Operating income outside of North America was 42% of total operating income in 1990, which included the gain on the sale of the European water management systems business, compared with 36% in 1989.

Total net assets increased $18.4 million, or 6%, over 1989. Higher currency translation rates accounted for $11.2 million of the increase in net assets outside of North America. Net assets increased in Western Europe and decreased in North America due to the net effect of acquisitions and divestitures. Corporate assets increased in North America and decreased in Western Europe as a result of the remittance of dividends and an increase in intercompany loans from Western Europe to North America. Other assets in North America include the investment in the joint venture with Solvay of $34.3 million in 1990. Net assets outside of North America were 39% of total net assets in 1990 compared with 26% in 1989.

### 1989 COMPARED WITH 1988

Net sales increased in North America in all product groups except the Specialty Plastics & Composites Group, which experienced a slowdown in the automotive market and competitive market pressures. Net sales increased 4% in Western Europe, despite an $18 million, or 2%, decrease in total net sales attributable to lower currency translation rates on international sales. Pacific Area net sales decreased 3%, primarily due to lower currency translation rates and the effect of a divested business at LTI. Net sales outside of North America were 28% of total net sales in 1989 and 1988. Export sales increased by $3 million to $57 million, representing 7% of consolidated net sales in 1989.

Operating income increased in North America in all groups except the Specialty Materials & Services Group. The disposal of a product line in 1988 and lower gross margins in the nonwovens business resulting from increased raw material and manufacturing costs caused the decrease in operating income in this group. Lower currency translation rates decreased operating income outside of North America. Operating income decreased 13% in the Pacific Area, primarily attributable to increased manufacturing and selling costs associated with new food packaging products in Singapore. Operating income outside of North America was 36% of total operating income in 1989 compared with 38% in 1988.

Total net assets increased $18.1 million, or 6%, over 1988, despite a decrease of $2.6 million in total net assets due to currency translation effects. Corporate assets decreased in North America principally due to the reclassification of the $10 million corporate investment in the cogeneration project at year-end 1988 which is included along with $47.6 million of property, plant and equipment in operating assets at year-end 1989. Additionally, $45.6 million of debt is included in liabilities in North America at year-end 1989 related to this project. Net assets in Western Europe increased principally due to higher cash and short-term investments at LTI included in corporate assets. Net of discontinued operations, net assets in the Pacific Area remained relatively constant. Net assets outside of North America were 26% of total net assets in 1989 and 1988.

# 1991 Annual Report The Dexter Corp.

| In thousands of dollars | 1991 | 1990 | 1989 | 1988 | 1987 |
|---|---|---|---|---|---|
| **NET SALES*** | | | | | |
| North America | | | | | |
|   Total Net Sales | $638,100 | $632,165 | $631,736 | $615,835 | $574,206 |
|   Intercompany Sales | 36,258 | 25,721 | 22,418 | 22,453 | 17,661 |
|   Net Sales | $601,842 | $606,444 | $609,318 | $593,382 | $556,545 |
| Western Europe | | | | | |
|   Total Net Sales | $290,118 | $256,548 | $195,661 | $188,311 | $169,450 |
|   Intercompany Sales | 11,036 | 2,526 | 2,485 | 1,850 | 2,487 |
|   Net Sales | $279,082 | $254,022 | $193,176 | $186,461 | $166,963 |
| Pacific Area | | | | | |
|   Net Sales | $ 56,810 | $ 47,480 | $ 46,230 | $ 47,423 | $ 34,202 |
| Consolidated | | | | | |
|   Total Net Sales | $985,028 | $936,193 | $873,627 | $851,569 | $777,858 |
|   Intercompany Sales | 47,294 | 28,247 | 24,903 | 24,303 | 20,148 |
|   Net Sales | $937,734 | $907,946 | $848,724 | $827,266 | $757,710 |

* Intercompany sales between areas are based on estimated market prices or on amounts computed to provide profits to each unit. Excluded from net sales is Dexter's share of the sales of 50% or less owned joint ventures which are accounted for under the equity or cost methods.

| | 1991 | 1990 | 1989 | 1988 | 1987 |
|---|---|---|---|---|---|
| **OPERATING INCOME (LOSS)** | | | | | |
| North America | $ (50) | $ 60,565 | $ 60,182 | $ 57,502 | $ 65,634 |
| Western Europe | 39,081 | 40,347 | 29,629 | 29,743 | 28,906 |
| Pacific Area | 3,195 | 2,993 | 4,413 | 5,099 | 3,064 |
| Consolidated, net of eliminations | $ 40,897 | $103,047 | $ 94,358 | $ 91,793 | $ 97,082 |
| **NET ASSETS AT YEAR-END** | | | | | |
| North America | | | | | |
|   Operating Assets | $454,280 | $431,017 | $477,387 | $408,780 | $383,383 |
|   Corporate Assets and Other* | 97,337 | 113,369 | 59,668 | 70,101 | 74,591 |
|   Liabilities | (372,894) | (334,403) | (295,738) | (250,453) | (248,740) |
|   Net Assets | $178,723 | $209,983 | $241,317 | $228,428 | $209,234 |
| Western Europe | | | | | |
|   Operating Assets | $187,785 | $173,813 | $101,273 | $ 98,175 | $100,394 |
|   Corporate Assets and Other* | 11,086 | 13,377 | 28,517 | 22,172 | 29,056 |
|   Liabilities | (81,806) | (70,930) | (61,826) | (59,616) | (61,259) |
|   Net Assets | $117,065 | $116,260 | $ 67,964 | $ 60,731 | $ 68,191 |
| Pacific Area | | | | | |
|   Operating Assets | $ 33,906 | $ 29,939 | $ 26,939 | $ 25,014 | $ 23,193 |
|   Corporate Assets and Other* | 77 | 868 | 706 | 2,149 | 1,900 |
|   Liabilities | (15,989) | (13,352) | (11,645) | (9,096) | (8,730) |
|   Net Assets | $ 17,994 | $ 17,455 | $ 16,000 | $ 18,067 | $ 16,363 |
| Consolidated | | | | | |
|   Operating Assets | $675,971 | $634,769 | $605,599 | $531,969 | $506,970 |
|   Corporate Assets and Other* | 108,500 | 127,614 | 88,891 | 94,422 | 105,547 |
|   Liabilities | (470,689) | (418,685) | (369,209) | (319,165) | (318,729) |
|   Net Assets | $313,782 | $343,698 | $325,281 | $307,226 | $293,788 |

* Corporate assets consist primarily of cash, securities and investments, including corporate assets of Life Technologies. Other assets include the investment in the joint venture with Solvay & Cie S.A. of $35,795 in 1991 and $34,347 in 1990 and the assets of discontinued operations in 1988 and 1987.

# INDEX OF COMPANIES REVIEWED AND INDUSTRY
## 1991–1992

|  |  |
|---|---|
| Abbott Laboratories | Health Care |
| Adobe Systems, Inc | Software/Data Services |
| Aetna Life & Casualty Company | Insurance |
| Addington Resources Inc | Nonferrous & Mining |
| Affiliated Publications, Inc | Media |
| Air Products and Chemicals, Inc | Specialty Chemical |
| Air & Water Technologies Corp | Environmental |
| Alaska Air Group, Inc | Airline |
| Albertson's Inc | Retail |
| Alcan Aluminium Limited | Nonferrous & Mining |
| Aldus Corp | Software/Data Services |
| Alexander & Alexander | Insurance |
| Alliance Capital Management LP | Financial Services |
| Allied-Signal Inc | Diversified Companies |
| Aluminum Co. of America | Nonferrous & Mining |
| Amax Gold Inc | Nonferrous & Mining |
| AMAX Inc | Nonferrous & Mining |
| Amdahl Corporation | Computer & Electronics |
| Amerada Hess Corp | Petroleum |
| American Barrick Resources Corp | Nonferrous & Mining |
| American Brands, Inc | Food, Beverage & Tobacco |
| American Cyanamid Co | Chemical |
| American Express Company | Financial Services |
| American General Corporation | Insurance |
| American Home Products | Health Care |
| American International Group, Inc | Insurance |
| American Management Systems, Inc | Software/Data Services |
| American Software Inc | Software/Data Services |
| Amoco Corporation | Petroleum |
| AMP Inc | Computer & Electronics |
| AMR Corporation | Airline |
| AmSouth Bancorporation | Banking |
| Anadarko Petroleum Corporation | Petroleum |
| Analysts International Corp | Software/Data Services |
| Anheuser-Busch Companies, Inc | Food, Beverage & Tobacco |
| Aon Corp | Insurance |
| Apache Corp | Petroleum |
| Apple Computer, Inc | Computer & Electronics |
| Archer-Daniels-Midland Co | Food, Beverage & Tobacco |
| Arkla, Inc | Natural Gas |
| Asarco Inc | Nonferrous & Mining |
| Ashland Coal Inc | Nonferrous & Mining |
| Ashland Oil, Inc | Petroleum |
| ASK Computer Systems Inc | Software/Data Services |
| Astra Pharmaceutical Products, Inc | International Pharmaceuticals |
| Atlanta Gas Light Co | Natural Gas |
| Atlantic Richfield Company | Petroleum |
| Attwoods PLC | Environmental |
| Autodesk, Inc | Software/Data Services |
| Automatic Data Processing, Inc | Software/Data Services |
| Avery Dennison Corporation | Specialty Chemical |
| Baker Hughes Inc | Petroleum |
| Baldor Electric Co | Electrical Equipment |
| Ball Corporation | Container & Packaging |
| B.A.T. Industries p.l.c. | Food, Beverage & Tobacco |
| Banc One Corporation | Banking |
| Bancorp Hawaii, Inc | Banking |
| Bank of Boston Corporation | Banking |
| Bank of New York Company, Inc., The | Banking |
| BankAmerica Corporation | Banking |
| Bankers Trust New York Corporation | Banking |
| BanPonce Corp | Banking |
| C.R. Bard Inc | Health Care |
| Baroid Corporation | Petroleum |
| Barnett Banks, Inc | Banking |
| Battle Mountain Gold | Nonferrous & Mining |
| Baxter International | Health Care |
| BayBanks, Inc | Banking |
| BB&T Financial Corp | Banking |
| Bear Stearns Companies Inc | Financial Services |
| Becton Dickinson and Company | Health Care |
| A.H. Belo Corp | Media |
| Bemis Company, Inc | Container & Packaging |
| Beneficial Finance | Financial Services |
| Betz Laboratories, Inc | Specialty Chemical |
| BMC Software | Software/Data Services |
| Boatmen's Bancshares, Inc | Banking |
| Boise Cascade Corp | Paper & Forest Products |
| Boole & Babbage Inc | Software/Data Services |
| Borden, Inc | Food, Beverage & Tobacco |
| Borland International | Software/Data Services |
| Bowater Incorporated | Paper & Forest Products |
| Brand Companies, Inc., The | Environmental |
| Briggs & Stratton Corp | Machinery |
| Bristol-Myers Squibb Company | Health Care |
| British Airways PLC | Airline |
| British Petroleum Co. | Petroleum |
| Broken Hill Proprietary Co | Foreign-Based Oil |
| Brooklyn Union Gas Co | Natural Gas |
| Brown-Forman Corp | Food, Beverage & Tobacco |
| Browning-Ferris Industries, Inc | Environmental |
| Burlington Northern Inc | Railroad |
| Burlington Resources, Inc | Petroleum |
| Cadence Design Systems, Inc | Software/Data Services |
| CAERE | Software/Data Services |
| Campbell Soup Company | Food, Beverage & Tobacco |
| Canonie Environmental Services | Environmental |
| Capital Cities/ABC Inc | Media |
| Capital Holding Corp | Insurance |
| Caterpillar, Inc | Machinery |
| CBS Inc | Media |
| Chambers Development Corp | Environmental |
| Champion International Corp | Paper & Forest Products |
| Charming Shoppes, Inc | Retail |
| Chase Manhattan Corporation | Banking |
| ChemDesign | Specialty Chemical |
| Chemical Banking Corp | Banking |
| Chemical Waste Management | Environmental |
| Central Bancshares of the South, Inc | Banking |
| Central Fidelity Banks, Inc | Banking |
| Chevron Corporation | Petroleum |
| Chubb Corp., The | Insurance |

Ciba-Geigy Corp. Inc . . . . . International Pharmaceuticals
CIGNA Corporation . . . . . . . . . . . . . . . . . . Insurance
Cincinnati Milacron Inc . . . . . . . . . . . . . . . Machinery
Citicorp, New York . . . . . . . . . . . . . . . . . . . . Banking
Clark Equipment Company . . . . . . . . . . . . . Machinery
Clean Harbors . . . . . . . . . . . . . . . . . . . . Environmental
CNA Insurance Companies . . . . . . . . . . . . . . Insurance
Coastal Corporation, The . . . . . . . . . . . . . . Natural Gas
Coca-Cola Company, The . . . . Food, Beverage & Tobacco
Coca-Cola Enterprises Inc . . . . Food, Beverage & Tobacco
Coeur d'Arlene Mines Corporation . . . . . . Nonferrous & Mining
Cognos Inc . . . . . . . . . . . . . . Software/Data Services
Columbia Gas System, Inc., The . . . . . . . . Natural Gas
Comcast Corp . . . . . . . . . . . . . . . . . . . . . . . . . Media
Comerica, Incorporated . . . . . . . . . . . . . . . . . Banking
Commerce Bancshares, Inc . . . . . . . . . . . . . . . Banking
Compaq Computer Corporation . Computer & Electronics
Computer Associates International, Inc . . . Software/Data Services
Computer Sciences Corp . . . . . . . Software/Data Services
Computer Task Group Inc . . . . . . Software/Data Services
ConAgra, Inc . . . . . . . . . . . . Food, Beverage & Tobacco
Conseco Inc . . . . . . . . . . . . . . . . . . . . . . . . Insurance
Consilium . . . . . . . . . . . . . . . Software/Data Services
Consolidated Natural Gas Co . . . . . . . . . . Natural Gas
Consolidated Papers, Inc . . . . . Paper & Forest Products
Consolidated Rail Corporation . . . . . . . . . . . . Railroad
Constar International, Inc . . . . . . Container & Packaging
Continental Bank Corporation . . . . . . . . . . . . Banking
Continental Corp . . . . . . . . . . . . . . . . . . . . Insurance
Cooper Industries, Inc . . . . . . . . . . Electrical Equipment
Adolph Coors Co . . . . . . . . Food, Beverage & Tobacco
CoreStates Financial Corporation . . . . . . . . . . Banking
Costco Wholesale Corp . . . . . . . . . . . . . . . . . . Retail
CPC International Inc . . . . . . . Food, Beverage & Tobacco
CRA Limited . . . . . . . . . . . . . . . . Nonferrous & Mining
Cray Research, Inc . . . . . . . . . . Computer & Electronics
Crestar Financial Corporation . . . . . . . . . . . . Banking
Crown Cork & Seal Co., Inc . . . . Container & Packaging
Crystal Brands, Inc . . . . . . . . . . . Apparel and Textiles
CSX Corporation . . . . . . . . . . . . . . . . . . . . . Railroad
Cummins Engine Co., Inc . . . . . . . . . . . . . . Machinery
Cyprus Minerals Co . . . . . . . . . Nonferrous & Mining
Dayton Hudson Corp . . . . . . . . . . . . . . . . . . . Retail
Deere & Company . . . . . . . . . . . . . . . . . . . Machinery
Delta Air Lines, Inc . . . . . . . . . . . . . . . . . . . Airline
Delta Woodside . . . . . . . . . . . . . . Apparel & Textiles
Dexter Corporation, The . . . . . . . Specialty Chemical
Dial Corp., The . . . . . . . . . . . . Diversified Companies
Diamond Shamrock Inc . . . . . . . . . . . . . . . . Petroleum
Digital Equipment Corp . . . . . . . Computer & Electronics
Dillard Department Stores, Inc . . . . . . . . . . . . . Retail
Walt Disney Company, The . . . . . . . . . . . . . . . Media
Dominion Bankshares Corporation . . . . . . . . . Banking
Dover Corporation . . . . . . . . . . . . . . . . . . . Machinery
Dow Chemical Co . . . . . . . . . . . . . . . . . . . . Chemical
Dow Jones & Co., Inc . . . . . . . . . . . . . . . . . . . Media
Dresser Industries, Inc . . . . . . . . . . . . . . . . . Petroleum
Dreyfus Corp . . . . . . . . . . . . . . . . . . . Financial Services
Dun & Bradstreet Corp., The . . . . . . . . . . . . . . Media
E.I. du Pont de Nemours & Co . . . . . . . . . . . Chemical
Easel Corp . . . . . . . . . . . . . . . Software/Data Services
Echo Bay Mines Ltd . . . . . . . . . . Nonferrous & Mining
Ecolab . . . . . . . . . . . . . . . . . . . Specialty Chemical
Edison Brothers Stores, Inc . . . . . . . . . . . . . . . . Retail
Electronics Arts . . . . . . . . . . Software/Data Services
Electronic Data Systems Corp . . . . Software/Data Services
Elf Acquitaine . . . . . . . . . . . . . . . . . . Foreign-Based Oil
EMCON Associates . . . . . . . . . . . . . . . Environmental
Emerson Electric Co . . . . . . . . . . . Electrical Equipment
Energy Service Company, Inc . . . . . . . . . . . Petroleum
Engraph, Inc . . . . . . . . . . . . Container & Packaging
Enron Corp . . . . . . . . . . . . . . . . . . . . . . Natural Gas
Enron Gas & Oil Company . . . . . . . . . . . . . Petroleum
ENSERCH Corporation . . . . . . . . . . . . . . Natural Gas
Enterra Corporation . . . . . . . . . . . . . . . . . . Petroleum
Environmental Elements Corporation . . . . Environmental
Equifax Inc . . . . . . . . . . . . . . . Software/Data Services
Equitable Resources, Inc . . . . . . . . . . . . . . Natural Gas
Ethyl Corporation . . . . . . . . . . . . . . . . . . . Chemical
EXEL Limited . . . . . . . . . . . . . . . . . . . . . . Insurance
Exxon Corporation . . . . . . . . . . . . . . . . . . Petroleum
Federal Paper Board . . . . . . . . Paper & Forest Products
Ferro . . . . . . . . . . . . . . . . . . . Specialty Chemical
Fieldcrest Cannon Inc . . . . . . . . Apparel and Textiles
Fifth Third Bancorp . . . . . . . . . . . . . . . . . . . Banking
Figgie International . . . . . . . . . . Diversified Companies
Firstar Corporation . . . . . . . . . . . . . . . . . . . Banking
First Alabama Bancshares, Inc . . . . . . . . . . . . Banking
First American Corporation, Tennessee . . . . . . . Banking
First Bank System Inc . . . . . . . . . . . . . . . . . Banking
First Chicago Corporation . . . . . . . . . . . . . . Banking
First Citizens BancShares . . . . . . . . . . . . . . . Banking
First Empire State Corporation . . . . . . . . . . . Banking
First Fidelity Bancorporation, Newark . . . . . . . Banking
First Financial Management Corp . Software/Data Services
First Hawaiian Inc . . . . . . . . . . . . . . . . . . . . Banking
First Interstate Bancorp . . . . . . . . . . . . . . . . Banking
First of America Bank Corporation . . . . . . . . . Banking
First Security Corporation . . . . . . . . . . . . . . Banking
First Tennessee National Corporation . . . . . . . Banking
First Union Corporation . . . . . . . . . . . . . . . . Banking
First Virginia Banks, Inc . . . . . . . . . . . . . . . . Banking
Fiserv Inc . . . . . . . . . . . . . . Software/Data Services
Fleet Financial Group, Inc . . . . . . . . . . . . . . Banking
Freeport-McMoRan Copper & Gold Inc . . . Nonferrous & Mining
Fruit of the Loom, Inc . . . . . . . . . . Apparel and Textiles
H.B. Fuller Company . . . . . . . . . . . Specialty Chemical
Gannett Co., Inc . . . . . . . . . . . . . . . . . . . . . . Media
Gap, Inc., The . . . . . . . . . . . . . . . . . . . . . . . Retail
GEICO Corp . . . . . . . . . . . . . . . . . . . . . . Insurance
General Electric Co . . . . . . . . . . . Electrical Equipment
General Mills, Inc . . . . . . . . . Food, Beverage & Tobacco
General Re Corp . . . . . . . . . . . . . . . . . . . . Insurance
General Signal . . . . . . . . . . . . . . Electrical Equipment
Georgia Gulf . . . . . . . . . . . . . . . . . . . . . . . Chemical
Georgia-Pacific Corporation . . . . Paper & Forest Products
Geraghty & Miller Inc . . . . . . . . . . . . . . . Environmental

Gerber Products Co. . . . . . . . Food, Beverage & Tobacco
Giddings & Lewis, Inc . . . . . . . . . . . . . . . . . Machinery
Gitano Group, Inc . . . . . . . . . . . . . Apparel & Textiles
Glaxo Holdings, p.l.c. . . . . . . . . . . . . . . . . Health Care
Global Marine, Inc. . . . . . . . . . . . . . . . . . . . Petroleum
BF Goodrich . . . . . . . . . . . . . . . . . . . . . . . . . Chemical
W.R. Grace & Co . . . . . . . . . . . . . Specialty Chemical
W.W. Grainger, Inc . . . . . . . . . . . Electrical Equipment
Grand Metropolitan PLC . . . . Food, Beverage & Tobacco
Great A&P Tea Co. Inc., The . . . . . . . . . . . . . . . Retail
Great Lakes Chemical . . . . . . . . . . . . Specialty Chemical
Groundwater Technology, Inc . . . . . . . . . Environmental
Guilford Mills, Inc . . . . . . . . . . . . . Apparel and Textiles
Halliburton Co . . . . . . . . . . . . . . . . . . . . . . Petroleum
Harding Associates Inc . . . . . . . . . . . . . . Environmental
Harnischfeger Industries, Inc . . . . . . . . . . . Machinery
Harsco Corp . . . . . . . . . . . . . Diversified Companies
Hartmarx Corporation . . . . . . . . . Apparel and Textiles
HBO & Company . . . . . . . . . . . Software/Data Services
Hecla Mining Company . . . . . . . Nonferrous & Mining
Heekin Can, Inc . . . . . . . . . . . Container & Packaging
H.J. Heinz . . . . . . . . . . . . . Food, Beverage & Tobacco
Hemlo Gold Mines, Inc . . . . . . . . Nonferrous & Mining
Hershey Foods Corp . . . . . . . Food, Beverage & Tobacco
Hercules Chemical Co., Inc. . . . . . . . . . . . . . Chemical
Hewlett-Packard Co. . . . . . . . Computer & Electronics
Hibernia Corporation . . . . . . . . . . . . . . . . . . Banking
Hoechst AG . . . . . . . . . . . International Pharmaceuticals
Hogan Systems Inc . . . . . . . . . . Software/Data Services
Home Depot Inc., The . . . . . . . . . . . . . . . . . . . Retail
Homestake Mining Co . . . . . . . . . Nonferrous & Mining
Household International, Inc . . . . . . . Financial Services
Honeywell, Inc . . . . . . . . . . . . . . Electrical Equipment
Horsehead Resource Development Co. Inc . Environmental
Huntington Bancshares, Inc . . . . . . . . . . . . . . Banking
ICF International, Inc . . . . . . . . . . . . . . . Environmental
Illinois Central Corp . . . . . . . . . . . . . . . . . . . Railroad
Imcera Group, Inc . . . . . . . . . . . . . . . . . . . . Chemical
Imperial Chemical . . . . . . . . . . . . . . . . . . . . Chemical
Inco Limited . . . . . . . . . . . . . . Nonferrous & Mining
Informix Corp . . . . . . . . . . . . . Software/Data Services
Ingersoll-Rand Co . . . . . . . . . . . . . . . . . . . Machinery
Intersolv . . . . . . . . . . . . . . . . Software/Data Services
Integra Financial Corp . . . . . . . . . . . . . . . . . Banking
Intel Corp . . . . . . . . . . . . . . Computer & Electronics
Interleaf Inc. . . . . . . . . . . . . . Software/Data Services
International Business Machines Corp. . . . . Computer & Electronics
International Paper Company . . . Paper & Forest Products
International Specialty Products . . . . . Specialty Chemical
International Technology Corp. . . . . . . . Environmental
ITT Corporation . . . . . . . . . . . . Diversified Companies
James River Corp. of Virginia . . . Paper & Forest Products
Jefferson-Pilot Corp. . . . . . . . . . . . . . . . . . . Insurance
Johnson & Johnson . . . . . . . . . . . . . . . . . Health Care
K mart Corp . . . . . . . . . . . . . . . . . . . . . . . . . Retail
Kaiser Aluminum Corporation . . . . Nonferrous & Mining
Kansas City Southern Industries, Inc . . . . . . . Railroad
Keane Inc . . . . . . . . . . . . . . . Software/Data Services
Kellogg Co . . . . . . . . . . . . Food, Beverage & Tobacco

Kellwood Co. . . . . . . . . . . . . . . Apparel and Textiles
Kemper Corporation . . . . . . . . . . . . . . . . . . Insurance
Kennametal Inc. . . . . . . . . . . . . . . . . . . . . Machinery
Kerr-McGee Corp. . . . . . . . . . . . . . . . . . . . Petroleum
KeyCorp . . . . . . . . . . . . . . . . . . . . . . . . . . Banking
Kimberly-Clark Corporation . . . . Paper & Forest Products
KLM Royal Dutch Airlines . . . . . . . . . . . . . . . Airline
Knight-Ridder, Inc. . . . . . . . . . . . . . . . . . . . . Media
KnowledgeWare, Inc . . . . . . . . . Software/Data Services
Kroger Co., The. . . . . . . . . . . . . . . . . . . . . . . Retail
LAC Minerals, Ltd . . . . . . . . . . . Nonferrous & Mining
Laidlaw Industries, Inc. . . . . . . . . . . . . . . Environmental
Landmark Graphics Corp. . . . . . . Software/Data Services
Lasmo plc . . . . . . . . . . . . . . . . . . . Foreign-Based Oil
LEGENT Corporation . . . . . . . . . Software/Data Services
Leslie Fay Companies, The . . . . . . . Apparel and Textiles
Liberty Corp . . . . . . . . . . . . . . . . . . . . . . . Insurance
Eli Lilly and Company . . . . . . . . . . . . . . . Health Care
Limited, Inc., The . . . . . . . . . . . . . . . . . . . . . Retail
Lincoln National Corp. . . . . . . . . . . . . . . . . Insurance
Liz Claiborne, Inc. . . . . . . . . . . . . Apparel and Textiles
Loctite Corp . . . . . . . . . . . . . . . . Specialty Chemical
Logicon Incorporated . . . . . . . . . Software/Data Services
Longs Drug Stores Corp . . . . . . . . . . . . . . . . . Retail
Lotus Development Corp. . . . . . . Software/Data Services
Louisiana Land & Exploration Co . . . . . . . . . Petroleum
Louisiana-Pacific Corp. . . . . . . . Paper & Forest Products
Lubrizol Corp, The. . . . . . . . . . . . . . Specialty Chemical
Lyondell Petrochemical Company . . . . . . . . . Chemical
Magma Copper Company . . . . . . Nonferrous & Mining
Marion Merrell Dow, Inc . . . . . . . . . . . . . . Health Care
Marsh & McLennan Corporation . . . . . . . . . . Insurance
Marshall & Ilsley Corp . . . . . . . . . . . . . . . . . Banking
May Department Stores Co . . . . . . . . . . . . . . . Retail
Maytag Corporation . . . . . . . . . . Electrical Equipment
MBNA Corp . . . . . . . . . . . . . . . . . . . . . . . Banking
Maxus Energy Corp . . . . . . . . . . . . . . . . . . Petroleum
MCN Corp. . . . . . . . . . . . . . . . . . . . . . Natural Gas
McDermott International, Inc. . . . . . . . . . . . Petroleum
McDonald's Corp . . . . . . . . Food, Beverage & Tobacco
McGraw-Hill, Inc. . . . . . . . . . . . . . . . . . . . . . Media
Mead Corporation, The . . . . . . . Paper & Forest Products
Mellon Bank Corporation . . . . . . . . . . . . . . . Banking
Melville Corporation. . . . . . . . . . . . . . . . . . . Retail
Mercantile Bancorporation Inc . . . . . . . . . . . Banking
Mercantile Bankshares Corp . . . . . . . . . . . . . Banking
Mercantile Stores Co., Inc . . . . . . . . . . . . . . . . Retail
Merck & Co., Inc. . . . . . . . . . . . . . . . . . Health Care
Meridian Bancorp, Inc. . . . . . . . . . . . . . . . . Banking
Merrill Lynch & Co., Inc. . . . . . . . . . Financial Services
Merry-Go-Round Enterprises, Inc . . . . . . . . . . . Retail
Michigan National Corporation . . . . . . . . . . . Banking
Microsoft Corporation . . . . . . . . Software/Data Services
Mid-American Waste Systems, Inc . . . . . . . Environmental
Midlantic Corp. . . . . . . . . . . . . . . . . . . . . . Banking
M.I.M. Holdings Limited . . . . . . Nonferrous & Mining
Minnesota Mining & Mfg. Co. . . . Diversified Companies
MNC Financial Inc . . . . . . . . . . . . . . . . . . . Banking
Mobil Corporation . . . . . . . . . . . . . . . . . . . Petroleum
Monsanto Company . . . . . . . . . . . . . . . . . . Chemical

|  |  |
|---|---|
| J.P. Morgan & Co., Inc | Banking |
| Morgan Stanley Group, Inc | Financial Services |
| Morton International | Specialty Chemical |
| Motorola, Inc | Computer & Electronics |
| Murphy Oil Corp | Petroleum |
| NAC Re Corp | Insurance |
| Nabors Industries, Inc | Petroleum |
| Nalco Chemical Co | Specialty Chemical |
| National City Corporation, Cleveland | Banking |
| National Fuel Gas Co | Natural Gas |
| NationsBank Corp | Banking |
| Navistar International Corp | Machinery |
| NBD Bancorporation, Inc | Banking |
| Neiman Marcus Group, The | Retail |
| Nerco, Inc | Nonferrous & Mining |
| Newmont Mining Corp | Nonferrous & Mining |
| New York Times Company, The | Media |
| NICOR Inc | Natural Gas |
| Nordstrom, Inc | Retail |
| Norfolk Southern Corp | Railroad |
| Norsk Hydro A.S. | Foreign-Based Oil |
| Northern Trust Corporation | Banking |
| Norwest Corporation | Banking |
| Novell Corporation | Software/Data Services |
| Occidental Petroleum Corp | Petroleum |
| Ogden Projects, Inc | Environmental |
| Ohio Casualty Corp | Insurance |
| OHM Corp | Environmental |
| Old Kent Financial Corporation | Banking |
| Olin Corp | Chemical |
| Oracle Corp | Software/Data Services |
| Oryx Energy Company | Petroleum |
| Owens-Illinois, Inc | Container & Packaging |
| Oxford Industries, Inc | Apparel and Textiles |
| PACCAR, Inc | Machinery |
| Pacific Enterprises | Natural Gas |
| PaineWebber Group, Inc | Financial Services |
| Panhandle Eastern Corporation | Natural Gas |
| Paramount Communications Inc | Media |
| Parker Drilling Company | Petroleum |
| Parker Hannifin Corporation | Machinery |
| Paychex, Inc | Software/Data Services |
| Pegasus Gold Inc | Nonferrous & Mining |
| J.C. Penney Company, Inc | Retail |
| Penn Central | Diversified Companies |
| Pennzoil Company | Petroleum |
| Peoples Energy Corp | Natural Gas |
| PepsiCo, Inc | Food, Beverage & Tobacco |
| Petrie Stores Corp | Retail |
| Pfizer Inc | Health Care |
| Phelps Dodge Corporation | Nonferrous & Mining |
| Philip Morris Companies Inc | Food, Beverage & Tobacco |
| Phillips Petroleum Company | Petroleum |
| Phillips-Van Heusen Corp | Apparel and Textiles |
| Pittston Company, The | Nonferrous & Mining |
| Placer Dome Inc | Nonferrous & Mining |
| Platinum Technology Inc | Software/Data Services |
| PNC Financial Corporation | Banking |
| Policy Management Systems Corp | Software/Data Services |
| Potlatch | Paper & Forest Products |
| PPG Industries | Chemical |
| T. Rowe Price Associates, Inc | Financial Services |
| Price Company | Retail |
| Primerica Corp | Financial Services |
| Protective Life Corp | Insurance |
| Quaker Oats Co | Food, Beverage & Tobacco |
| Quantum Chemical | Chemical |
| Questar Corporation | Natural Gas |
| Ralston Purina Co | Food, Beverage & Tobacco |
| Reliance Electric Co | Electrical Equipment |
| Repsol S.A. | Foreign-Based Oil |
| Republic New York Corporation | Banking |
| Reuters Holdings | Media |
| Reynolds Metals Co | Nonferrous & Mining |
| Rhone-Poulenc Rorer, Inc | International Pharmaceuticals |
| Riggs National Corporation | Banking |
| Rite Aid Corp | Retail |
| RJR Nabisco, Inc | Food, Beverage & Tobacco |
| Roche Holdings AG | International Pharmaceuticals |
| Rockwell International Corp | Diversified Companies |
| Rohm and Haas Co | Chemical |
| Rollins Environmental Services, Inc | Environmental |
| Rowan Companies | Petroleum |
| Royal Dutch/Shell Group | Petroleum |
| RTZ Corp. PLC, The | Nonferrous & Mining |
| Russell Corporation | Apparel and Textiles |
| SAFECO Corp | Insurance |
| Salomon Inc | Financial Services |
| Sandoz Ltd | International Pharmaceuticals |
| Sanifill, Inc | Environmental |
| Santa Fe Energy Resources, Inc | Petroleum |
| Santa Fe Pacific Corporation | Railroad |
| Sara Lee Corp | Food, Beverage & Tobacco |
| Schering-Plough Corp | Health Care |
| Schlumberger Ltd | Petroleum |
| Scott Paper Co | Paper & Forest Products |
| E.W. Scripps Co | Media |
| Seagram Company Ltd. (The) | Food, Beverage & Tobacco |
| Seagull Energy Corp | Natural Gas |
| Sealed Air Corporation | Container & Packaging |
| Sealright Co. Inc | Container & Packaging |
| Sears, Roebuck & Co | Retail |
| SEI Corporation | Software/Data Services |
| Shared Medical Systems | Software/Data Services |
| Shawmut National Corporation | Banking |
| Sigma Aldrich Corporation | Specialty Chemical |
| Signet Banking Corporation | Banking |
| Smith International, Inc | Petroleum |
| SmithKline Beecham Corp | Health Care |
| Society Corporation | Banking |
| Software Publishing Corp | Software/Data Services |
| Software Toolworks Inc | Software/Data Services |
| Sonat Inc | Natural Gas |
| Sonoco Products Company | Container & Packaging |
| SouthTrust Corporation | Banking |
| Southwest Airlines Co | Airline |
| Spiegel, Inc | Retail |
| Springs Industries, Inc | Apparel and Textiles |
| St. Paul Companies, Inc | Insurance |

Star Banc Corp . . . . . . . . . . . . . . . . . . . . . . . . Banking
State Street Boston Corporation . . . . . . . . . . . Banking
Sterling Software Inc . . . . . . . . . Software/Data Services
Stone Container . . . . . . . . . . . Paper & Forest Products
Stratus Computer Inc. . . . . . . . . Computer & Electronics
Structural Dynamics Research Corp . . . . . . Software/Data Services
Sun Company, Inc . . . . . . . . . . . . . . . . . . . . Petroleum
Sungard Data Systems . . . . . . . . Software/Data Services
SUN Microsystems Inc . . . . . . . . Computer & Electronics
SunTrust Banks, Inc . . . . . . . . . . . . . . . . . . . . Banking
Super Valu Stores, Inc . . . . . . . . . . . . . . . . . . . . Retail
Symantec Corp . . . . . . . . . . . . . . Software/Data Services
Symix Systems . . . . . . . . . . . . . Software/Data Services
Syntex Corp . . . . . . . . . . . . . . . . . . . . . . . Health Care
Systems Software Associates . . . . Software/Data Services
Systems Center, The . . . . . . . . . . Software/Data Services
Tandem Computer Inc . . . . . . . . Computer & Electronics
Tele-Communications, Inc . . . . . . . . . . . . . . . . . Media
Teledyne, Inc . . . . . . . . . . . . . . . . Diversified Companies
Temple-Inland Inc . . . . . . . . . . Paper & Forest Products
Tenneco Inc . . . . . . . . . . . . . . . . . . . . . . Natural Gas
Texaco Inc . . . . . . . . . . . . . . . . . . . . . . . . . Petroleum
Texas Instruments . . . . . . . . . . . Computer & Electronics
Texfi Industries, Inc . . . . . . . . . . . . . Apparel and Textiles
Textron Inc . . . . . . . . . . . . . . . . . Diversified Companies
Tidewater, Inc . . . . . . . . . . . . . . . . . . . . . . . Petroleum
Tiffany & Co . . . . . . . . . . . . . . . . . . . . . . . . . . Retail
Time Warner Inc . . . . . . . . . . . . . . . . . . . . . . . Media
Times Mirror Company, The . . . . . . . . . . . . . . . Media
TJX Companies, Inc., The . . . . . . . . . . . . . . . . Retail
Torchmark Corp . . . . . . . . . . . . . . . . . . . . . . Insurance
Total Compagnie Francaise . . . . . . . . Foreign-Based Oil
Toys R Us Inc . . . . . . . . . . . . . . . . . . . . . . . . Retail
Transamerica Corp . . . . . . . . . . . . . . Financial Services
Transco Energy Co . . . . . . . . . . . . . . . . . Natural Gas
Travelers Corp., The . . . . . . . . . . . . . . . . . . Insurance
TRC Companies Inc . . . . . . . . . . . . . . . . Environmental
Triad Systems Corporation . . . . . Software/Data Services
Tribune Company . . . . . . . . . . . . . . . . . . . . . . Media
TRINOVA Corporation . . . . . . . . . . . . . . . . Machinery
TRW Inc . . . . . . . . . . . . . . . . . . Diversified Companies
Tultex . . . . . . . . . . . . . . . . . . . . . . Apparel & Textiles
Tyco Laboratories . . . . . . . . . . . . Diversified Companies
Tyson Foods, Inc . . . . . . . . . Food, Beverage & Tobacco
UAL Corp . . . . . . . . . . . . . . . . . . . . . . . . . . Airline
UGI Corp . . . . . . . . . . . . . . . . . . . . . . . Natural Gas

UJB Financial Corporation . . . . . . . . . . . . . . Banking
Unifi Inc . . . . . . . . . . . . . . . . . . . . . Apparel & Textiles
Union Camp Corporation . . . . . Paper & Forest Products
Union Carbide Corp . . . . . . . . . . . . . . . . . . Chemical
Union Pacific Corp . . . . . . . . . . . . . . . . . . . . Railroad
Union Texas Petroleum Holdings Inc . . . . . . . Petroleum
Universal Corporation . . . . . . Food, Beverage & Tobacco
Unocal Corp . . . . . . . . . . . . . . . . . . . . . . . Petroleum
UNUM Corporation . . . . . . . . . . . . . . . . . . Insurance
Upjohn Company, The . . . . . . . . . . . . . . . Health Care
USAir Group, Inc . . . . . . . . . . . . . . . . . . . . . Airline
USF&G Corporation . . . . . . . . . . . . . . . . . . Insurance
USLife Corp . . . . . . . . . . . . . . . . . . . . . . . Insurance
U.S. Bancorp . . . . . . . . . . . . . . . . . . . . . . . Banking
UST Inc . . . . . . . . . . . . . . . Food, Beverage & Tobacco
Valero Energy Corporation . . . . . . . . . . . . . Petroleum
Van Dorn Company . . . . . . . . . . Container & Packaging
Varity Corporation . . . . . . . . . . . . . . . . . . Machinery
VF Corp . . . . . . . . . . . . . . . . . . . Apparel & Textiles
Waban Inc . . . . . . . . . . . . . . . . . . . . . . . . . . Retail
Wachovia Corporation . . . . . . . . . . . . . . . . . Banking
Walgreen Co . . . . . . . . . . . . . . . . . . . . . . . . Retail
Wal-Mart Stores, Inc . . . . . . . . . . . . . . . . . . . Retail
Warner-Lambert Company . . . . . . . . . . . . . Health Care
Washington Gas Light Co . . . . . . . . . . . . . Natural Gas
Washington National Corp . . . . . . . . . . . . . . Insurance
Washington Post Co . . . . . . . . . . . . . . . . . . . Media
Waste Management, Inc . . . . . . . . . . . . Environmental
Wellcome PLC . . . . . . . . International Pharmaceuticals
Wells Fargo & Company . . . . . . . . . . . . . . . Banking
Western Mining Corporation Holdings Ltd . Nonferrous & Mining
Western Waste Industries . . . . . . . . . . . . Environmental
Westinghouse Electric Corp . . . . . . Electrical Equipment
Westmoreland Coal Co . . . . . . . . . Nonferrous & Mining
West One Bancorp . . . . . . . . . . . . . . . . . . . Banking
Roy F. Weston, Inc . . . . . . . . . . . . . . . . Environmental
Westvaco Corporation . . . . . . . . Paper & Forest Products
Weyerhaeuser Co . . . . . . . . . . Paper & Forest Products
Wheelabrator Technologies Inc . . . . . . . . Environmental
Whirlpool Corporation . . . . . . . . . Electrical Equipment
Willamette Industries, Inc . . . . . Paper & Forest Products
Williams Companies, The . . . . . . . . . . . . . Natural Gas
Winn-Dixie Stores, Inc . . . . . . . . . . . . . . . . . . Retail
F.W. Woolworth Corporation . . . . . . . . . . . . . . Retail
Xerox Corporation . . . . . . . . . . Computer & Electronics
Zenith Electronics Corp . . . . . . . . Electrical Equipment